ALAN EREIRA

THE
ELDER
BROTHERS

Alan Ereira is a historian and award-winning film-maker whose documentary *From the Heart of the World* aired on public television in the United States. Like *The Elder Brothers,* it chronicled his work with the Kogi. Mr. Ereira lives in London, where he is currently at work on a film series about the Crusades.

THE
ELDER
BROTHERS

THE
ELDER
BROTHERS

ALAN EREIRA

VINTAGE DEPARTURES
Vintage Books
A Division of Random House, Inc.
New York

FIRST VINTAGE DEPARTURES EDITION, DECEMBER 1993

Copyright © 1990 by Alan Ereira

A portion of the royalties for this book go to the Tairona Heritage
Trust, a charity that the author established to help protect the Kogi.

Library of Congress Cataloging-in-Publication Data
Ereira, Alan.
[Heart of the world]
The elder brothers / Alan Ereira. — 1st Vintage departures ed.
p.   cm. —(Vintage departures)
Originally published: The heart of the world. London: J. Cape, 1990.
Includes bibliographical references (p.   ) and index.
ISBN 0-679-74336-7
1. Kagaba Indians—Philosophy.   2. Man—Influence on nature—
Colombia—Santa Marta Range.   3. Kagaba Indians—Social
conditions.   4. Kagaba Indians—Religion and mythology.   5. Santa
Marta Range (Colombia)—Description and travel.   I. Title.
[F2270.2.K3E74   1993]
986.1'16—dc20   93-10502
CIP

Author photograph © Jerry Bauer

Manufactured in the United States of America
10   9   8   7   6   5   4   3   2   1

Contents

Acknowledgments

A large number of people have contributed their time and energy in order to help me bring the words of the Elder Brothers to the attention of the world. My wife Sarah and daughters Kate and Ros have lived with this project for three years, and have not only tolerated my own obsession with it but have shared it, travelling to Colombia and working with me.

This book is an account of the making of a television film. The BBC and the Goldsmith Foundation both put their full backing into what I was doing, and I am grateful to them for that and for permission to quote from translations of interviews which I conducted and recordings I made in the course of working on the film. The film crew, Bill Broomfield, John Cridlin and Bruce Wills, and the two anthropologists on the project, Dr Graham Townsley and Felicity Nock, endured the tough bits without complaint, made sure that everything happened the way it was supposed to happen, and looked after me most carefully. The constant reassuring support of people whose reliability and good nature were as important as their professional skill and were never wanting no matter what happened, made what could have been a very difficult experience seem easy.

The importance of the help of many others will be obvious. The staff of Asuntos Indígenas, the Office of Indian Affairs, in Santa Marta, all contributed in a very substantial way, and even allowed Dr Townsley to live in their office. Alec Bright looked after my interests in Bogota with unstinting dedication. The Museo del Oro, Cano the replica-maker and Helicol the helicopter company made sure that I had what I needed, when I needed it. And, of course, as the story I tell makes clear, the contributions of the people who physically cared for us, Ricardo Nuñez and Frankie Rey, went far beyond simply cooking and making camp – though these in themselves were no mean feats, and it is a great compliment to them that we all ended healthier and fitter than we had been at the start.

I would also like to thank the Colombian government's representatives in London, Ricardo Samper, who was for a while acting Ambassador, and Dr Cepeda, Ambassador Extraordinary, for their willingness to intercede on my behalf with the authorities in Bogota whenever I was running into bureaucratic difficulties. Without their help nothing would have been possible.

Dr Graham Townsley helped me greatly in writing this book, and made a substantial contribution to it. He spent considerably longer in the Sierra than I did, and stayed behind after I had left to supervise the work of translation. This is, however, a personal account for which I take responsibility.

Colombia is a troubled country, with an unhappy reputation abroad. Wherever I went I met help, encouragement and interest. The politicians and public officials that I met were concerned about the indigenous people and doing a great deal – in some cases an extraordinary amount by any standards – to help them retain their integrity, security and privacy. They need and deserve all our support. They have to have great courage to carry out their work; we do not need to be brave, just to be responsible.

THE
ELDER
BROTHERS

I

The Sierra Nevada de Santa Marta

We are the Elders.
We were the Elders of all
With greater knowledge, spiritual and material.

The speeches of the Elder Brothers are rooted in an archaic past. For four centuries these people, the last surviving high civilisation of pre-conquest America, have watched in silence from their hidden world in the mountains of Colombia. They have kept their world alive and intact, and kept their distance. Now, in what they fear may be the closing days of life on earth, they have summoned us to listen.

The words of the Elder Brothers need to be taken seriously for a number of reasons. They provide a unique insight into the thinking which lay behind the cities and the gold that dazzled the Spanish conquerors, and which today stand before us mutely. They offer us a way of understanding our own past, and insights into the real meaning and profundity of archaic religious thought.

But above all, we need to listen because of the importance of their message. The Elder Brothers believe that they are the guardians of life on earth. They see the world as a single living being which they have to look after and care for. Their whole way of life is dedicated to nurturing the flora and fauna of the world; they are, in short, an ecological community whose morality is wholly concerned with the health of the planet. Now, the Elder Brothers have seen the changes start which mark the end of life. The world is beginning to die. They know that we are killing it. That is why the Elder Brothers have spoken. They wish to warn us, and to teach us.

We are already aware of the signs that our environment is likely to change catastrophically, and that we ourselves are creating that change. But our response is to look for the technological 'fix' that will stave off disaster: lead-free petrol and catalytic converters for our cars, 'scrubbers' to clean up factory emissions, perhaps more use of nuclear power in place of coal. None of these proposed solutions offers any real hope, if the Kogi are correct, because they are products of the same attitude which has created the problem. We have to learn to understand the world in a different way. That is why they are desperately anxious for us to listen.

They say that it is not yet too late. They also say that they will not speak again.

Santa Marta

The nearest 'civilised' city to the Elder Brothers is Santa Marta, a steamy, violent little community wedged between a mountain and the Caribbean sea. Its links to the rest of Colombia are fragile. The telephone system is frequently blocked and liable to sudden collapse. The few scheduled flights are always late and often cancelled. The railway station is more of a local monument than a gateway to the world. Trains no longer run to Bogota: the only overland transport is a bus, which slowly plods the 700 miles. Permanently stranded in the sidings are two locomotives, named after the city's two most famous brothel 'madams'. Their funerals were attended by the largest crowds in the city's history.

The Samarios, the people of Santa Marta, have evolved a way of life well suited to a city difficult to scrutinise. Their economy has been based for centuries on smuggling and banditry. A bottle of good malt whisky costs less in Santa Marta than in any duty-free shop in the world. Until a few years ago, when the United States swooped in with planes carrying defoliant, it was also the centre of the Columbian marijuana trade. I have a friend who was a mule-driver on the last marijuana caravan to come down to the coast. Twelve hundred mules descended the mountain, each with two sacks of leaves, and six hundred men and boys accompanied them with shotguns. It was, he says, a beautiful sight.

The army, the police chief and the local officials had all been paid off in advance. But as the leaders of this endless line came around a bend in the track they were nevertheless confronted by three policemen.

Three policemen facing six hundred guns. The proposition they put forward sounded suicidal. They wanted three million pesos to stand aside. Otherwise they would arrest the mule train. The gamble was, in its way, heroic. If the money was not paid, the policemen would have to be shot, and that would draw the attention of the government in Bogota to what was going on.

The policemen got their money – half on the spot, and half when they revealed the name of their informant. Santa Marta values obscurity and revenge more highly than money.

The history of the city is mysteriously difficult to sort out. It seems likely that this is where the continent of South America was first discovered by Europeans.

In 1493, Columbus brought 1,200 men to settle on a Caribbean island which he called Hispaniola. Five years later one of those settlers, Alonso de Ojeda, sailed south looking for gold, pearls and slaves.* It is probable that he sailed along the beaches of Santa Marta,† and found a continent.

Another man, in another ship, travelled with him. They split up to trace different sections of coast. The other ship went east along the coast of Venezuela. Amerigo Vespucci publicised his finds and became known as the discoverer of the continent. Alonso de Ojeda did not.

Santa Marta was founded in 1525, which makes it the oldest surviving Spanish town in South America. It is controlled to this day by five old families from the Spanish colonial period. They are an autocratic, almost feudal élite, living in staid and faded grandeur with vast land-holdings. The rest of the population has to get along as best it can.

When I first arrived there, in January 1988, the marijuana boom had ended. But there was an even bigger business requiring quiet obscurity. Colombia had become the world's largest supplier of cocaine, and Santa Marta had adapted its traditional role to this new trade. Some of

* Reichel-Dolmatoff, 1951, p. 3
† Aguado, 1906, vol. XXXI, p. 138

the leaders of the infamous Medellin cartel had their holiday ranches in the area, and the airport was in constant use by small aircraft shuttling backwards and forwards to Miami. The biggest houses along the beach belonged to more junior figures, and the town was informally run by José Abello, 'El Mono', 'The Beau', who came from a middle-class family and had become a cocaine multi-millionaire.

The belt of land behind the town, in the mountain foothills, was not easily crossed. It belonged to the *narco-traficantes*, the drug traffickers, and I was warned to keep well clear. This was a problem, because my destination was the mountain.

The mountain

The Sierra Nevada de Santa Marta is a very strange mountain. Steep and rugged, it rises straight out of the Caribbean. Its two peaks stand side by side, almost exactly the same height, nearly 19,000 feet above the sea and only 26 miles inland. This is the highest coastal mountain in the world, a landfall visible far offshore.

The Spanish never really subdued the mountain. Even today parts of it are almost impenetrable. The lower part, at least on the north face, is still wrapped in dense jungle, and even in the short dry season much of the terrain is too steep for mules. If you do not have the help of the Indians, the distance you can travel is limited by the food you can carry, and the going is slow.

Geologically, it is an oddity. The Sierra stands near the northern limit of the Andes, but it is not a fold mountain like that great chain, and it is made of a different rock. Shaped as an almost perfect triangular pyramid, with each side 90 miles long, it seems to be a tectonic island – a mini-continent, floating alone on the great subterranean ocean of magma which supports the earth's crust, and attached by a passing chance to South America.

It is close enough to the equator to have no seasons, and for day and night to be of equal length all year round. Well watered by heavy downpours, the only change you notice in the course of a year is that there are two periods, called 'summers', when less rain falls – one in June, and another between December and February.

The mountain

As it rises from Caribbean beaches and burning desert at the base to eternal snows at the top, the Sierra Nevada embraces every kind of climate to be found between the equator and the poles, and every kind of landscape too. There are dense tropical rain forests, cloud forests, open woodlands, alpine meadows, high tundra — and a variety of animals and plants to match. Bears, tapirs, deer, jaguars and pumas still live in the forests, with multitudes of smaller creatures: monkeys, armadillos, ocelots, wild pigs and wild cats, turkeys and alligators, are just a few examples. In the air are pelicans and condors, storks and macaws, mockingbirds, hummingbirds and hawks. There are few plants, animals or birds which cannot find an appropriate niche in the infinite variety of the Sierran habitats.

As the mountain folds and twists, it offers slopes which face in all directions, each with its own little climate and its own ecosystem. Because it stands alone, divided by sea or a baking plain from any other high ground, the dense variety of living things that can only survive in the cooler conditions above its base are imprisoned there. Only the birds can leave, and many forms of plant and animal life are unique to this mountain.

As an ecological laboratory, rich in all forms of life, it is intriguing enough. But the Sierra Nevada de Santa Marta has a greater significance. Columbus and his successors, the European invaders of America, destroyed the world they found. The civilisations of America crumbled and vanished as Europe advanced. Only here are there towns, cities, farms, priests, temples, dances and education carrying on along lines established before Columbus came: towns without the wheel, farmers without the plough, educators without the written word, priests with the power of government. The Sierra is not just a reserve for wildlife: it is a philosophical reserve, home to a society which guards the mental landscape which Europeans reworked over all the rest of America.

This is the land of the Kogi, the people who call themselves the Elder Brothers of humanity. We are their Younger Brothers.

To walk to the Sierra

It seems absurd that these people should have preserved their isolation when they are so close to the raucous, violent energy of Santa Marta. Twenty miles separate a Kogi temple or ceremonial house from Santa Marta cathedral. But for us, the Younger Brothers, those 20 miles are as hard to cross as a minefield. Nature, the Colombians and the Kogi have conspired to keep this sanctuary well protected.

One problem is the terrain. A strong, fit person with a good guide and a machete can cover little more than 5 miles a day. There is a rich abundance of venomous snakes and spiders, and some more exotic natural hazards (my favourite is the rabid vampire bat). These are worrying, but do not amount to an insuperable barrier.

The cocaine ranches may sound like a bigger problem, but with good information you can find a route that evades the dangerous patches (and if you are really lucky, the private armies of the *narco-traficantes* may be put out of action by the Colombian government, though I would not count on that).

A few more hazards still await you, of course. If you try to find an easy route, using dirt roads to take you as far as possible, you will find yourself in bandit country. There is a way in to Kogi territory from the north-east side of the mountain, but you have to pass through the ramshackle towns of the Guajira desert, whose murder rate is the highest in Colombia (which means the highest in the world), and where a stranger is sometimes seen as a useful opportunity to see if a gun is working properly.

Or you may simply be stripped of your pack, your boots, your money and your clothes. That happens to many travellers.

Next come the guerillas. The largest guerilla group, until recently, was M19. They staged a spectacular coup a few years ago by seizing the Justice Ministry in Bogota and holding the judiciary hostage. The government responded with vigour, shelling the Ministry and killing judges and guerillas alike. The leaders of M19 seem to have been deeply impressed by this. They have now come down from the mountain and taken seats in the Senate. But that still leaves the ELN and FARC. FARC control the peasant areas in the west of the Sierra. You do not want to meet them. The ELN control the peasant areas in the south and

6

part of the east. You *really* do not want to meet them.

Did I mention the gangs of tomb-robbers? They value their privacy, and you may stumble across them even in the most civilised parts of the countryside. Try not to.

If you are still walking (the temperature is around 37 degrees centigrade, the humidity around 90 per cent), you will probably meet a small, dark-skinned man dressed in a loose white cotton tunic and rolled-up trousers. He may ignore you completely, but if he speaks a few words of Spanish he might offer the traditional Kogi greeting: 'When are you leaving?'

The Kogi do not like visitors. They saw the Spanish arrive in the sixteenth century, and they remember vividly what followed. They know what the Younger Brother is doing at the base of the mountain, and they regard him with deep mistrust. We are the cocaine growers, the mercenaries, the guerillas, the hired assassins. We are thieves, murderers, the destroyers of people, of culture, of the world. The indigenous people of America were once hospitable. They have learned that hospitality is the most dangerous virtue on earth.

If you keep going – and you will find the walking very difficult – you may eventually reach a village of circular huts with strangely thatched roofs. The village will be clean and tidy, but all the doors will be closed, and there will be no one around.

You may wait here a few days, if you have brought enough food. If you are lucky, no one will come and you can go back. A German anthropologist recently got this far and was unlucky. She was surrounded by a screaming, enraged crowd and locked in a hut.

A fellow film-maker, Brian Moser, had a similar experience shortly before I first went to the Sierra. Brian had been there before with a friend, and seen a little of the Kogi: his experiences are described in *The Cocaine Eaters*. Everyone who becomes involved, however slightly, with the world of the Kogi understands at once that these are very special people, and Brian decided to go back and film them for television. He was beaten, and violently ejected.

The Kogi are not a violent people: they see that as being our speciality, and they disapprove of it. But alone among the peoples of South America, they have maintained their world intact, with its secrets, through periods of Spanish conquest, of colonial and post-colonial war, and barbaric slaughter of Indians in order to clear their land (a process which still continues in other parts of South America). When uninvited visitors prove stubborn, they can expect to be handled roughly.

The last Taironas

The Kogi are not hunter-gatherers, or a wandering tribe. They are a nation whose fields have been continuously cultivated and towns continuously occupied for more than a thousand years. Fragments of related civilisations, Maya and Inca, live on in isolated communities in the Andes and Central America, but they are fragments, co-existing with our world and all, to a greater or lesser extent, reshaped by it. The Kogi alone survive as a proto-state, maintaining the authority of their own theocratic institutions, exerting the power of their ancient laws, living in a universe which they perceive in an utterly different way from us. These Elder Brothers look on us as children, dangerous, irrational and essentially helpless. In Spanish, they call us 'civilizados', the civilised people. It is an expression of deep irony.

The Kogi represent the most complete surviving civilisation of pre-Columbian America. But they are not fossilised, and their society is not a museum. When the Spanish first landed, they encountered a civilisation here which they called 'Tairona'. In fact, Tairona was the name of one people among many in the Sierra, but all these peoples formed a single, tightly interconnected civilisation. Today archaeologists still use 'Tairona' as the name for the whole of that civilisation.

The encounter with the Spanish was ultimately to prove extremely destructive, as it was for all the cultures of South and Central America. The unique achievement of the Taironas was that, by a combination of their own inner strengths and their extraordinary geographic position, they were able to survive the encounter. But the culture was very nearly destroyed, and Kogi society was created as the Taironas' response to this catastrophic crisis.

Their culture has changed over five centuries – though considerably less than our own. And they have been in control of the changes. Faced by the threat of complete destruction, they were forced to decide what was really central to them, what it would mean to survive. The survival of a culture is not the same as the survival of individuals: it is the survival not of the body but of the mind. And the emphasis of Kogi society became, and remains, an emphasis on the life of the mind – a life which is almost incomprehensible to us.

Fundamental to that survival is the maintenance of a physical separation between their world and our own. Every intrusion made into their territory – by tourists, by anthropologists, by robbers, by peasants, by seekers after wisdom or profit – is a threat. They are hidden, and have developed a culture of silence and secrecy. Communication with the outside world is taboo: children are taught to hide from strangers, and adults regard all outsiders as dangerous. Everything about the Kogi is concealed.

Why me?

I am not an experienced explorer. I am an historian of sorts, who makes television programmes. I do not relish danger and detest discomfort, I have never thought of myself as physically tough and prefer a comfortable chair to even a short walk. I have no particular knowledge of anthropology or archaeology, and had never been to South America before.

But the Kogi have decided that they have to break their long silence. And I was the person they decided could best help them.

The Kogi were forced into this position by the same logic that imposed secrecy on them for so long, the logic that says they have a duty to survive. It is a duty created by being the Elder Brothers.

It is a fundamental belief among the Kogi that they are the guardians of life on earth. That is what it means to be an Elder Brother. They order reality, and engineer the fertility and fecundity of nature. They have been sustained in this conviction by the extraordinary vitality of the Sierra Nevada, by the powerful contrast between their own well managed landscape and the havoc at the foot of the mountain, and by their own longevity. We reckon the normal human life to be three score years and ten. They have another twenty years: at eighty, a Kogi expects to be fitter and more vigorous than we do at fifty, and I know several active, energetic Kogi around a hundred years old.

In believing themselves to be responsible for the well-being of the world, they take on responsibility for the well-being of the Younger Brother. That requires nothing from us. So long as the Kogi are able to survive and continue their work, the world is fundamentally safe.

Up to now we have ignored the Younger Brother. We have not deigned even to give him a slap.

But they can ignore the Younger Brother no longer. The Younger Brother has got out of hand: he has begun to undermine the structure and stability of the whole world.

The leaders of this extraordinary society decided that we must be warned. We must be shown what we are doing, and made to understand the catastrophe coming rapidly upon us. It is, in their view, the only hope for us and for them.

But now we can no longer look after the world alone. The Younger Brother is doing too much damage. He must see, and understand, and assume responsibility. Now we will have to work together. Otherwise, the world will die.

The difference between my experience and Brian Moser's was probably just a matter of timing. Had he arrived a year later, perhaps he would have met a gentler reception.

It was very difficult for the Kogi to make the decision to work with me. It was hard enough for the leaders to make the decision in principle: it was even more difficult for them to carry that decision through, and convince all their people that they must overcome carefully cultivated habits of suspicion and secrecy. Nothing less than absolute terror can explain it. The Kogi have risked everything: they are quite convinced that the risk must be taken.

Ramón, a Kogi who is very important in this story, once asked me to bring him a globe of the world. 'I know', he said, 'that the world is round, as an eye is round and a head is round and a house is round. And you know that the world is round. But you know it in a different way from me. So bring me a globe, so that I can understand what you know.'

I picked up an orange and drew the continents on it. Here, I said, is a globe: this is the world, here is America, here is the ocean, here is my country England far in the north. Here in the centre, between North and South America, between the two great oceans, is the Sierra Nevada.

Ramón stared blankly at the orange. All this was obvious nonsense. But plainly it meant something to me. And if I thought the world was somehow like an orange, then perhaps I could be taught something by using it. He bent his arm, pointed his elbow towards me, and balanced the orange on it.

'The world is balanced on an elbow. It is very delicately balanced. It gets more delicate every day. You are shaking the world. And if you shake it any more' – he touched the orange lightly with a finger tip – 'it will fall.' The orange fell, and Ramón stared at me, wondering if I understood.

I have just been watching a movie called *Network*. Peter Finch, a newscaster at the end of his career, hears a voice in the night which is not the voice of God, and the voice tells him to speak the truth to the world. Filled with awe, Finch asks, 'Why me?' And the voice, which is not the voice of God, answers, 'Because you've got sixty million viewers, dummy! You're on television!'

The Kogi asked me to carry their message to the outside world because they wish us to be saved from what they see as imminent, and almost inevitable, destruction – and because, although they have never seen television or opened a book, they know that these forms of communication, whatever they are, are their only way of being heard.

It is important to understand that this is not an appeal to 'save the Indians' or 'save the rain forest'. It is true that the Kogi are in danger, and true that the rain forest which forms part of their domain is threatened. But the Kogi are concerned to save us – our survival is at stake.

The Trust

The Kogi do have their own needs. I have established a charitable trust, The Tairona Heritage Trust, which works with the Mamas. Part of my advance for this book has already gone to that Trust, and if the book earns any royalties, part of that money will go to it. When the television film was made, a lump sum was given to the Kogi by the BBC. The film was co-produced with money from the Goldsmith Foundation, and part of any income accruing to this organisation from the sale of the film will also go to The Tairona Heritage Trust.

The objects of the Trust are to assist in the reacquisition of the Indians' ancestral land, to support medical projects, and to help to stabilise the frontier between the indigenous people of the Sierra and the outside world. I hope that this frontier can become a point of exchange, where the Kogi can sell their own produce and buy the things they need, such as iron tools, from us. It should also be a place of cultural exchange, for they have much to teach us if we are prepared to listen, and they do not want us to enter their territory.

These are expensive projects in local terms but not in global ones; given the continuing support of the Colombian government, the Trust could do all that is currently possible for the price of a Rolls-Royce. If anyone wants to support its work, by making a donation through the publisher, that would of course be very deeply appreciated.

But the Kogi do not believe that the world can be saved by giving them money. They see us as moral idiots, greedy beyond all understanding. Over and over again they speak of us sacking, looting the planet, tearing at its flesh without respect. The highest morality is understanding that for everything that is taken, something must be given back. We have got away with it for a long time, but time has run out now, and we cannot solve the problem by charitable donations alone. The Kogi demand that we behave responsibly, that we begin to take care of the world. They are demanding an ethical revolution on our part, in which greed and selfishness are tempered by awe, and by a sensitivity to the earth as a living—and now perhaps dying—totality.

If we fail to respond, they say, all life will be destroyed very soon. They have seen the signs, and they are profoundly fearful. Since I have lived with them, I have learned to trust their judgments.

2

First Contact

I first became involved with Colombia in January 1988, when I was filming the story of the Spanish Armada. The gold of the New World was at the heart of sixteenth-century Spain, and I was following the story of that gold. That is how I was led, as the conquistadors were led, to the Taironas of the Sierra Nevada.

It was a story that began on the Caribbean island called Hispaniola, Columbus's first colony. There was gold there, but in a few years it had all been exhausted and its population exterminated. Hispaniola became the base from which voyages of exploration and conquest were launched to the shores of America.

It became the focus of European rivalries; France captured one half of the island, and to this day it is divided between the Spanish-speaking people of the Dominican Republic and the French-speakers of Haiti. My interest was in a raid by Francis Drake, one of the provocations which led Spain to launch its great crusade against England. That took me to the capital of the Dominican Republic, Santo Domingo.

The heart of that city remains much as it was when it was built, a few streets of fine sixteenth-century Spanish houses, a fort, and a cathedral (the oldest cathedral in the Americas). It still suggests the military power and wealth of the world's greatest empire, one which laid claim, within a hundred years of Columbus, to all the Americas, to Africa and Asia, to Jerusalem and half of Europe. The architectural trinity of the conquest was forged here: fortress, church and viceregal palace. This was the workshop where the New World was shaped.

By the time Drake arrived the gold of Hispaniola was no more than a memory, and he sailed on to what is now Colombia. I would have to go there too, because the best collection of American gold is in the Museo del Oro in Bogota. I was pursuing the relics of a vanished world, and, like the men who looted there three centuries before, I did not understand what these relics meant. I only knew that they were gold, and this gold had changed the history of Europe.

Gold made the Spanish crown wealthy enough to finance huge armies and vast fleets. The Most Christian King of Spain transformed the sacred gold of Incas and Aztecs into Christian coin; he bought himself the title of Holy Roman Emperor, and paid for Christendom's reconquest of the Mediterranean from the Turks. Armies of mercenaries were gathered to destroy the Lutherans of Germany. New powers, new technologies, new wars flowed out of the molten gold, and the ships of Europe were drawn across the Atlantic by the magnetic pull of the golden motherlode.

If that motherlode ever had a name, it was El Dorado. But El Dorado was not a place; it means 'The Golden Man'. At his accession, a Muisca chieftain was covered in gold and ceremonially carried on a raft into the centre of a lake, to dive into the water. There he surrendered his offerings of gold and jewels.

The conquest of South America was a man-hunt, the pursuit of El Dorado. He was run to ground at Bogota, high in the mountains of the Andes. In 1538 two separate expeditions met here: Gonzalo Jiménez de Quesada had set out with half the population of Santa Marta and arrived after 500 gruelling miles with seventy starving soldiers, while Sebastián de Benalcázar had come 500 miles from the south, from the ruins of the Andean citadel of Quito which had been burned to thwart him of plunder, and his ragged forces of 160 had been three years on the march driving a herd of pigs.

This was the home of El Dorado; the sacred lake stood in the bowl of a volcano. On the floor of the valley, the conquerors built their cathedral, their fortress, their palace. Santa Fé de Bogotá was a city created by desperate men pursuing fantasies of wealth at the end of the world.

Today El Dorado is an airport. But the man-hunt for wealth still goes on. Everyone had stories to tell me about Bogota. It was universally agreed to be the most violent city in the world. This is not true, but it is all right as an approximation. I was warned by friends and fellow-passengers, and as my destination grew closer the warnings grew more detailed. Do not walk alone in the centre of the city, even in daytime. Do not accept anything to eat, drink or smoke from a stranger because it may be coated with a nerve poison, and you will wake up two days later stripped in a gutter. Do not make casual friends. Robbery is normal, murder is commonplace. Stay away from the slums: stay away from the down-town area: lock yourself in your room and don't go out.

When I arrived at El Dorado, I was met by Alec Bright, who had recommended himself as a local 'fixer'. Alec was an expatriate from the Isle of Wight who seemed to know everything and everyone and who increased my anxieties by telling me how dangerous it is even being in the airport. He looked terribly out of place among the Colombians, dressed in his English tie and tweed jacket, moving around with precise, delicate steps and a harassed, anxious expression. I later discovered that Alec had tunnel vision, and must have been continuously haunted by his vulnerability to armed bandits standing slightly off to one side.

It was a relief, and in some ways a disappointment, to discover that my hotel and Alec's home, on the north side of the city, were in comfortable and expensive streets considerably less dangerous than the ones where I live in North London. Alec's house was surrounded by orchids and visited, at set times every day, by a couple of hummingbirds. My hotel, the Charleston, was as luxurious as any in the world, a quiet, civilised place that reminded me of some of the small expensive hotels in Washington. The neighbours were evidently prosperous. Later I discovered that many of them were very prosperous indeed. Billionaires. White powder billionaires. But, at this stage, I wandered around in happy ignorance.

Down-town Bogota had a tenser atmosphere, not helped by Alec's insistence that any walking should be brief, brisk, and carried out firmly gripping our cases. Perhaps it really is that dangerous. There have certainly been times when I have felt uncomfortable on the street, and the sight of a residential block guarded by a ragged man with a machete does make me feel anxious. Yet in the heart of the city there is one of the greatest treasures in the world, a building filled with more than fifteen thousand pieces of pre-Columbian gold.

The core of the museum is an immense room built as a time-locked safe. You step through the 2-foot-thick steel doors, and then into a dark inner chamber. You are locked inside. Slowly, the lights come up revealing a vast hoard of gold objects – necklaces, bracelets, crowns, masks and strange images of people that are not people, animals that are not animals.

The finest of these, cast in a very distinctive way, are the objects labelled 'Tairona'. They have a baroque richness, a fullness of form which is to my eye lacking in much of the rest of the display.

The Lost City of the Taironas

Shortly before leaving London, I had been given a photocopy of an article about a recently-discovered Tairona city.* Apart from its archaeological site-name, Buritaca 200, it was known only as La Ciudad Perdida – 'The Lost City'. Covering 3 square miles of mountainside, it was apparently located in a jungle area encouragingly known as 'El Infierno' – Hell – because it was somewhat difficult to move through. The BBC had suggested that, since I was in Colombia anyway, I might take a day and see if the Lost City should be filmed for an archaeology programme.

I had never heard of the Taironas before. It only gradually dawned on me that what I knew of the conquest of South America had filtered down not through the chronicles and history books but through archaeology. Archaeologists had found the great cities of the Aztecs and the Incas and the Mayas, and so I knew about these. But this was the first discovery of a monumental Tairona site. The Taironas had just entered history.

Yet the chronicles of the conquistadors contain descriptions of elaborate Tairona cities. Capital cities, Bonda, Betoma, Pocigueica, and hundreds of smaller towns, are mentioned in the bizarre rhyming descriptions which the Spanish scribes felt inspired to write. Taironaca, for instance, was:

* 'La Ciudad Perdida – Major Colombian Archaeological Find', *Colombia Today* XIV, no. 4, New York 1979

The Lost City of the Taironas

City of thatch, but firmly founded,
Crumbling on the eastern side,
A triangular court compounded
Of great stone slabs flat and wide.
Each edge of the space is bounded
By a hundred-pace-long side
And at the corners three great dwellings
And their kings live in these buildings ...
These are also roofed with straw
And many go to dine inside
And some three hundred or still more
Soldiers may sleep there beside.*

The Taironas were not an imperial society, and their isolated location was out of reach of the Incas to the south and the Aztecs to the north. But they formed part of a larger culture which can be traced through northern Colombia and Central America, and which was fully established fifteen hundred years ago. This network of complex societies had developed large-scale stone engineering to construct mountain terraces and architecture and extensive irrigation and drainage systems. There was a hierarchy of villages, towns and cities and specialised pottery and metal-working, with extensive exchange of produce and manufactured goods. At first the gold pieces produced by the various societies of the area, which included the Muisca, Quimbaya, Sinu and Tairona, were quite primitive and very similar to one another, indicating a close similarity of belief and ritual. There is evidence that many of these similarities extend to a much greater area, from Ecuador in the south, northwards into Central America.

Around one thousand years ago, the archaeological record suggests that these societies became technically more sophisticated and their gold-work becomes more easily differentiated. By the time the Spanish arrived, the Taironas had been a highly developed and complex society for some five centuries. They were exchanging goods over a wide area, as far afield as Costa Rica. Their golden objects, double-headed animals and strange homunculi speak of a rich symbolic world, and the triangular courtyard in Castellanos's description of

* Castellanos, 1886, 8, 322

17

Taironaca sounds like a representation of the triangular base of the Sierra.

It seems that the core of the Tairona world remained unharmed for rather longer than the other civilisations of the Americas. The great empires folded up very quickly: the Mayans had collapsed long before the Spanish arrived, the Aztec and Inca empires were destroyed in 1521 and 1535 respectively. The immediate relatives of the Taironas, such as the Muiscas, were conquered and enslaved just as fast. But although Santa Marta was founded in 1525, the Taironas continued to co-exist with the Spanish for about seventy-five years more. And when the final struggle broke out and the Indians were defeated, they did not become unwilling subjects of a Spanish administration. They withdrew, and disappeared.

In fact the tide of history was simply running in another direction. The flow of gold from South America faded to a trickle soon after the first unbelievable torrent, but at Potosí in Bolivia there was a mountain made of silver, and the Potosí silver mines kept Spain busy digging a grave for its own economy.

The Taironas may have worked gold, but they did not seem to have any gold mines. The Sierra Nevada had thin mountain soil covered, on the lower slopes, with dense jungle, and it was very hard going because of the steep rugged slopes. It really was not worth getting involved, when the pickings were so much easier and richer elsewhere. The Spanish were happy to use the natives close to Santa Marta as a slave labour force, but saw no reason to penetrate any distance into the mountain.

So long as the Indians there were not causing any trouble, no one really cared whether they lived or died, or what they were up to.

And so history flowed around the bottom of the Sierra, lapped at its base, but left the Indians alone.

Simón Bolívar, the great liberator, set out from the Magdalena river that flows along the western side of the mountain pyramid. At the beginning of the nineteenth century he liberated Gran Colombia from the Spanish, and then returned to Santa Marta as the new America disintegrated into a set of squabbling republics. He died there, having transformed the history of a continent. But 20 miles away, behind the jungle wall, life carried on unchanged.

In the 1870s a priest, Father Rafael Celedón, went in to the Sierra to make converts among the Indians and produce a catechism in their language. He succeeded in writing the catechism, and even produced a book of their grammar, an achievement which has never been repeated, but he was not successful in making converts or any other kind of inroads. He was not welcome, and was constantly confronted with sullen passivity. The Kogi did not resist him in any way, they simply made it clear that they did not like him being there. In 1915 the anthropologist Konrad Preuss spent a few months in their lowest-lying community. Most of this time he was lying ill in a hammock, and he reported a complex mythology of 'demons'.

In the early twentieth century the United Fruit Company arrived from the United States and set up a system of serf labour, growing bananas at the southern foot of the Sierra and shipping them out, by slow steam trains, down the western side to the ports of Baranquilla and Santa Marta. Peasants flocked to the plantations, centred on Fundación and Valledupar, and the easier southern slopes of the mountain were deforested to make way for the new cash crop. Santa Marta became a prosperous city, Fundación and Valledupar became oppressed ones. But when the banana boom collapsed and the United Fruit Company left, the northern side of the Sierra was still mysterious.

In the 1940s two government anthropologists, a Russian *émigré* called Geraldo Reichel-Dolmatoff, and his wife Alicia, penetrated more deeply into the region. They discovered there the most complete cultural survival of pre-Columbian America: a society which not only maintained the rituals of a vanished world, but which appeared to sustain them on a basis of intellectual analysis and systematic learning. They had entered the world of the Kogi.

I had read some of Reichel-Dolmatoff's work, and it seemed plain that the Kogi were the intellectual descendants, and possibly the actual descendants, of the Taironas. There were two other tribes living in the Sierra, called in the literature Ika and Sanka (I was to get to know them as Asario and Arhuaco), but they were both said to be more acculturated. They inhabit the southern and western sides, which are more vulnerable to settlement. It was the Kogi who would be interesting, and the Lost City appeared to be in Kogi territory.

They were plainly a deeply mysterious people. Twenty years after he began writing about them, Reichel-Dolmatoff thought that there might be perhaps two thousand Kogi hidden in the Sierra.* By 1987,

* Reichel-Dolmatoff, 1967, p. 57

though still speaking of them as a 'small' group, he had trebled his estimate.* I was beginning to hear of even larger numbers. In fact we now know of the presence of approximately eleven thousand Kogi. They outnumber the Asarios and Arhuacos combined in the Sierra, and it is an indication of their successful isolation that such a large population should have remained undetected until they chose to make themselves known. These are, after all, settled farmers, and every family also has a house in a Kogi city.

Everything I heard in Bogota increased my interest. The Kogi were well known by repute: I was told of their deliberate remoteness, their determination to have nothing to do with the outside world. I was told stories about them being masters of levitation and telepathy, with a direct link to supernatural powers in the spirit world, and that they are the repository of a secret knowledge.

There was also a certain amount of more concrete information. Alec Bright had worked as an architect, and had played a part in designing the Museo del Oro. (He had not designed the security system, which had been devised after a careful study of the robbery in the movie *Topkapi*.) He had himself taken an interest in certain kinds of Tairona gold-work. In fact Alec had a theory that the mushroom-shaped extrusions surrounding the heads of the crouching, bat-faced figures so commonly found are actually connected with magic mushrooms, and represent a hallucinogenic mental explosion.† Alec tried to explain to me, with elaborate diagrams, the Kogi perception of the world as a quartered circle, a disc-world with other disc-worlds above and below.

The centre of Kogi life, he told me, is the circular ceremonial house, whose floor has four fires and which represents this earth. Above, its conical roof symbolises the whole of the top half of the universe and contains representations of the disc-worlds above. Below, conceptually at least, the cone is mirrored as a series of underworlds. The Kogi priests, the Mamas, sit in the ceremonial house as though it were a womb, and they are at the foot of an umbilical cord reaching down from the centre of the roof.

---

* Reichel-Dolmatoff, 1987, p. 73
† Richard Evans Schultes and Alec Bright, 'Ancient Gold Pectorals from Colombia: Mushroom Effigies?' *Botanical Museum Leaflets*, vol. 27, nos 5–6, pp. 113–41, Harvard University, Cambridge, Mass. 1979

Tairona gold

Very little if any of the gold in the Museo del Oro was discovered by the Spanish: their finds were melted down and sent to Spain as ingots.

The gold objects in the museum were generally found by tomb-robbers within the last fifty years. Tomb-robbing is a large-scale activity among Colombian peasants. In fact it is so large-scale that in 1972 they tried to win legal recognition for a *sindicato de guaqueros*, a tomb-robbers' trade union, with over ten thousand members. Exactly who the tomb-robbers felt was exploiting them I do not know, but there have been and still are some very large operators in the business. One of the largest, incidentally, was Guillermo Cano, who owns the most prestigious souvenir shops in Colombia, selling exact replicas of his own finds. Cano had the shrewdness to sell his personal collection to the museum after making moulds of every object. That is why Cano is able to make the best reproduction pre-Columbian gold.

Tomb-robbing has a peculiar status in Colombia. There are laws about it, but they are like the speed limits: everyone supposes they exist, but no one I have heard of has actually fallen foul of them or could say with confidence what they are. Cano's customers can sit in comfortable leather arm-chairs, in between browsing among the cases of golden replicas, and watch an expensively-produced video showing exactly how to pillage an archaeological site.

Generally speaking, of course, the gold was produced by cultures which have vanished from the face of the earth. But Tairona graves are claimed by the Kogi, and there is some embarrassment about Tairona gold. As a gesture of respect, Alec told me, the museum sent presents to the Kogi Mamas: some stone beads, which they believed to be Tairona, and some salt. Eventually the beads were returned to the museum, with a message.

Thank you for the salt. It comes from a region from which we have had no salt for four hundred years. But we know nothing about the beads. They have no place here.

El Dorado

My immediate task, having seen the museum, was to visit the Lost City. I was already quite certain from everything I had heard that what made the city interesting was the presence of the Kogi. Here was something unique: a monumental archaeological site, with a native tradition still surviving around it. Though there was one obvious problem: the natives would be most unlikely to have anything to do with me.

There was another problem too. I was ignorant of the basic facts of life in the Andes. I knew nothing about mountains, about jungle, about Indians or about the ancient culture of the people. I had nervously equipped myself with stout boots and a huge bag of medicines, and felt desperately ill prepared.

To break me in gently, Alec and his sons suggested going a few miles out of Bogota to take a look at Guatavita, the legendary site of El Dorado. This is the dark, circular lake that still holds the fabulous treasure of the Muisca Indians. The original conquerors were unable to get their hands on the gold. It was beyond their reach. Within a few decades a huge wedge was cut out of one side of the mountain rim, lowering the lake by 60 feet and revealing some treasures, but the centre was untouched. In the early years of this century the lake was undermined to drain the water off, but the bottom set as hard as concrete, the sluices jammed with mud, and the lake filled up again. Recently a model raft, made of gold, with gold figures on it, turned up in a tomb and can now be seen in the Museo del Oro.

It is easier to reach Guatavita than it was in 1538, but it is still a challenge. It might be easy in a four-wheel drive vehicle, but the Colombians stick to the view that the best all-terrain vehicle is a twenty-year-old Packard. We got out of Bogota safely, and on to the side of the Guatavita reservoir, created to supply Bogota with electric power, but the climb up from there to the volcanic lake, on a steep dirt track, was too much for the taxi. Fortunately there were four passengers, and with the driver remaining gamely at his post we got it up there.

So I had a chance to work my boots in, walking around the rim of the lake, a chance to work my lungs in, gasping in the thin air, and a chance to work my head in. There was a path around the lip of this perfect cone. It was rather like walking around the top of a giant Pavlova cake, with a neat slice carefully taken out by the treasure hunters. There were light grasses, and shrubs down the side of the even slope that led to the black circular pool in the centre. It felt domesticated; a place for a Bogota picnic. Whatever mystery had once been practised here had been extinguished long ago. Looking at the lake, the only insight that came to me was that all I could see was a circular lake, so geometrically perfect that it seemed man-made. And although I had read about the legend, and seen the model raft, I really had no idea what it was all about. Perhaps it would be the same with the Lost City.

The Kogi have some connection with El Dorado: they are, like the Muisca, a Chibcha people, and their language belongs to that group. I suppose that they are the best hope we have of understanding why the offerings were made at Guatavita, as they are the best hope we have of understanding so much of what has been lost. But I could not then think of any reason why they should want to tell me about it.

In this frame of mind, Alec and I flew up to the coast for my day trip to the Lost City.

Bureaucracy

It had taken quite some organising.

Immediately after the city had been found, there had been some hope that it might draw tourists to the region, as the monumental cities of Peru, Cuzco and Machu Picchu have drawn swarms of prosperous back-packers. Santa Marta and its resort satellite Rodadero are popular places for holidays despite the difficulty of getting there and the greater problem of leaving. The airport is filled every night during the New Year holiday season with patient holidaymakers whose air tickets were valid for planes which never came, and whose hotel rooms have been turned over to other people. Nevertheless, more tourists seemed like a good idea, and helicopter trips were laid on from the hotels to the Lost City. They soon had to stop.

In the maze of interlocking bureaucracy, it was surprising that the

Lost City had ever been investigated. The jungle of the Sierra is theoretically controlled from the equally dense jungle of Bogota, where the overlapping, intertwined jurisdictions of the Indian Affairs Office, the National Parks Agency, and the Institute of Anthropology and Archaeology strive to throttle each other and break free into supremacy. And just in case they should ever work in harmony, a Foundation for the Sierra Nevada, independent of government, at that time had vague authority granted by the President.

Briefly, in the first rush of enthusiasm after the discovery of the city, there really had been cooperation between all these outfits. But because in Colombia anthropology and archaeology are regarded as the same subject, anthropological projects in the Amazon were closed down to finance the dig at the Lost City. Trouble followed when an Amazon anthropologist, from one of these discontinued projects, was promoted to run the Indian Affairs office. And more trouble came when the head of the Institute of Anthropology and Archaeology took over the National Parks Agency. And more when the Foundation for the Sierra Nevada, created by one President, looked for support from his successor.

The Lost City was shut. There were no longer any archaeologists allowed to work at the site. And I had to have permission from all these competing agencies to set foot in the place.

There were no helicopter tours on offer any more. It was possible to walk, but the 20-mile hike from Santa Marta would take at least four days each way, and the area around the site was controlled by guerillas. There was no practical alternative to hiring my own helicopter from Medellin and having it flown 400 miles to the coast. Alec negotiated his way through all the permissions, and we flew north to meet the helicopter.

Cartagena and Ciénaga Grande

The conquerors of Colombia had melted down its gold and sent it to Cartagena on the Caribbean coast. From there it was shipped to Spain. When Francis Drake found nothing at Hispaniola, he moved on to Cartagena and stormed the port. Before going to the Lost City, I also had to go to Cartagena, to arrange filming there for the Armada project.

Bogota is rather a dour, serious city; but the *costeños*, the coastal people of Colombia, are much more Caribbean in temperament. The transition from the cool heights of Bogota to the constant heat and the noise of the coast was startling. Even at night the temperature hardly drops at all. But the old Spanish colonial heart of Cartagena, with its narrow streets, tall buildings and overhanging balconies, did offer shade, and was very beautiful.

When Drake arrived Cartagena was still young, and its simple defences collapsed before him. Later on, a complete system of fortifications was constructed to defend the harbour against English pirates, and this is still intact. But by then there was no significant quantity of gold being exported – it had gone. It had done massive damage to the society which stole it. Castile had used the gold to sustain a rigid aristocratic society and was left crippled; its great sheep farmers had been ruined, its agriculture devastated. The ingots were turned into coins – 'golden raindrops', they were called, because when they touched the hot soil of Spain they evaporated in a cloud of debt, condensing again in the pockets of northern European bankers. As the gold flowed through the rest of Europe, it created massive inflation and threw ordered kingdoms into confusion. A new order gradually emerged in which Spain was a very minor power indeed. Cartagena had become a monument to the pursuit of luxury and the defence of wealth, and it survives as a monument because Spain was left with neither money nor reason to develop it further.

Once I had done my lightning tour of the old city and the forts, we hired a taxi to drive along the coast to Santa Marta. The helicopter was to meet us just after dawn, so we set out in the dark. The roads, for once, were good, and it was an easy trip. As the sky lightened we crossed the shore-line lakes of Ciénaga Grande, where villages on stilts house communities of fishermen. The water and the misty air merged completely in the morning light, so that everything was a single gleaming vaporous space. The sky and the water were one. The dugout canoes seemed to be suspended, silhouetted against the bright light, the fishermen almost naked. From time to time one would stand up, swirl a small circular net overhead and cast it into the light, where it vanished.

These lakes were, until recently, freshwater lagoons. The road was built along the narrow strip of land – no wider than a dyke – that ran between the fresh water and the salt. Somehow, it seems, the road has upset the balance of drainage, so that salt water is now seeping into the lagoons. The dense forests that grew there are now dead, and we drove in the pale light of dawn through silver jungles of skeletal tree-trunks, rising into the mist from the shining, poisoned water. It was an eerie and disturbing journey. And all the time we were driving towards the mountain, the dark, sudden, steep Sierra.

Visit to the Lost City

Santa Marta airport is at the edge of the sea, a single runway and a small terminal building. The helicopter arrived on time, and we worked out a route with the pilot. Although the Lost City is so close to the airport, this was fairly complicated, because we had to avoid flying over any known cocaine ranches.

The journey was spectacular. The Sierra rises immediately behind the airport, and in a couple of minutes we were over dense jungle. The mountain consists of a series of ravines, rising sharply and then falling away steeply to the next valley and the next ridge. Trees cover the lower slopes, and they stand proud along the tops, reaching 100 feet or more into the sky.

Suddenly a bare patch appeared. A huge system of walled terraces had been built along a sharp ridge, with large stone circles grassed over. They were the only flat ground visible. The biggest of these was an ideal landing pad, offering itself to the sky in the middle of this thick jungle. It was so striking from the air that it really looked as though the Lost City was made for helicopters.

As we came down, we could see a complex of these circles, all on different levels, connected by large, well made stairways. In the middle of one terrace was a wooden shed, and a couple of men in uniform emerged. These were policemen who had been left to guard the site.

By the time we touched ground, the entire complement of guards had turned out: three men in jungle green with cheap rubber boots, and one in a T-shirt who was their cook. They seemed disappointed to see us. Apparently they had been placed here for a one-month tour of duty three months ago, and when they heard us coming they assumed that we were their relief. Alec had anticipated this, and brought a bottle of rum as consolation.

The soldiers showed us around, commenting from time to time on my boots. I was glad to have them. But somehow my stout rubber, steel-supported soles did not provide the firm grip I had expected. The whole city was a network of ancient narrow steps and steep stone tracks. The constant drip of the foliage in the dark green light of the jungle meant that the stone-work under foot was slippery and treacherous.

The largest terraces, up on the ridge, were evidently the foundation of a complex of ceremonial buildings and open spaces; below, the smaller terraces and circular stone bases represented domestic and work areas, and tiny fields. The stairways in the ceremonial area were fine and broad, but further down they were cramped and awkward. I had to move up and down crab-wise: the steps were far too narrow for my boots. It gradually dawned on me that they were designed for bare feet: they were ideal for someone who moved on the balls of his feet.

The more I saw, the more I became aware of how carefully everything had been thought out. Every house had a stone drainage channel around it, feeding the water away to a lower level: even now, four hundred years after it had been abandoned, the city was well drained. The terraces had overhanging stone lips, so that the water would not wear away the walls below.

The stones were roughly dressed, but cut accurately enough to make 30-foot-high walls without mortar. The general air of the place was both monumental and rustic. And overwhelmingly, I was conscious of this being a city built in an area of abundant water and vigorous fertility. It had disappeared into the jungle (which could reclaim a cleared site within two years), and withstood colossal downpours of rain for four centuries, and yet it could be reoccupied at any time.

But what was it? Surely it had at least a name? The Spanish chronicles describe a number of large Tairona cities, but none of them seems quite to fit the description of this location. What kind of life had gone on here? What were the buildings that once stood on these foundations – were some of them ceremonial houses, as Alec had described? And how had the city died?

Archaeology had not produced answers to any of these questions. But from everything I had heard, it seemed the Kogi knew. They had been unhappy at the archaeology, and had protested that this was one of their sacred sites. To them, there was no difference between archaeology and tomb-robbing – and the idea of tourists trampling over their ancestral places was anathema to them. Things had turned out to their advantage: the political squabbles had shut down both tourism and archaeology, and Martín von Hildebrand, the Amazonian anthropologist who now ran the Office of Indian Affairs, had used their criticism as an argument for returning research money from the Sierra to the Amazon. The Kogi had no reason to explain anything.

But perhaps I could make contact. One of the policemen seemed rather closer attuned to the place than his colleagues: having nothing else to do, he had taken up birdwatching and settled more comfortably into the jungle than the others. We talked about the Kogi, and he made me a present of a little gourd. This, he explained, was a poporo. It was about 6 inches long, a tube with a bulb at one end: it looked like a little beige penis.

The Kogi use it when they chew the leaf of the coca bush. They place powdered sea-shells in the gourd, and then dip a stick in it. Licking the stick gives them enough lime to activate the coca. Then they wipe the stick on the top of the gourd, gradually building up a yellow 'calc' of lime and spittle. This becomes a thick deposit, sometimes 2 or 3 inches thick, in the form of a cap or a wheel.

The coca leaf is the source of cocaine, but chewing it has a very different effect from ingesting the refined powder. The leaf is a little smaller and brighter than a leaf of privet. It takes more than 6 pounds of leaves and a complex chemical transformation to make a single ounce of the commercial drug. The Kogi chew constantly on small quids of the bitter, dried leaves. In this tiny quantity, released very slowly, the coca acts as a mild stimulant and a medicine. In good hotels in Cuzco, Peru, where visitors are likely to suffer from altitude sickness, new arrivals are given a cup of coca tea to steady them. Chewing the leaf dulls sensations: it stops a person feeling tired or hungry, and it enables the Indians to walk long distances, work long hours and go without sleep for nights on end. It has been used all over South America for at least a thousand years. There is no evidence that chewing coca leaf, or drinking coca tea, is in any way harmful.

A poporo is the mark of a man among the Kogi: it is not used by women or children. This one was unused: a poporo for someone about to grow up.

I asked whether the soldier knew of anyone who spoke both Spanish and Kogi. Yes, there was a man, called Ramón. I should look for him in Santa Marta, at the Casa Indígena – the Indian House.

It was time to go. The early morning in the Sierra is usually cloudless, but towards midday the clouds build up and we could not take the chance of being stranded. Clutching my virginal poporo, I climbed in the helicopter with Alec and flew away.

Eventually, a relief party did arrive to take over from the policemen. They found three corpses: two policemen and the cook. There had, it seemed, been a gun battle. It was assumed for a few months that the third policeman had murdered his colleagues and fled, but then his body turned up too, further down the mountain. Current rumour has it that they had fallen in with tomb-robbers, and then fallen out. The story of gold, blood and death seems to continue. It casts rather a cloud over my little, pure poporo.

It was noon when we landed. I had one afternoon to get my film off the ground.

The Casa Indígena

The soldier had mentioned the Casa Indígena. I did not know what this might be, but a taxi-driver at the airport said he knew the way. We drove along the coast road, past luxury hotels, over the low ridge of a Sierra foothill, and Santa Marta was spread before us.

On a flat wedge of land between two arms of the mountain, it was a huddle of low buildings with a white cathedral rising from the centre. On the far side were industrial docks, on the near side single-storey shacks, and between, the remnants of the old colonial city.

The taxi-driver soon got lost, but eventually found his way up an unmade side-street to a high wire fence with a large wire gate. It was locked. Inside was a compound, containing a number of circular white-walled huts with conical asbestos roofs, and a square block that was evidently offices. An Indian approached warily from the offices.

He was about 5 feet tall and dressed in pure white: a white cotton jerkin with loose sleeves, and baggy white trousers that were rolled up to mid-calf. He wore a straw cowboy hat, from which his hair hung, black and straight, to his shoulders. In his hand he carried a poporo, the wood worn to a rich brown by his hands and an inch-thick ring of calc around the top. A long thin stick protruded from it. Across his body woven bags were slung – one under one arm, two under the other, all white with coloured bands around them. He was also wearing a black plastic Casio digital watch and a pair of scruffy black leather shoes.

The taxi-driver, who understood roughly what I wanted, told him imperiously that I wanted to see someone in authority. 'There's no one here.' Alec and I intervened to stop a bad situation from getting worse. The Indian was avoiding looking us in the face. I tried to explain why we wanted to come in. We were looking for a man called Ramón. 'We don't want gringos in here.'

I was under the impression that 'gringos' meant North Americans, so I vigorously explained that the term did not apply, I was not a gringo, I was from England. Later, of course, I found out that 'gringos' includes Europeans, but my ignorance was a distinct advantage. The Indian did not know what England was, and let us in, stone-faced.

The taxi-driver and Alec were both eager to find someone who looked official, but I wanted to talk to the Indian. With Alec interpreting into Spanish, I explained that we had come directly from the Lost City. Did he know it? 'Yes, I have a farm there.' This was news. Did that mean that it was not wholly abandoned? 'It is near there. Very near.' I was a film-maker interested in the Lost City and wanted to speak with the Kogi. 'I am Kogi.'

Alec and the driver looked suspicious. I explained my idea, the reason why I had come. Did he think I could put this idea to the Kogi Mamas? He shook his head. No. The Kogi Mamas would not be interested. Who else is here? Only the cook. He turned away. In the whole conversation, he had never looked at my face.

The cook emerged from the office block, and I explained again why I was there. It was Sunday, could I come back tomorrow? No, I was leaving for Bogota immediately. Well, today is Sunday, so the Director is at home ... In a few minutes, the taxi-driver had the address and we had travelled a few blocks to a quiet residential street, where Amparo Jiménez Luque, the Director of the Ministry of the Interior

Office for Indian Affairs for the provinces of Magdalena and Guajira, Sierra Nevada de Santa Marta, had just finished lunch with her parents.

On the way, I worried about the bad impression we had made on the Indian. Alec was full of reassurance. He had been too acculturated, with his shoes and watch, he spoke Spanish too well, his clothes were too clean and his hat too stylish – he was probably not a Kogi at all. He was a city Indian, a man of no consequence. But I had an uneasy feeling that nothing was inconsequential around the Sierra. We had to be very careful.

This time Alec was under strict instructions to translate exactly, without any interpretation of his own, and the taxi-driver was to stay well clear. If anything went wrong now, I would know that it was entirely my fault.

The woman who came to meet me looked about forty, compact and strong with a long, serious face. She looked at me very directly, and listened intently as I spoke.

I had, as usual, no idea who I was speaking to. Of all the tough, determined people I would meet in Colombia, Amparo is the toughest and most determined. Like many thinking people who had grown up in the 1950s and 1960s, she had become politically radical as a student. These were the savage final decades of *La Violencia*, the hundred-year-old civil war between Liberals and Conservatives in which some quarter of a million people were killed for their political opinions. The state, weak and corrupt, had nothing to offer its citizens; it could not provide economic help to the poor, or justice, or fair treatment from the police. Castro's emergence in Cuba seemed to offer hope of a revolution that would end violence and injustice, and offer a future to the poor.

Amparo was one of many thousands who as students shared that hope, and the ideal of social justice still burns fiercely in her. When, by a stroke of chance, she was offered her present job she knew virtually nothing about Indians but she learned fast and recognised that here was a cause to which she could and should devote herself.

She has made many enemies. Hardly a week goes by without some intrigue to remove her, or some denunciation against her to the government or to a gang of ideological bandits, but at the time of writing this she is still holding grimly on to her place and her mountain. The Kogis are her responsibility, and she fights for them as a tigress is supposed to defend its cubs. When she was appointed to the job she went up the mountain as the emissary of the government in Bogota and she offered them all her energy in their support. The Kogi looked at her, liked what they saw, and decided that here, perhaps, they had a friend in the world of the Younger Brothers. Amparo is trusted as no other outsider is trusted by the Kogi. And Amparo would fight anyone, including the government that employs her, who would do them harm.

At the time, I knew nothing of this. I explained simply that I thought it possible that the Kogi Mamas might want to speak to the outside world. Perhaps they might see it as a way of allowing the Younger Brother in without having to tolerate tourism. Perhaps they might feel that they needed something from outside, and this would be a way of communicating. Perhaps they might be prepared to explain their own culture and the meaning of the archaeological sites, and offer that as a substitute for allowing in an endless stream of researchers. For surely there must be pressure for tourism and for academic research!

And I had heard a story that the Kogi believed that their days were numbered. Perhaps they might feel that they should pass on some of their knowledge before it is too late.

The main point was that this would be their film, made in collaboration with me. I did not want to make a film *about* the Kogi, I wanted to make a film with them. They would decide its message, and I would help them turn that into a television programme. Could Amparo find a way of passing this suggestion to the Mamas? I would not want to meet them myself unless they had already heard the proposal, and invited me in.

Amparo's reply astonished me. Many television companies had come — from Europe, from North America, from Japan – wanting to film the Kogi. All had sought her help, for without her permission no cameras could go into the Sierra. And she had turned them all down, until today. But this was different. This was the first time anyone had proposed a collaboration with the Kogi – not to make a film about them, but to make a film with them. Yes, it was a good idea. She would support it. Of course, she did not know what the Mamas would say. But she would ask them. Yes.

Of course, there would be a language problem. She herself spoke no Kogi, and she did not know of any Colombian who had learned the language. But Ramón – his name was Ramón Gil – would be able to translate. Ramón, apparently, was a Kogi with fluent Spanish. She would arrange for Ramón to translate my proposal, and tell me the Mamas' reply.

My day in the Sierra had ended well.

Professor Reichel-Dolmatoff

I went back to Bogota, wanting now to talk to the Reichel-Dolmatoffs, the people who had studied the Kogi and could help me understand how they think. But they were not at home, and I did not have time to go to find them. The film crew had arrived for the project I was there to work on, the Spanish Armada. There was a small technical problem with the filming permission – somehow Colombian bureaucracy had snarled up – but we managed to find a way round it. I never quite understood what happened, but we were in, and the Museo del Oro laid on a wonderful supply of objects for us to film.

We then had to film the spots I had reconnoitred in Cartagena, but by now Avianca, the airline, was on strike. We would have to drive 800 miles up the Andes. This seemed an awful prospect, until I discovered that it would give me a chance to meet the Reichel-Dolmatoffs after all. They were in Villa de Leyva, about 100 miles from Bogota, and close to the road north.

Villa de Leyva is high above the main road, in an arid region where many dinosaur bones have been found and several Westerns filmed. It looks like a stage set. Built in 1572 as a retreat for the Viceroy, it is a perfectly preserved colonial town of pure white buildings with a huge open square, the biggest in the country. Just off the square is the large, low old house where the professor was living.

Geraldo Reichel-Dolmatoff is the great figure of Colombian anthropology. He did pioneering field-work all over the country and became an aristocrat of social science. Wearing a white pith helmet and blazer, setting up a formal table each day for tea in the jungle, he and his wife Alicia studied the archaeology and the people of the Sierra. Virtually everything known about the Kogi came from that work.

Alicia had given up her academic career many years ago to raise their children and support him.

We were greeted courteously, and sat in the courtyard of the house, in the shade of the veranda, while Alicia arranged for tea and biscuits, and I explained what I wanted, and what I had done so far. Reichel was not impressed, and had never heard of Amparo. The Kogi would be impossible to film, even if they let me in. He himself had laboured under terrible difficulties there. So far as I was aware, his main informants had been young men, and he did not seem to have been allowed full access to the Kogi world, but I was surprised to learn how hard they had made things for him.

'They do everything at night: they never speak in the daytime. Inside the houses, lying in hammocks, in the dark – that is when they talk. And you cannot understand them half of the time; they speak with a mouthful of coca leaves, and they mumble. That is why no one has been able to learn their language. Some of them speak Spanish, but very badly. I had to make notes by torchlight, lying in a hammock, and hardly able to understand what was being said to me. You can't make a film out of that.'

Reichel was a tall, well built man with white hair and a neat white moustache. Everything about him was precise: his manners, his dark blazer, his clipped, highly elocuted, immaculate English. I tried to imagine him making notes in a hammock. Presumably the torch would have been in his mouth, so that he would not have been able to speak and make notes simultaneously. This would not have been a very happy time for him.

There was, he assured me, nothing to film. This was a people with no visual art: their whole culture was one of pure intellect. He told me of one occasion when he had asked if they had carved images of animals. 'Oh yes,' he was told, 'we have a huge carved stone jaguar.' Enthusiastic to see it, he was taken on a tough four-day walk over the mountain. Eventually they stopped near a large black rock. He looked around. 'Where is the jaguar?' 'Here, don't you see? Don't you see its eye?' Reichel peered at an insignificant mark on the shapeless black rock. 'Oh yes. Yes. I see.' I did not like to ask whether the Kogi had a sense of humour, but I was certainly getting the impression they had not given him an easy time. Whenever he approached, he said, people had stopped talking, stopped working. Why didn't I film the

Arhuacos? They are much more approachable.

But surely, I said, the Arhuacos are more acculturated, more affected by the outside world? It is the Kogi who keep their culture intact, undamaged. It is the Kogi who can show us what the Lost City means. Yes, he agreed. But I would fail.

Still, if I wanted to try, he could give me some advice. It is important to take the right presents. Take sea-shells, for their poporos. They have been cut off from the sea. And go in the right frame of mind. Do not think that you are visiting some poor simple people who need our protection and help. The only thing they need from us is medicine, and to be left alone.

We parted on friendly terms, and I promised to stay in touch and ask for further help as things developed. Reichel had convinced me that the Kogi were indeed very special people. He himself was convinced that they have a depth of understanding from which we have much to learn. But why had he never heard of Amparo? Perhaps she was not, after all, in real contact with the Kogi. I resolved that when I got back to London I should try some other leads.

The invitation

I had picked up one other name: Javier Rodríguez, a linguistic anthropologist, was supposed to be working on the Kogi side of the mountain. Apparently he was once a Jesuit priest, a missionary, working in the Sierra among the Arhuacos. But in 1973 the Arhuacos threw out the missionaries: after listening to them for four hundred years, they had come to the conclusion that the missionaries' information was wrong and told them to go. Javier preferred the Arhuacos to the priesthood, gave up his vocation, and stayed. Obviously I would need someone who spoke Kogi: if he was really working among them now, he might be just the man.

I also met a Colombian film-maker in London, Patricia Castaño, who told me about an architect-turned-explorer, Bernardo Valderrama. Valderrama knew the Sierra better than anyone; Valderrama had been on the original archaeological expedition to the Lost City; Valderrama knew sites and cities that no one else had ever seen. Both

Valderrama and Rodríguez were willing to help.

I sent them letters to take to the Mamas, and photographs of myself. I was told that these were to be used for divination, when the Mamas consulted their ancestors to decide what to do. And then I received a message from Amparo. 'I have spoken with the Mamas. They say they are ready to work with you. You must come.'

3

Travelling to the Heart of the World

I returned to Colombia exactly a year after my first visit. Once more I went as the Spanish had gone, beginning my journey in Hispaniola. But this time I came from the other end of the island, from Haiti. Last time I had been following the trail of gold; now I was looking at the spirit world.

The Spanish found gold in Hispaniola, and stripped it away, and killed the inhabitants. The French found rich agricultural land, and shipped in African slaves to work plantations there. The largest and most profitable slave plantations in the world, two hundred years ago, were in Haiti. In the eighteenth century this was the richest colony of all, richer even than India. It produced sugar and coffee on a scale large enough to supply the whole of France.

Europeans were civilised people. The Spanish were Christians, and they brought the message of salvation to the people they killed. The French were philosophers of Enlightenment, and they brought the message of Liberty to the people they enslaved. I was visiting Haiti to explore the meaning of that message, on the two hundredth anniversary of the French Revolution.

Slavery was not abolished by the French government until Robespierre was at the height of his power and the Jacobins of Paris were at war with the 'moderate' revolutionaries of the provinces – the period called 'The Terror'. But by then, the slaves had broken their own chains. Haiti was created by a huge slave revolt, and, unlike the French, the Haitians were not reconquered by the armies of the ancien régime.

In fact Napoleon tried to invade Haiti and reimpose slavery, but failed. His army was confronted by a people bound together by a new religion, which was forged in the fire of the Haitian revolution out of materials drawn from the utterly different worlds of West African tribal ritual and French political argument. This bizarre alloy, which has proved indestructible, is called Voodoo. I wanted to illuminate the passion of the Terror with the fires of Voodoo.

We arrived in Port-au-Prince in the early evening, passing through a huge slum of decaying buildings, dirt roads, tense crowds and groups gathered round tables covered with candles. There were no shops in the normal sense: only stalls and booths. The driver assured us that the city had settled down a lot in the last few weeks – 'not many shootings' – but everyone was waiting for the next explosion of violence.

We were to stay in the Hotel Splendid, a small palace with pillared porticoes, sweeping stairways and a huge panelled dining-room. This was the height of the tourist season throughout the Caribbean, but we were utterly alone in there.

The hotel was owned by a German who had come to the island in 1940, and who was a collector of local paintings. These were exuberant, colourful, often primitive and frequently depicting a Haiti which only exists in the memory: a Haiti of tropical lushness, dense jungle and rich animal life. The hotel had its own well, but for most of the population there was neither clean water nor electric power. Haiti is the poorest country in the western hemisphere, and its poverty is all the greater because it is thoroughly westernised. More densely populated than the Netherlands, its people have consumed the land, totally deforesting the hills. They have little hope of feeding themselves from their own agriculture. They flock to Port-au-Prince, where there is nothing but the hope of a shack, a little rice, and water from a gutter.

Political turbulence and AIDS have smashed Haiti's tourist trade, its last remaining source of income. The Club Méditerranée on the northern coast has closed and during our stay in Haiti we did not see another visitor from outside.

Haiti had been ruled for years by the grim figure of François Duvalier, 'Papa Doc', a black man in a black suit with a black Homburg and a black heart. Papa Doc had twisted the dark side of Voodoo into a system of tyranny: he was Baron Samedi, the frock-coated master of death. He encouraged stories that his army of thugs, the Ton-Ton Macoutes, were zombies, corpses raised from their graves and reanimated with spirits under Baron Samedi's control.

Papa Doc had been succeeded by Baby Doc, who lacked the menacing charisma of his father, and who was swept aside by the military. The Haitians, who are proud of their history as a free people, celebrated the dawn of democratic opportunity with vigour. But the promised elections had been aborted while I was in Santo Domingo, and now General Prosper Avril was trying to hold on to power through the army.

The army was divided and sporadically fighting itself, unit against unit, while the civilian population would occasionally spot a member of the disbanded Ton-Ton Macoutes and prove, with the aid of a little paraffin and a box of matches, that the spirit inside him could be released and his body restored to its status as a corpse.

As a starting-point for a journey to the Kogi, Haiti was ideal: these are two worlds which are polar opposites. Haiti, reduced from wealth to wretchedness, represents the most absolute failure of European colonisation. And since this is where Columbus first established Spanish power in the New World, this island is part of the Kogi's history too.

Columbus did not go to the Sierra, but for the Kogi every conquistador was Columbus. Columbus, to them, is not simply the name of a man. It is a role, like Caesar. Every galleon that carried a cross on its sail, bearing priests and gold-fever, was manned by Columbus.

A few years ago, archaeologists discovered the site of Columbus's original settlement at Cap Haiti, close to the desolate site of the failed Club Méditerranée. It was excavated by North Americans from Florida, and then a State Visit was arranged for the President of France.

Baby Doc sent out the order to his provincial governor to make the site clean and tidy for this official trip, and his order was promptly obeyed. When the helicopter carrying Baby Doc and the French President landed, it came down on a large area of tarmac. The site had been bulldozed, flattened, and covered. It was very tidy indeed. When the news reached Florida, the archaeologist in charge of the project was struck dumb for a fortnight.

Haiti's revolution against slavery began with a Voodoo ceremony, the ceremony of Bois Caiman, 'The Crocodile Wood'. I was there to hunt out the remnants of that ceremony. I had begun my preparations for this trip by visiting Haitians in Paris, *émigrés* who were generous with their help and with introductions. They were concerned that I should understand that Voodoo is more than a folk cult for the poor: it is the very centre of Haitian culture. I did not know it then, but it was also to be my introduction to a knowledge shared between Africa and America, knowledge that the world is a single body of spirit.

Voodoo

We drove out through the crowded city, with its dense jams of brilliantly-painted buses, on past scrub-like plantations with lines of people washing themselves and their clothes in the ditch water at the roadside, until we reached a village of single-storey houses. The temple compound was in the centre of the village: a long, low building containing the shrines, and at one end, at right angles to it, the temple floor. This was an open veranda about 40 feet square.

There were low walls on the north and south sides of the veranda, and a flat roof over it; the east and west walls rose to the roof. On the west wall was painted Golgotha, the scene of Christ's Crucifixion. From the roof hung rows of brightly coloured paper ribbons, thousands of them, about 6 inches long, and from a small square green pedestal in the centre of the floor rose a red pillar.

The priest was a small, thin, middle-aged man, wearing a shabby suit and collarless shirt. He seemed quite happy for me to film the night's festivities. As darkness fell, a huge fire was lit in the yard in front of the temple. Large men with bull-whips guarded it, pouring on paraffin and cracking their whips to keep away evil spirits. They were stripped to the waist, and their black skin glistened with sweat in the light of the flames.

On the floor, an elaborate painting was being constructed with coloured sands. While the drums beat out their constant, rapid throb, a carpet of images began to creep over the veranda. This was the gateway to the spirit world: the elaborate doorway, with locks and keys, that would allow ancestral spirits, those of the place and those that had come with the transported slaves from Africa, to participate in the dance.

It was a laborious process, taking several hours. And then, when it was complete, matting was laid over it. The dance floor was ready.

Now the priest and his acolytes, a band of women with embroidered blue skirts and red headscarves, emerged from the temple in a dancing procession. The priest carried a huge cross studded with burning candles, and on either side were flag-bearers, with colourful, decorated banners carrying symbols of the spirit-gods. The women, representing the slaves they were descended from, carried sacks of maize on their heads. Barefoot, they surged back and forth around the fire to the pulsing rhythm of the drums. There were now two or three hundred villagers here; rum was being passed around, and everyone was fully immersed in the drama. The night was hot: the fire was ferocious: the drums, hypnotically throbbing hour after hour, had worked their way into everyone's bones.

The procession moved on to the dance floor. And now everyone joined in the dance, the priest standing on the central pedestal, filling his mouth with a mixture of rum and herbs in great swigs from a bottle, and spraying the dancers from his mouth. At one end of the floor was a barrel into which the maize was poured, and pairs of people took it in turns to crush the grain with a huge pestle while the dance went on. It was a swaying, awkward dance: the dance of people with manacled feet.

And then, as the night went on, the dance progressed: the invisible shackles were broken, the dancers became free. Work was transformed from oppression into liberty. The acolytes began to be taken over by spirits which used their bodies to join in the dance. Some of these spirits are kept in bottles in the temple shrine, and when the acolytes die they can expect their own souls to be guarded, in a used rum or Coca-Cola bottle, in the care of the priest.

Voodoo has no concept of sacred or profane, no sense of holiness. A Voodoo shrine is bizarre in the extreme: a human skull may be surrounded by bottle-tops, plastic dolls, a gaily-coloured toddler's bicycle, labels and trinkets. It dawned on me that here all life and all death are seen as belonging together in a single seamless web, which is the spirit world, ultimate reality. In normal life, as we go about our daily business, we are detached from this web, but through the trance induced by drumming, dancing, drinking, chanting, human beings can re-enter the real world.

The night was thick with the visceral energy of the ritual, a ritual designed to bypass the intellect and seize the body. By the time I came to leave, the priest had gone, his body inhabited by a powerful spirit that could not quite work his eyes, or keep his head from lolling. But it had the strength to accept my donation to the temple, and see me on my way with an assurance that I would return. I hope that it was right.

Gonavindua Tairona

I said goodbye to my film crew and flew on to Bogota, the drums still throbbing in my head. As soon as I arrived, I crumbled: the combination of altitude, a catastrophic meal on a Panamanian aircraft and culture shock sent my stomach into spasms. Twenty-four hours recovering in the cool sheets of the Charleston Hotel was absolutely necessary.

Alec had a terrible time getting hold of a helicopter, but he eventually succeeded and I flew up to Santa Marta. I was accompanied by an anthropologist, Felicity Nock, who had studied Andean textile work and was working on anthropological films for the BBC. She was my Spanish interpreter and anthropological advisor.

Something strange was obviously happening among the Kogi. All three contacts, Amparo, Javier and Bernardo, had gone into a different part of the Sierra, and each had come back with the same reply – an invitation. I had been working on the assumption that this was a fragmented society, in which different villages would have different reactions, but there seemed to be a common purpose.

Gradually I pieced together the story. Apparently the Mamas had decided that a major crisis is approaching, which threatens the survival of the planet. They had made a policy decision to speak to the Younger Brother, and my message arrived at the moment when they were looking for a way of carrying out this policy.

I was now going to visit all three areas, and see whether any of them would actually work with me. The first trip would be Amparo's. Felicity and I went to the Casa Indígena to find out what was going to happen.

We were met by a small committee: Amparo, two Indians and two Samarios. I recognised one of the Indians at once: he was the man who had treated me with such suspicion a year ago. I was now formally introduced to Ramón Gil. The other was called Adalberto.

Felicity had tried to prepare me for the shock of going among indigenous people, warning me not to react visibly to disease and premature old age, brought on by poverty and deprivation. I had composed myself accordingly, and now I was confronted by two people who were plainly in much better condition than I. Ramón, dressed as he had been a year ago, was lithe and alert, and Adalberto was tall, well muscled and had a healthy bloom to his skin. He was wearing a white toga-like garment, with a woven red stripe and a woven belt over white cotton trousers like Ramón's. His black, curly hair poured down to his shoulders from a hat shaped as a flat-topped cone – almost a helmet – also woven from white cotton. The pure white of his hat, the black of his superb hair, and his glowing dark face created an impressive picture.

Adalberto is an Arhuaco. He too had a poporo – Asario, Arhuaco and Kogi, the three peoples of the Sierra, share a common culture – but he spoke no Kogi and moved and looked physically more like a dark-skinned European.

The atmosphere was tense and awkward. Neither Indian would look at my face. The other people there were Carlos, a sturdy *costeño* who worked at the Casa Indígena, and Margarita, his wife, a smartly turned-out young lady in blouse, skirt and court shoes who is in fact Adalberto's sister. Carlos had grown up in Minca, a town just behind Santa Marta in the Sierran foothills, yet like many *costeños* had reached adulthood without even knowing that any Indians lived in the mountain. He had originally come to work in the Casa Indígena without understanding what it was. Margarita, on the other hand, was the daughter of an Arhuaco Mama, and had left the Sierra to become fully integrated in Santa Marta. She had come to the Casa Indígena as just one more secretarial job. But she had now been drawn back to her roots, while Carlos had learned about them for the first time and become enchanted. They are a delightful couple, and very protective of the Kogi. They were deeply suspicious of me.

I explained that I did not come with any plan of a film. I would simply ask the Mamas if they wanted to work with me on a film about themselves, if they wanted to use this way of speaking to the Younger Brothers. I would consult, I would listen, I did not want to force myself where I was not wanted. Gradually, the atmosphere relaxed. And gradually I began to learn what had been happening.

Ramón was the Cabildo Gobernadór – the Governing Councillor – of an organisation called Gonavindua Tairona, a legally constituted body which the Mamas wanted to use as a channel of communication with the outside world. The Arhuacos had already established such an organisation, and it had been effective in giving them a political presence in Colombia. That was the key to their successful expulsion of the missionaries, and to the progress they were making in obtaining funds for various projects.

The Kogi, having much less to do with outsiders, had to find people with the expertise to organise this on their behalf. So the Mamas had found Adalberto, who had been involved in the Arhuaco organisation. And they had found Ramón.

Ramón is not a full-blooded Kogi. His mother was Kogi, his father was a Mama of the Asarios. So was his grandfather. He had grown up as an Asario, in a community with extensive contact with the world of Santa Marta, speaking a little Spanish, good Asario, and having learned Kogi from his mother. Ramón has a quick mind and he is a good linguist. He had a reputation as a political activist, taking a leading role in attempts to turn back the tide of peasant infiltration and land-seizure in the Sierra. His engagement in this made him many enemies: settlers tried to kill him and his brother, who followed a different route into political action and is a member of a guerilla army, became his mortal enemy. But any kind of public stance makes you enemies in Colombia, and Ramón enjoyed the sense of being involved in big issues, and even the danger.

Once the Kogi Mamas had decided to speak to the outside world, they identified Ramón as their most important tool. He was summoned, and told that great and unusual powers, held by his grandfather, had not been passed to his father but were now in their safe keeping. These they would give to him, but first he must be prepared for the great work that lay before him.

For fourteen months, Ramón was spiritually prepared for his task. During that time he was not allowed to live with his wife or have any sexual contact – a considerable strain on both of them. He was being given a crash course in Kogi culture, geared to the specific task of turning him into a cultural interpreter. He had to understand enough of

Kogi wisdom to find metaphors that the Younger Brother could understand. They also sent him to Santa Marta to learn to speak Spanish properly.

'You ask "What is the Law of the Mother?" ' There is a long pause for thought. 'How can I explain? Put the brakes on. That is the Law of the Mother. Put the brakes on your tongue, on your mind, on your sex. That way, you save your gasoline, and your car will go a long way.' I was going to have reason to be grateful to Ramón, because he was the one person who could really move between our two utterly different mental worlds, and build conceptual bridges.

I was, and remain, acutely conscious of the depth of the chasm which separates my way of understanding the world from the Kogi's. The secret powers which were ultimately vouchsafed to Ramón make no sense in our world: the power to open hills, and the power to levitate. Somehow ideas like this are easier for us to cope with in more 'primitive' societies, where they are part of the stock-in-trade of people who we, at various times, have called witch-doctors, medicine-men and shamans. But the Kogi are very sophisticated. They believe in the power of the mind, intelligent spirit, as the underpinning of the world, and the gifts handed over to Ramón are not to be understood as tricks or delusions. They have meaning, but not the simple meaning that springs to the Younger Brother's mind and makes him want to say 'Show me!'

They were most anxious to teach me about Gonavindua Tairona, because it was important that I should work through this organisation. The contacts I had made through Javier and Bernardo were dangerous for the Kogi, because these involved me in a process of dealing separately with different communities. I might thus become the cause of a fragmentation of the Kogi world, and that could be fatal. The only chance, in their view, for the Kogi to sustain their civilisation while opening up new outside contacts was for those contacts to be passed through a single channel, ultimately controlled by the Mamas.

I assured them that I was very happy to work through Gonavindua Tairona – in fact it was exactly what I needed. I would still want to make the visits arranged by Javier and Bernardo, but I would want Ramón to come with me.

So it was agreed that I would be taken to the meeting with the Mamas that had been arranged through Amparo.

Pueblo Viejo

Five of us made the trip: Amparo, Ramón, Adalberto, Felicity and myself. The helicopter flew a careful route, intended to avoid over-flying cocaine ranches, and on the way Ramón pointed out a clearing where he lived. There stood two circular thatched huts.

Pueblo Viejo, where we landed, was not what I expected. The town is about 3,000 feet above sea level, where the jungle has given way to open wooded grassland, and the stifling heat of the coast has cooled to an easy temperature. This was very different from the Lost City. The morning sun was warm, the sky was clear, the mountain was stunningly beautiful, rising in small peaks and ridges around the town. From the helicopter we could see the drop away to a river on one side, with a timely-constructed log bridge spanning it. The word for such a bridge is *chinchorro*, a hammock. It did look like a wooden hammock.

The town was in two parts. One part was Kogi, a group of some thirty huts, mostly circular but a few square. Generally it is the Arhuacos who build square houses. The other part was plainly 'civil-ised', a small group of breeze-block farm buildings with tin roofs, and one very long single-storey building. This belonged to the nuns, missionaries. We landed in a field next to the nuns.

A group of Kogi were waiting around the landing area, and more appeared when we had touched down. The Kogi do not care for helicopters; they regard them as pollutants, irritations, part of that class of objects which has no place in the Sierra. They call all our gadgets 'moths', and believe that it is part of the Law of the Mother that such things should be kept away. But they were prepared to make an exception for this occasion.

The Kogi men were wearing white tunics and trousers, like Ramón, and were barefoot. All were carrying poporos, and wearing woven bags, *mochilas*, slung across their chests. The women wore a single, flowing white garment, bound round at the waist, and necklaces of red beads. All of them had small children or babies, and most of them looked pregnant.

Ramón greeted the men formally. Instead of a handshake, the Kogi greeting is to transfer some coca leaves from your *mochila* to the other person's while saying, usually silently, words to the effect of 'May each leaf be a blessing.' Silent speech is commonplace among them, and the film crew and I were to be constantly confused by it. It does make it very hard for a Younger Brother to know what is going on.

I was introduced to a few of the Kogi men, in particular to the Cacique Mama and the Jefe Mayor of a town called San Miguel. San Miguel is a major political and religious centre, so these were plainly important men. Everyone was introduced with Spanish names, and all towns were referred to in the same way. There are Kogi names, of course, but I was not to use them. Those names were generally kept private, and I was eventually asked not even to reveal the locations of Kogi communities which I have visited. That is why this book does not contain a detailed map of the Kogi world.

Felicity and I were introduced as 'The BBC'. Whatever 'The BBC' meant, we were it. I had been told that it was a distinct advantage that we were of different sexes – a balance of gender is fundamental to the Kogi understanding of the world, and it would be taken as a good sign that 'The BBC' was both male and female. But we were also very puzzling. Felicity was not my woman, I was not her man. No one asked directly about this odd union, but it was clear that everyone would like to know. And we wanted to know who they were, too.

Jefe Mayor, 'Great Chief', seems a clear enough designation, but what was a Cacique Mama? Cacique means 'chieftain', 'overlord': the gilded man of Guatavita, El Dorado, was a newly-appointed cacique. Was this man such a figure? He was small among the small: most Kogi are only about 5 feet tall, and the Cacique Mama was smaller. His face was wrinkled, his nose stubby and he generally reminded me of ET. Surprisingly, he had a thick greying moustache, though there was no sign of a beard. On his head was a pointed cap like a gnome, and his eyes glittered. His *mochila* was unlike any other: instead of plain bands of white and brown, it was brightly decorated with red and yellow symbols. He was called Mama Valencia.

Outwardly, the brilliant *mochila* and the goblin hat were the only signs of his authority; the Jefe Mayor, Juan Jacinto, had even less to mark him out. These are people without outward show: Ramón had used an expression I had once heard used by the Amish, the dour fundamentalist Pennsylvania Dutch community which does not use metal buttons and regards chrome fenders as sinful – 'We are a plain people'. The Jefe Mayor's long face and delicate, restrained gestures had an aristocratic quality, but he dressed exactly like everyone else, in plain, pure white. Only a narrow black striped band woven into the side of his tunic signified his lineage: it was a simple heraldic device, a South American tartan.

There were Younger Brothers here too: two settlers were working with some mules, and there were three nuns and a medical orderly called Andrés. This was a frontier, a meeting place of two worlds.

Andrés had been sent up here by the government. Colombia forces a compulsory service on medical students, sending them to remote spots where they have to live with minimal support and no money whatever. The Colombian government tends to have good intentions which it cannot back up with money or organisation. Andrés was completely broke and out of most medicines. He had to leave for a few days, and asked if he could travel out in the helicopter. In exchange, he offered accommodation in the medical post.

The nuns also offered accommodation: in fact they had our rucksacks carried through to rooms in the mission. But I was constantly nervous about the implications of every act I performed up here, and decided to move into the medical post instead. I was happy, though, to accept the nuns' offer of refreshment. This was a very good idea, as it introduced me to lulu juice, which is as close as I can imagine to nectar, the drink of the gods.

A juice sharp as grapefruit but as sweet as fruit squash, utterly refreshing and capable of truly satisfying a thirst, so that no matter how thirsty you were to begin with, you would stop long before you were full and say, 'I have had enough.' I had expected to find something of Paradise in the Sierra, and it had begun.

The nuns brought me lulus from the trees, small fruit like tangerines or Israeli sharon fruits, which when opened revealed a dense mass of seeds like a miniature pomegranate. These seeds, unlike the pomegranate's, are pulpy: you can make lulu juice with your bare hands. It hardly lasts at all – two days, and then it becomes undrinkable.

Andrés took me up to the medical post where he introduced me to his medical assistant, a Kogi called Arregoce. Arregoce would look after us in here, I was assured. There was the luxury of a tap and a flushing toilet, with water being fed by hosepipe from a stream in the hill above the building. That was the theory, but in fact the tap was dry, and Arregoce went off to hunt for the break in the hose. Meanwhile Andrés warned me about the snakes. 'We have every species of snake here except the cobra.' Snakes were ever the trouble in Paradise. Most of the victims are women, working in the gardens, and children.

There was ample room for Amparo, Felicity and myself to set up hammocks in the medical post. Never having been in a hammock before, I had been as nervous about this as about anything else, and friends had warned me how badly the back suffers if you sleep longways like a banana. The trick, I had been told, is to lie diagonally across it. I found it the most comfortable and relaxing position imaginable.

I had arrived feeling less than wonderful. My illness in Bogota had left me weak and suffering from a steady ache in one kidney. I thought it possible that a kidney stone might be about to launch its attack. I was also affected by the sudden switches in altitude. When I had got out of the helicopter my pulse had been racing and I had found it hard to catch my breath. Now the hammock, the lulu juice and the benevolent climate were beginning to restore me. Eventually I would learn from the Kogi the idea that physical well-being is a state of harmony with the world, and I would not find that difficult to understand. I felt as though I was in a place that was good for me. I was not passively relaxed – my antennae were fully extended, trying to gauge the feelings of the people around me – but a deep contentment was growing.

The ceremonial house

We went down to the village for Amparo to sort out some official business. This was to be done in one of the Kogi's few square houses, a large mud-walled building with a thatched roof. Like most Kogi buildings it had no windows, and it had two doors opposite each other. The floor was pounded earth, the roof was held up by stout wooden poles which acted as hammock supports.

There were three hammocks slung there. One was occupied by Mama Valencia and one by a man called Manuelito, who was not at all well. Manuelito had influenza and a blinding headache, and wanted sympathy and aspirins. I tried to grasp what was going on, but I was finding it all very difficult. I had never been in such a place before. And I knew that every move I made, every gesture, was being watched.

Body-language among the Kogi is a real language. They read a man like a book, because every physical act is writing in the air. Just as a graphologist knows that handwriting tells the story of the whole person, so the Kogi know that the slightest bodily movement is shaped by attitudes, experiences and character. A standard Kogi response to 'How are you?' is 'I am well seated'. The speaker may be walking along at the time. What he means is that he is at ease in his proper place, in balance and harmony with the world. That is how a man should be.

I knew enough of the Kogi to have picked up a few fragments of how they read body-language: the significance, for example, of crossing one's legs, which is a white man's act indicating tension, a slight withdrawal, perhaps a lack of frankness. I knew enough, in short, to know that there was nothing I could deliberately do to create a good impression. I did not know how to behave, how to stand, how to sit, where to walk. I decided that the Kogi would have to take me as I come. I would just have to relax and leave them to make what judgment they might.

We left Mama Valencia and Manuelito, and Ramón took me to a large circular building with walls of woven palm. This was the men's house, the ceremonial house. In Kogi it is called *nuhue*, the world-house. I had seen the foundations of such buildings in the Lost City: here the Lost City still stood and functioned, albeit without the large ceremonial platforms, and in a much more comfortable environment. Here debate goes on all night, night after night, without sleep. With the endless stamina that comes from constant coca-chewing and 'eating the poporo', issues are pursued exhaustively.

During the afternoon, a cloud had slowly come down the mountain and settled low over the town. It was so low that the tops of the houses were inside the cloud. The lumps and curves of the mountain seemed to blend with the village. One nearby ridge in particular, very close to the village, echoed the form of the houses.

There were four fires, one in each quarter of the circular floor. A few men were sitting around the fires, and some were lying in hammocks. The central passageway between the doors was clear, and on either side of it were long benches. The top of the thatched roof was entirely hidden in smoke. In fact the smoke inside exactly mirrored the cloud that clung to the outside.

Ramón told me that the mountains were the original ceremonial houses. Now I began to understand what was meant by the power to open mountains. If Ramón had been identified as the master of and been taught how to use that power, the power to link reality and the spirit world together and to create a world-house, a place which is both of this world and other worlds, then his words would carry great weight here. And Ramón was going to act as my interpreter.

He explained that here the higher worlds were represented: the Kogi universe rises through lower worlds until you reach our level, the ninth world. Beneath us, in the world of spirit, the ceremonial house is mirrored upside down. Our world is not only the highest of the nine lower worlds: it is the lowest of the nine upper worlds. The *nuhue* portrays the upper worlds as bands around the inside of the roof. Ramón called them planets, as part of his attempt to make me understand, but I do not think the Kogi identify them with lights in the sky. They are not seen with the eyes.

The whole universe, of upper and lower worlds, is contained in this womb-like enclosure, with humanity at the centre, between birth and death.

It was extraordinarily comfortable in there. This was where the men would sleep and talk when they were in town, sitting with their poporos constantly working, leaving their women and children in the family's town house. The smell of wood smoke, the relaxed atmosphere, were all very attractive.

But I had to go back to the medical centre to wait. The meeting would be held the next day, and we would be summoned.

Organisation of the town

The nuns, as isolated from the outside world as the Kogi, were living in a mission that had been established in the eighteenth century. At that time it was called San Antonio de Yucal. It was so ineffectual that in 1787 the missionary there could only suggest forcibly resettling the Indians on the coast. Every time their ceremonial houses were burned down, they simply rebuilt them!* A century later a fire destroyed the

---

* Reichel-Dolmatoff, 1953, pp. 60–1

whole town (whether this was a further effort at conversion is not recorded), and the Kogi moved away to establish a new settlement on the other side of the river. That is still there, and is known simply as San Antonio.

The old site was taken over by Colombian peasants, 'colonos', and it became known as Pueblo Viejo, 'Old Town'. The advance of the colonos was driving the Kogi off the fertile lands which grow cotton, and lately even higher, towards regions where plantains cannot grow and life cannot be self-sufficient.

Ramón had been influential in reversing the tide of encroachment. Amparo had obtained government money to buy out most of the colonos, and Ramón had resettled Kogi in Pueblo Viejo. There were now only a handful of colonos left.

The nuns — there were five of them — had seen all this as a challenge to their own influence. The colonos had been 'their' Christians, and Amparo was helping Indians who have no wish to give up their paganism. The nuns hated Amparo. And the Kogi of San Antonio detested Ramón, because he had moved his own people on to land to which *they* had ancestral claim. The remaining colonos told them that Amparo and Ramón wanted to turn the Kogi into the government's slaves, and they were inclined to believe it. This naturally created an alliance between these Kogi and the nuns. The nuns ran a school, and a number of San Antonio children were attending it. There were no Kogi converts to Christianity, but the nuns offered medicine, and occasional feasts, and would buy coffee for cash, which could be exchanged for machetes, axes and iron cooking pots. There was now an uncomfortable divide between the nuns and San Antonio on the one hand, and Pueblo Viejo on the other.

As with all Kogi towns, Pueblo Viejo is not permanently inhabited. The Kogi are farmers, and they live on their farms. They usually have a number of farms at different altitudes, growing the various crops appropriate to each level. On each farm there are two houses: one for the man, and one for his wife and children. But when the summons goes out they have to move to the family's town house and participate in the business of the meeting.

The Mamas run this world as priests and judges. They are the educated people, masters (and mistresses, for there are female Mamas) of the Law of the Mother. They are specialists; although they have the same core knowledge, they have from childhood developed their own areas of expertise and concern. Thus one Mama may have particular knowledge of a group of birds and animals, another of history, another may be particularly concerned with harmony in the community and so on.

They operate through the *comisarios*, town commissioners whom they appoint, whose tasks are to ensure that roads are maintained, that towns are kept neat and in good repair, and that public order is upheld. These *comisarios* are helped by *cabos*, constables. Perhaps it is easiest to think of the *comisarios* as sheriffs and the *cabos* as their deputies. But they exert an authority which no normal white community has experienced. There is a sense in which the Kogi are like members of an isolated sect which has chosen to hide itself away from the corrupt world and live under the strict regime of its religious leaders.

The object of life for ordinary Kogis is not to achieve personal enlightenment or salvation; it is simply to live, to farm, and to obey the Mamas' guidance in right living. In their search for Spanish terms to describe their society, the Kogi chose to describe the mass of their society as *vasallos*, vassals. There are also secular Lords, such as the Jefe Mayor, but these no longer wield the authority which they must have exerted as warrior chiefs before the conquest. Jefe Mayor is also a Mama, and without that badge of wisdom I doubt whether he would be so significant a figure.

This is entirely a masculine structure of power; women are never *comisarios* or *cabos*. Although there are a few women Mamas, these are necessarily isolated from public life, as the stage on which a Mama performs in public is the *nuhue*, the world-house, which is closed to women. Women do have an assembly house of their own, but that is an enlarged version of a domestic dwelling. It has one door, and is dominated by the single central hearth; women meet in there to talk, sometimes cooking together. The *nuhue* is a much more formal space, where the work is political and deliberately educational. Here the business of the town is carried on alongside a series of lectures – 'giving advice' – by the Mamas, teaching the vassals obedience to the Law and elucidating its meaning. These sessions are compulsory. The *cabos* go round the town with sticks, yelling at men who are tardy in coming. If someone has not come down from his farm, the *cabos* are quite likely to set off in the night and fetch him by main force.

Today, however, the town was filled with an unusual population. There had been no summons to the vassals. Mamas and *comisarios* were gathering from a number of different parts of the Sierra to decide on the film. Amparo had no idea who would come, or what the outcome might be.

Arregoce

The next morning, Arregoce offered to take me and Felicity for a stroll to look around. We climbed the hill behind the medical post. It was very steep, and the early morning sun was hot. Arregoce watched me in amazement. 'You don't know how to walk! Don't you have to walk in your country? In your cars and aeroplanes, don't you walk?'

On the way up, we could look down on San Antonio, a cluster of some forty houses. Visually it had a purity which Pueblo Viejo lacked: there was no trace of colonos, and no mission.

The hill had few trees but there was dense undergrowth, and many snakes. Eventually we reached the summit, which was crowned by Arregoce's house. It stood alone, and his son was there, a child of about eight.

Arregoce spoke Spanish. He had been educated by the nuns and was proud of it: 'My father was an ignorant man. He did not even know how to speak.' This confused me. Generally speaking it was easy to see how the Kogi had retained their culture: they are proud of it. Most Indian societies collapsed not simply because of conquest, but because their individual members, when offered the choice, wanted what the white men could offer: ready-made cloth, metals, guns, alcohol and medicines. The Indians came to doubt the value of their own society, to accept the Christian valuation of it as primitive and backward. This remains true of most indigenous communities today. Very few Indians would reject factory clothing, or a bicycle, or an outboard motor for a canoe. But the Kogi are different. They choose to be who they are.

They see us as primitive and backward, and themselves as the guardians of profound knowledge. They speak of us not as *hermanos menores*, which would simply mean 'younger brothers', but as *hermanitos menores*, a diminutive, 'very little brothers'. They recognise our technological skills, and appreciate the usefulness of some of what we make, but anything which represents a threat to the way in which they live (including our clothing and our transport) is firmly rejected. Arregoce was a puzzle. If he really regarded a man who spoke only Kogi as a man who 'did not know how to speak', what was he doing there? And, come to think of it, why had the nuns never made a convert? And why had I never heard of a Kogi permanently leaving the Sierra?

Perhaps it is just too beautiful to leave. Looking across the river valley, with Pueblo Viejo, San Antonio, and one other Kogi town spread out below, the view was spectacular. The mountains rose sheer all around, the morning light striking patches of jungle and bare rock, wisps of cloud hanging around the peaks.

'It is very beautiful.'

'Yes,' Arregoce replied. 'It is a dream world.'

The meeting

In the afternoon the summons came. We walked down the track to the silent town. The meeting was to be held in the church, a square thatched structure which had been erected in the days when this was San Antonio, and was now only used to store tools and do business with Amparo. It was a place connected with the Younger Brothers, a kind of no-man's land.

The building was full. There were a few benches, but most people were standing. They had been arriving, on foot and on horseback, during the night and morning. I had seen some crossing the river: shining white clothes, shining black horses, red woven harness. Others had walked for two days barefoot over the mountains.

All faces were turned towards me. The elders of the Tairona civilisation, in their white robes, holding their poporos, were waiting for me to speak.

Amparo introduced me, offering assurance that I was an honest and serious person from a highly respected organisation, the BBC. The problem of trust was obviously significant. What did the Kogi know of the Younger Brother, except that he was a conquistador, a robber, a murderer, a stealer of land? They had encountered a few who seemed to be less dangerous – the nuns, Amparo, Andrés – but the majority of these were women. It would be difficult for them to trust a white man. And it was still not at all clear to them what 'The BBC' was. Some clearly formed the view that it was a kin-group of some sort. That would explain why I did not speak Amparo's language.

Speaking was laborious. First I delivered a sentence in English, then Felicity spoke in Spanish, and finally Ramón gave it in Kogi.

I began by trying to explain what a film was. To my amazement, there was an immediate reaction. A film, I was told, was not the truth. The Kogi did not want to be involved with something that was not the truth.

I could not escape the certain instinct that they were talking from some knowledge about movies. I was completely baffled. How did they know about movies?

Later I discovered how. The Mamas exercise their authority through a system of examination. (Since their Spanish tends to draw on the language of the Catholic church, they translate this as 'confession'.) When someone feels unwell, or is troubled by headaches or bad dreams, or has some crisis in his life, he will go to a Mama for help. The Mama will ask him to describe all his experiences over a long period in exact detail, a process which will last for many days. Out of this he hopes to find the key to the problem, the action which has thrown this person out of balance with the world.

The Mamas thus learn everything known to any individual Kogi, and they share this knowledge. They collect all the information they can about the outside world, and one of Ramón's duties, as an emissary in that world, is to keep them informed. If at any time any Kogi has visited Santa Marta – and a few, like Ramón, have been further afield, to Bogota – he may have seen television or even visited a cinema. What one Kogi experiences, all the Mamas learn. They had never seen television or a movie themselves, but they knew very well what I was talking about.

No, I assured them this film would be the truth. It would be a partnership: it would have to be. I knew nothing of them and their world; I would not know what should be said, what should be shown. They would decide what needed to be said, and we would decide together how it should be shown.

Ramón's translation had a rhythm and authority that seemed to go well with my own deliberate pattern of speech, and enhanced it. I just hoped that he was actually conveying what I was saying. Sometimes he could not grasp a concept, and Amparo had to reinterpret Felicity's Spanish, shaping it in a way that made sense to him. As we went on, the mood of the meeting changed and became more positive. When I said that I would consult at every stage with the Mamas, and only work through their organisation, Gonavindua Tairona, there was a mass chant of assent and a rattle of poporo sticks.

I explained that I could see dangers as well as benefits in making a film. It might attract tourists. It would be important to say in the film that people should not come to the Sierra. The Younger Brother should know that the Elder Brothers have retained, alone among the indigenous people of America, the world of their ancestors, and they have done this by cutting themselves off. Their isolation must be respected. Another rattle of assent.

They must decide whether a film is a good idea, and they would decide for reasons which I would not understand. Another rattle. But they should also know what would be involved. We would have to come with our machines. We would have to arrive in helicopters. We would need a generator to make light, and we would need to put lights in the ceremonial house. The camera cannot work in the dark. It would be noisy, there would be many people, they would have to work with the film camera and work to a schedule. If they were going to say yes, they must be prepared to let all this happen. Otherwise it would be better to say no.

Finally, I produced a small domestic video camera and explained the idea of a film image – an eye with a memory, which is not a very good eye and needs bright light to see well. If anyone wanted to see more, he should come outside into the light and take a look.

About two-thirds of the assembly were sufficiently interested to come outside, and I showed them how to use the camera. No one asked any questions: they simply looked through the viewfinder and at a playback of themselves. Some plainly found it amusing, others retained their *gravitas* throughout.

I had finished. The Mamas would talk all night, and in the morning they would go to the mountain top and divine.

At dawn, the Mamas were clearly visible on the hillside opposite.

The mountain top was obviously conceptual. By mid-morning they were back, and we were summoned again. Rows of benches were drawn up, and I was asked if I had any way of making a record of the meeting. I produced a tape recorder, explained what it was, and was told to turn it on.

One after another, the Mamas rose to speak. Their speech was rhythmic, emphatic, heavy with repetition. It sounded almost a different language from that I had been hearing.

> All of those who are present here
> from the community of the Mamas
> made divination up there on the hillside
> with their knowledge.
> They concentrated and analysed.
> They said up there:
> Now we will say to the Younger Brother
> We were the elders.
> We are elders of all,
> with greater knowledge, spiritual and material.
> Serankua tells us
> that he created us
> that he created the earth
> that he made the sky.
> He is called Serankua.
> He made us to care for the creatures, flowers, nature.
>
> Thus it was.
> The Elder Brother was there to protect the earth,
> because the earth,
> it is our Mother, earth.
> Without earth we cannot live.

The idea that the earth is the mother of all life is common throughout Indian societies, in North and South America. But I was deeply impressed by this sense of responsibility. These people truly believe that they were created as the guardians of the world. That establishes the basis of their lives, and of their history. Ramón's translation carried the force and rhythm of the speeches, in Spanish which was hypnotically powerful.

The meeting

All Colombia was Elder Brother
who knew how to dance with his mask,
with his feather,
with his gold,
with his clothing, his habit,
with all his riches of gold.
All, all of Colombia was sacred,
sacred land,
Mother Earth.

After centuries and centuries of years
the Younger Brother passed from the other country,
says the Mama.
Señor Christopher Columbus came to this land
and immediately saw the riches
and killed, shot, many natives.
He took the gold which had been here.
Sacred gold, gold of masks,
all kinds of gold.
They took so much.
So much.
So much.

So the native people who lived close to the shore,
all natives, went.
They ascended up above.
So above they remained without gold.
Almost weak, where there was no food,
they climbed up.
For them the trees were like people.
They did not fell them.
They took little pieces.
There they sowed.
But then the Younger Brother arrived.
Immediately he began to multiply
and went about felling the forests,
and the natives moved a little nearer the mountain tops
with hunger.
Some died from hunger, weakness.

> They had nothing to eat,
> they died.
> But in this time there was no help.
> Not from anyone.
>
> The Mama says: I stayed without gold,
> I remained without anything,
> but with thought strong, profound,
> still esteemed.
> A system.
> 'Let us keep these customs.
> Keep the tradition.
> Let us keep it.'
> We respect the Mother Earth.

The more I came to understand what was being said, the more I realised that here was the key to the survival of the Kogi. Their respect for the earth is a responsibility for it. The Mamas believe that without them the earth would not be cared for. They are not concerned with personal survival, but with the survival of their system, customs, tradition – their knowledge of the world, and how to take care of it. They call this the Law.

The Law has been kept safe by isolation. But now, isolation is not enough.

> Today the water is drying up.
> There's no longer sufficient water,
> so the Mama says.
> Who is at fault?
> The Younger Brother is at fault,
> because he drove me higher up,
> and now he is chopping down the forest,
> he is felling it.
> Who is at fault?
> The fault is with the Younger Brother.
>
> Now he has to open his eyes,
> look to the problem.
> Today he has to help me to clean below,

that there will be animals, plants, nature,
that there will be deep water,
sufficient water,
water.
So that there will be all types of nature.

This, then, was why they wanted to make a film. They had something to say, and this was the way to say it, to reach the Younger Brother. But it was not intended to be a general opening up to the world.

The Mama also says,
the Mamas say,
they don't want other types of people,
or other organisation that comes to work with us,
but only the BBC.
Many have come here,
they say:
I too am government.
I too was sent by Bogota.
I too.
This they do not want.
Only with the BBC.
And the BBC takes on the responsibility
of telling the rest of the world
that something should be done.
They don't want other people to come here
to talk with them
but only your person.

4

Planning

The Mamas had done more than agree to a film: they had commissioned one. We sat down together and I tried, groping, to establish what we could film and how it would tell the story that they wanted. I had now evidently been accepted, and was able to hold some of these conversations more casually, with Ramón's help, in the ceremonial house. They were very practical about the work, and seated on a stool, with the Kogi sitting around the four fires and lying in hammocks, I felt relaxed and at peace.

I explained that the Younger Brother expects not only to be told things but also to see them. This, they said, they had anticipated, and they would expect me to film at archaeological sites, to film dances and the teaching of an initiate and so on. About all this they had already divined. I was impressed by their seriousness, and by the quickness of their intelligence. They had immediately grasped the nature of my work, and the idea of constructing an argument by using a camera. They were also quite clear about the responsibilities which they would bear in making the film, and how they should be divided.

I was surprised to discover that one of their main concerns had been that no harm should come to anyone working on the film, and that had been one of the matters on which they had divined and pondered. I began to trust the Mamas; to trust their judgment and to trust their divinations.

At the end of our discussions they insisted on drawing up a formal specification for the film. Although they do not use writing themselves, they presume we take things more seriously if they are set down on paper. So Amparo had to make a copy of our agreement in Spanish, and then, during the night, all the Mamas and *comisarios* there came out of the ceremonial house to put their thumb-prints to it. One by one they gave their names to be written under the marks, and so we learned who these people were. They came from almost every Kogi community.

Felicity and I took many photographs while we were there, but it was obvious that photography was a strain for them. I assumed that this was because they might believe that in taking their image we were taking something from them. I had heard such stories of other Indian groups. But no, Mama Valencia explained, that was not quite right.

Everything we do is an event not only in the physical world but also in the spirit world. We live in a world shaped in spirit. Every tree, every stone, every river, has a spirit form, invisible to the Younger Brother. This is the world of *aluna*, the world of thought and spirit. *Aluna* embraces intelligence, soul and fertility: it is the stuff of life, the essence of reality. The material world is underpinned, shaped, given life and generative power in *aluna*, and the Mama's work is carried out in *aluna*.

We have no grasp of this. We see only the dream world, the shadow world of materials. That is why we cannot grasp the significance of our actions, or understand their effects.

To take a photograph, like any other activity, is an act in *aluna* as well as in the physical world. In photographing a Mama, I am making him participate in an action both spiritual and material. But my camera was made without thought for its essential structure, and I use it without understanding what I do. The result, said Mama Valencia, is like a blow to his spirit, a punch in the guts of his soul. He was visibly tired by the repeated clicks of the shutter.

I was worried by the implications of this for a filming schedule, but I was told not to worry. The Mamas would work to strengthen themselves for the ordeal: they would make preparations.

Obviously it would be an ordeal: people, lights, cameras, tape recorders are difficult enough to cope with on the physical level, without seeing everything we do as heavy-footed, blindfold blundering through the landscape of *aluna*. Every footstep we took in this garden of the spirit would crush something.

I knew that we would not film for a year, because I wanted to return in this, the driest season, when the working day is longest. I suggested that a year might give them enough time to make the spiritual preparation necessary.

I was told that I too had a great deal of preparation to do in my head: I too would have to work in *aluna*. This would be much harder for me, because I had had no training. I would have to start at the beginning. For the Kogi six months would be sufficient. But a year was good. I would need all that time. At the end of a year, Mama Valencia suggested, I would be ready to make the film.

I promised to return in nine months to finalise arrangements, and went back to Santa Marta in a daze. We brought Manuelito down with us, to see a doctor. He was very sorry for himself, feeling that his illness was the result of overwork. He too was an official of Gonavindua Tairona, given the job because he had been one of its most outspoken critics. He described his life as one of constant travelling on behalf of the Mamas, ordered around without pause or rest. 'I am their errand boy. They say, "Manuelito, go there! Do this! Quickly!" And so I must. My head hurts terribly. I am sick.' Ramón often spoke the same way. Both men felt they needed to spend some time in retreat from the world, recovering their balance. Personally, I did not think my balance would ever be quite the same again.

A Kogi dispute

Bernardo Valderrama had walked a great deal of the Sierra. He believed that he was descended from one of the conquistadors, Don Palomino, who gave his name to the Palomino river, where he had been swept to death in a torrent. Bernardo was now devoting his life to retracing the steps of his ancestor, and in the process was exploring regions which white men have not visited for centuries.

He was very excited at having recently discovered a Tairona city occupied by Kogi, and believed that he was the first outsider to find it. This was where we were going: a city on stone foundations, with high terrace walls, with a shaped stone bench, and with a population who needed medical help. They were suffering badly from worms, and I was to take up a consignment of worm tablets.

Ramón was not happy about this proposed trip, or about my insistence that he should come with us as the representative of Gonavindua Tairona. His mother's family was in dispute with the community we were going to visit.

The story appeared to go like this. The town in question was indeed ancient, and had been continuously occupied until about sixty years ago, mainly by the extended family of Ramón's mother. But then, at a major festival, there was an outbreak of food poisoning which had killed some thirty people. The town was abandoned.

A few years ago a different clan decided to colonise the ruins. Their Mama, a member of the clan, divined that it was all right to do this, and also that it was permissible to bring some of the terraces back into cultivation. Counter-divinations by Ramón's mother's family produced very different instructions. We were walking straight into the middle of a feud.

Arguments of this kind, especially disputes over land, are quite central to Kogi society. Their intensity and bitterness are so strong that I wondered how this society had managed to survive. Surely, too, the idea of different Mamas producing different results from divination undermined its very basis. If the voices that come from the spirit world are merely the tools of factions, what use are they? And why did the Kogi world not fragment at any time in the past?

I had seen the answer at the meetings in Pueblo Viejo, though it took me a while to understand it. There had been representatives of many communities there, most of them at odds with one another. But underneath the tensions and arguments there was a basic sense of a common purpose: the survival of the world, and the responsibility of the Mamas to continue their work of looking after it. Few societies have ever displayed the ability to make a common decision and put it into action without upheaval. But at times when critical decisions have to be made, the Mamas are capable of holding a shared divination, of reaching a conclusion, and of seeing that it is carried through.

Divination

Divination is a formalisation of the link between the world of *aluna* and the physical world. It may be understood as speaking with ancestors, because physical death is not the extinction of life, only its transition from the body, but that alone would be a travesty of it. Nor is it enough to understand divination as a way of receiving messages from gods, though *aluna* is the Mother, and the Mother is listened to by divining.

Divination is the reading of signs. Since everything that happens is an event in the world of *aluna*, everything that happens also reflects that world. To put a question is an act in *aluna*, an act of pure thought, and if it is properly put then its answer is instantaneously present, here in the physical world as well. Divination is the mental process of properly shaping a question, and the highly formal process of reading the answer.

This is not a new idea to us: we have remnants of it in reading the cards or tea-leaves. To us, divination has an air of mystery, and we tend to respond more cautiously, more nervously towards it the more mysterious its trappings, and the more complex it is made. The tarot, rich in complex symbolism, seems deeper than reading tea-leaves; the I Ching, with its elaborate volumes of interpretation for the fall of a few yarrow stalks seems even more impressive.

For the Kogi, anything that is unpredictable could serve as an instrument for reading the answer to a question. Even drumming the finger-tips together may offer a slight element of chance that can be interpreted. But the most highly formalised system of interpretation has been developed for reading bubbles in a bowl of water. A hollow Tairona bead is carefully lowered into the bowl, and from the bubbles that appear on the surface the answer is known.

If the interpretation is a device, an invention, a way of justifying and mystifying authority, then all this is quite meaningless. That might be the conclusion to be drawn from the divinations and counter-divinations that surround disputes like the one over Bernardo's town. But the Kogi world has not fragmented into factions, and disputes over divinations are resolved by further divinations. The Kogi themselves do not regard most Mamas with anything approaching awe; they will commonly complain that a Mama is ignorant and worldly (the two main criticisms which they regard as significant). If a Mama was using divination in an obviously self-interested way, that would be recognised. In fact divinations are seen as having straightforward practical utility in daily life, and not as especially mysterious or mystifying.

Divination would also, of course, be meaningless if there were no higher reality, no world of *aluna* where all things have their essence and all things are bound together in a single life. Our whole intellectual tradition, scientific, rational, seems to demand a rejection of *aluna*. But ours is a tradition which says there is only one ultimate test: not 'does it make sense?' but 'does it work?'

Our scientific world-view had no trouble believing in aspirins and electricity because they worked, not because they made sense. The Kogi make all decisions on the basis of divination, and their society has continued to function in the face of pressures which few societies have ever been able to withstand. For them, it works. We have no other way of commenting on it. The question that confronts us is whether our view, that there is nothing beyond the biological and chemical machine, works. Up to now it has seemed to produce spectacular results. But the Kogi see these as short-term benefits on the way to a catastrophe. We are, to them, like people who have jumped off a mountain and, falling fast, are proclaiming our ability to fly. They believe they can see further, and that their own old-fashioned ideas will prove to be right. Unfortunately, they also believe that they are roped to us, and will shortly be yanked to destruction.

Shell gathering

I wanted to take some shells to Bernardo's community, as Reichel had suggested. The Kogi need shells for the poporo: they burn them to produce the lime powder that goes into the gourd. But they no longer have access to the sea. They had spoken to me about the urgent need for this access: it would provide salt and fish, as well as shells. More than this, it would allow them to continue with their work of bringing the different areas of the Sierra, which are the different areas of the world, into harmony.

Early in the 1970s, a coastal road was constructed along the northern side of the Sierra. This road, which enabled the exploitation of the minerals in the Guajira desert, opened the lower part of the northern Sierra for colonisation. Everyone refers to the small farmers who flooded in not as *campesinos*, 'country people' (i.e. peasants or small-holders), but as *colonos*, settlers, colonisers, the latest wave of new-comers following in the wake of Columbus. They deforested the land near the road to make fields, which lasted only a few years before the soil was eroded away. And so they move on to new patches, and spread the disaster.

With conventional agriculture failing, many turned to marijuana and later cocaine. This created a ribbon of badlands along the coast, too dangerous for the Kogi. It would be a nice gesture to bring them shells. Ramón and Adalberto were enthusiastic about a shell-gathering expedition, and Carlos offered to drive us in his truck.

I had expected us to be going to a beach close to Santa Marta, but the beaches there were either lacking in shells or were closed by *narco-traficantes*. We had to drive the whole length of the Sierra, through the increasingly ramshackle mestizo towns, until we reached Dibulla on the edge of the Guajira.

On the way we stopped in Mingeo, a clutch of single-storey shop-fronts along the road, where we picked up an Arhuaco Mama and his pupil who had walked for four days to reach the beach, and were grateful for the lift. This was a bi-annual pilgrimage for the Mama, difficult, dangerous, but necessary.

There is no sea on the other side of the mountains. The people from there have to come down here to collect shells. That's why the ancestors made roads that came right down here to the sea.

Ramón also took advantage of the stop to put out a contract on the life of a large iguana that we had seen crossing the road. He hoped to collect a large iguana steak on the return journey. The Kogi's respect for nature does not make them vegetarian. As with all the indigenous people of the Americas, hunting and fishing provided their protein before the Spanish brought farm animals to the continent. Iguana is still a delicacy.

Dibulla is not a comfortable place. It has a reputation as a place of casual killings. The most prominent feature of Dibulla is its cemetery, with a large ornamental entrance.

Strangely, just outside the town a luxurious private club has been erected, with a swimming pool and comfortable bars. It reeks of money behind a high wire fence and an elaborate security system. Dibulla reeks of poverty, hopelessness and raw sewage.

We did not stay long. We were left in peace on the dirty, windswept beach, and though it was poor in shells everyone's *mochila* was soon filled. When we got back I succeeded in exerting enough moral pressure for some to be left with me as a present for the community Bernardo would be taking us to meet.

The following day, despite Ramón's obvious anxieties, we climbed into the helicopter with Bernardo and set off. The town was on the far side of a steep ridge in the mountains, and the top of the ridge was at the upper limit of the Bell Ranger's endurance. As we struggled over, it was plain that the valley on the far side was filled with cloud. We could not descend.

The pilot tried a number of ways to get into this closed valley. One of them brought us into a blind canyon, which steadily narrowed as its sides rose above us. It soon became clear that we were in trouble: the sides were too high for us to get out, and the canyon had narrowed to less than a hundred feet across. Below us was thick cloud. We were all white-knuckled as the helicopter turned to escape, with just enough room for the rotor blades.

Back at the airport I was ashen, but Ramón was grinning. 'Serankua has decided. Serankua says we should not go.' I asked him to go up on foot later, when he could, and take the shells and worm medicines. He said he would, and I never heard any more about that town.

I found Ramón's confidence in Serankua infectious, and easily slipped into a kind of fatalism. The Mamas had laid a great responsibility on me, a responsibility which I could not bear alone. I needed to believe that their own divinations had meaning, and that, so long as I played my part, Serankua would ensure that events fell out properly. I already trusted the Mamas. Now I began to trust in something more.

By boat to Pueblito

My fatalism was about to be severely tested. There was one more visit planned to the Kogi, with Javier Rodríguez. Javier was a kindly, eager man who had spent so long with the Arhuacos that he really wanted to be one. He thought of himself as a trainee Mama, and carried a *mochila* and poporo. This evidently annoyed Ramón, who had little time for him.

Javier's visit would be to a town on the south side of the Sierra. That is more accessible than the north, and we would not need the helicopter. But first, I planned a visit to Pueblito.

Pueblito was one of the early Tairona sites to be discovered, close to the coast. It had been excavated in the 1920s and 1930s, and its main structure revealed by Reichel-Dolmatoff. He had determined that its occupation had ended early in the seventeenth century. It was evidently not on the same monumental scale as the Lost City, but I ought to go there. Ramón and Javier agreed to come too.

There were two access routes to Pueblito. One involved striking off across country from the coast road, heading towards the sea for about three hours. The other meant following the road until it reached the beach, then walking along a shore path for about two hours and climbing a stone stairway which leads straight up to the city. I decided on a third way. We would take a boat direct to the bottom of the stairway.

Astonished, now that I had the idea, that no one else seemed to have thought of this, I dispatched Felicity to hire a boat.

The natural starting point for this journey was Taganga, a small fishing port just to the east of Santa Marta. Taganga is either charming or wretched, according to your point of view. Taxi-drivers all believe that it is charming, and never fail to comment on its beauty as they come over the rise that conceals it. Nostalgic Colombians remark on the superb cooking at its one hotel, the Blue Whale, which was set up by a Frenchwoman who came as a hippy and stayed. They seem not to have noticed that the Frenchwoman no longer runs the Blue Whale, and its menu is brief, dull and utterly Colombian. But it is cheap, the bay is pretty, there is good fishing and diving on the nearby coral reefs, and hard-up archaeologists like to stay there. With a little imagination and a desensitised nose, Taganga can be transformed from a waterside slum into an off-beat resort.

There are other drawbacks to Taganga. Taxi-drivers from Santa Marta do not like travelling there after dark, because of bandits on the road. It was a major centre for the shipping of marijuana, and some of the friendly fishermen have been involved in long-running land disputes with the *narco-traficantes*; one such dispute in a nearby town led recently to nine men being killed. But that's Colombia.

We had already met Pedro the Fisherman, a tall, seriously underdressed, very black Tagangan, when he was providing beach entertainment for the toddler child of a holidaying archaeologist. I had vaguely expected Felicity to have hired one of the large motor vessels moored out in the bay, but she thought I had struck a deal with Pedro, and, trusting my supposed good judgment, agreed a fee for his boat. It was a 20-foot-long, open vessel with an outboard motor, called *Gairaca*, the name of one of the beaches along the coast. This was an encouraging sign, as it suggested that Pedro had covered the distance before. Included in the price was lunch, and a crew of two baling with tin cans.

A crude shelter had been rigged against the beating sun, and once we cleared the headland at the entrance to the bay a huge wave crashed down on it. So did the next, and the next, and so on.

Ramón, who had never been to sea before, sat in his white robes with a stoic detachment as the sea rose up and fell on him. Perhaps, I speculated, he thought this was the way it should be. Later I discovered that he was composing himself for death. The rest of us were baling like crazy.

The fishermen took it all quite equably, and were baffled when I announced that I was not going back in their boat. It took far longer than anyone anticipated to reach the beach, and I could see that, even if I could endure it, we would not get up to Pueblito and back in time to make Taganga before nightfall. The fishermen agreed that trying to round the unlit headland and cross the coral in the dark probably was not a good idea.

We dried off on the beach, which happened to be the most perfect beach I had ever seen: pure, clean sand, clear blue sea, and jungle coming right down to the shore. With the mountain rising directly from the beach, it looked exactly as it must have looked when Alonso de Ojeda first discovered this coast in 1498.

The first colonists

On 12 June 1514, a Spanish galleon arrived to start the process of colonisation. The Indians came down to the shore to look. They had dressed lightly, and covered themselves in the red juice which acts as a mosquito repellent. The commander sent a small party to land, but the Indians ran up to the landing boats 'and with their bows and arrows and with a courteous manner, showed us that they would have to resist our landing.' A lengthy document had been prepared to read to the assembled crowd. It began:

> On the part of the most high and most mighty and most catholic defender of the church, always conqueror and never conquered, the great King Don Fernando (fifth of that name), King of the Sicilies and of Jerusalem, and of the Indies, islands and dry land of the Ocean Sea ... dominator of barbarous peoples; and of his most high and most mighty lady Queen Doña Johana, his very dear and very daughter, our masters: I Pedrarias Dávila, their subject, messenger and captain, notify and would have you know that God our Father, the one and the trinity, created the skies and the earth, and a man and a woman, of whom you and we and all the men of this world are descendants and offspring, and all those who will come after us. Because of the multitude which from the generation of these has grown over five thousand years and more since the world was created, it was necessary that some men went in one direction and others in others, and that they divide themselves in many kingdoms and provinces, for in only one they could not be sustained.★

It went on to explain the fundamental doctrines of Christianity, including the doctrine of the Trinity and the position of the Pope, which led on in a natural and interesting way to the theory of European political structures and the Divine Right of Kings. The logical and

★ Oviedo, 7, 121–34. This document, edited by Dr Palacios Rubios and approved by a committee of Spanish theologians and prelates, had to be carried and read out by all expeditions of conquest. Oviedo was himself responsible for proclaiming it on this expedition.

obvious conclusion was that the listening Indians were now to consider themselves subjects of the Spanish crown and should begin taking instruction for baptism. As a treatise in late medieval political theory and theology it was a well considered speech. In case the Indians could not understand Spanish, it was repeated in Carib, the language of the natives of Hispaniola. It was a thoughtful touch, though the native people of Colombia understood it no more than Spanish.

The Indians, having failed to grasp their proper duty as the Spaniards understood it, fired some arrows towards the landing craft. This was interpreted as an act of rebellion against their new rulers, and the Spanish attacked.

When the Spaniards' scribe protested that the Indians had not understood a word that had been said to them, the soldiers laughed at him. After all, it did not really mean anything.

One among the many bizarre features of this moment is that the Indians also tried to explain something to the Spanish. It is even possible that they may have been saying something rather similar. Certainly they are saying something along the same lines today. One of the speeches made to me by a Mama seems like an answering echo to the Spanish argument, that the way the world and humanity were created leads to political duty.

The world was made in the beginning, and we made afterwards.

Then Serankua looked at the earth which we have. He said to the humans, 'You are beings created to protect it, to maintain the balance, to care for the world, the universe. Concentrate and take care of it.'

Our history, the history of the Mama, says that in this land all people held the same beliefs as one another. We were all Elder Brothers. When we collect firewood it is paid for, bought, like buying rice, like buying clothing. We pay Serankua for firewood, for water, for the air we breathe, for what we need to live, for every little animal. We have always known that there is a payment to be made for everything.

Then a Younger Brother was given knowledge of mechanical things. And because this land was very sacred, if Younger Brother stayed here he would do harm to Mother Earth. He would not have respected Mother Earth, he would only ever tear out the eyes of the

Mother, he would only ever tear out the guts of the Mother, without compassion, without feeling pain.

Thus the Younger Brother had less understanding. Then Serankua said, 'Let us send them away to the other side and, so that they respect us and so that they shall not pass, I make a division – the sea.'

But the Mamas say the Younger Brother came back across to this side, thinking he had learned, had studied, and was wise.

They came and started to tear out the blood of the Mother Earth, started to tear out the eyes of the Mother Earth without respect.

Serankua said very clearly, 'Elder Brother must respect Younger Brother and Younger Brother must respect Elder Brother. Do not come here, I have created a division.' But Younger Brother did not respect it, he came and violated the law, the original spiritual law of Serankua, and today the people here, the Mamas, say that Younger Brother must listen to us, that he must learn to respect us. Thus speak the Mamas.

The Spanish proclamation ended more fearsomely. If the native people did not submit,

I assure you that with the help of God I will enter powerfully against you, and I will make war on you in every place and in every way that I can, and I will subject you to the yoke and obedience of the church and their highnesses, and I will take your persons and your women and your children, and I will make them slaves, and as such I will sell them, and dispose of them as their highnesses command: I will take your goods, and I will do you all the evils and harms which I can, just as to vassals who do not obey and do not want to receive their lord, resist him and contradict him. And I declare that the deaths and harms which arise from this will be your fault, and not that of their highnesses, nor mine, nor of the gentlemen who have come with me here.

The Spanish fired some powder shots into the air and the Indians disappeared from the beach. The Spanish landed at last, went to a hut near the beach, and Dávila began symbolically cutting at the branches of trees with his sword, claiming possession of the land in the name of the King of Castile. He made further proclamations, which he had taken down in writing, and he 'asked for witness'. There was no Indian in sight.

Pueblito

Felicity, Javier and I followed Ramón into the jungle. The trail led to a rock wall, with shaped stone panels standing against it. It looked like a dead end. 'These are guards,' said Ramón. 'They are stone people. We must go past them.' Squeezing through the gap between them, we were on a continuation of the path. Immense cut slabs formed walls on either side, then there was another squeeze under a low roof, and we were at the start of the stairway.

Rising 700 feet through dense jungle, this stairway is deeply impressive. We began climbing it at midday, when the air was at its hottest and most humid. Ramón bounded up the slabs, nimbly crossing huge breaks where trees had uprooted chunks of stone. 'Be careful, you could break an ankle here. I can climb this in twenty minutes. For you, an hour.' For me, nearer two. I had assumed that Ramón was in his mid-thirties. He would run up a section, then rest and wait for me. He was, in fact, fifty-six. The Kogi are not like us.

By the time we reached Pueblito I was shattered. And now Ramón showed us round. Broad highways ran between low walls, with well-shaped kerb-stones leading into the foundations of ceremonial houses. 'This was the men's house. This was the women's house. This was the Place of the Sun. Here was the Mama's office. And here was the place for speaking to other towns with your mind: the telephone exchange.' Telepathy is not regarded very highly among the Kogi: it is relegated to minor figures, Mamalitos. They seem to take it for granted, and I have never wanted to know about it. If it does not work I shall be disappointed, and if it does I shall be confused.

Pueblito was quite different from the Lost City. Not only was it lower down the mountain and much flatter and more open, it was also constructed of well-dressed stone, altogether less rustic and more polished. In many ways a less ambitious construction, in a less demanding environment, it conveyed affluence and expertise in stone-working. Some of the stones were very large indeed: 20-foot slabs had been cut square and smoothly finished.

We began our walk out, towards the highway. As we walked, we talked. Ramón spoke about the loneliness of the Elder Brothers, their sense of being the last survivors. 'The Mamas used to travel in *aluna* and meet other people from other places there. But as the years passed, there were fewer and fewer people who reached the spirit world to talk with them. Now there is no one. It is deserted.'

What did he mean? Mama, I discovered, means the sun: the Mamas are Enlightened Ones. And there were once other Enlightened Ones, indigenous to other countries, so Ramón assured me. Quite recently, the last ones disappeared. They have stopped visiting the spirit world.

We talked about our families: I said that when I returned, I would bring my wife. Ramón said ruefully that this would be better than a lot of money, to have one's wife. His own marriage had broken up because he was away working so much. His wife had divorced him.

She was Kogi. Divorce among the Kogi is very simple: a woman simply switches her allegiance to another man, and symbolises that by accepting a piece of meat from him. Ramón had remarried, but he missed his first wife.

We talked about walking. The Kogi walk all the time, criss-crossing the Sierra on their way from farm to farm, from town to town. This is a vital part of the life of the Sierra. Movement from one area to another, carrying produce and seeds, stones and shells, is essential to the harmony of life. The roads were made by the ancestors, hundreds of miles of them, and they are sacred, and must be maintained, and must be walked. The ant is an Elder Brother who walks the roads, said Ramón.

Then we sat down to rest, and he pointed to a tiny speck moving across my shoe. 'A garrapata. He too is walking.' What, I asked innocently, is a garrapata? Ramón and Javier explained.

It is a tick. Garrapatas hang in a dense cluster from the leaves, a ball of black unpleasantness which shatters on contact with an animal into hundreds of tiny hungry insects. Attaching themselves to any creature that walks through the undergrowth, they seek out the one spot on its body that is protected from the brushing leaves, which is warm and moist and has a good blood supply close to the surface. The genitalia are garrapata heaven, and that is where they go.

They bury their heads deep in the flesh, and grow big and fat. If you pull them off, the head is left behind, under the skin, where it festers.

Once gorged, the garrapata works its way back to the outer part of the creature, to be brushed off on to a leaf and give birth to a clutch of eggs that hatch and wait for the next ride.

They have a profound understanding of clothing, seeking out any gap – down the belt, perhaps, or around the socks – that will let them reach their target.

Physically, the garrapata is no threat at all. Psychologically, I just cannot cope with it.

Physically, the walk out to the road was the finish of me. Ramón was plainly worried by my exhausted robotic stumble as the afternoon went on: 'The BBC is dying,' he announced. I felt that he had put his finger on it. We reached the road at nightfall, and waited for a *rápido*, a bus, to Santa Marta. Two passed without stopping, and it gradually dawned on us that the drivers were frightened to stop after dark. Eventually, however, one took the risk and we got back. I hurried to my room and covered myself in rubbing alcohol, the one sure way to remove garapatas. Rubbing alcohol on the groin gives a strange burning sensation. I would have to find some other way of getting the film crew to Pueblito.

Signs and omens

Over the next few days, Javier was a mine of information about the Kogi. He told me that Mamas are educated from infancy in the dark, and only allowed into the light when their education is complete, after two periods of nine years. Nine is the number required for completeness, as a foetus spends nine lunar months in the womb, and there are nine worlds. There are also characters called *moros*, he said, whose education continues for two more periods of nine years. These I would never meet: they live high in the Sierra, and speak only with Mamas. These are the oracles who determine ultimate policy. These creatures are the ones who have seen the approach of the end of the world. I later discovered that *moro* is the word for any pupil studying to be a Mama. It does seem quite possible that some students are not released into the light until they are over thirty. These strange figures would be polluted by contact with anyone impure. The Kogi are profoundly ascetic, and prepare themselves for important moments by fasting, meditation and sexual abstinence; contact with anyone who is still locked into the gross physical world can, they believe, render this preparation useless. Javier's *moros* would be in this heightened state all their lives, and it would therefore be impossible for me ever to set eyes on them, but he suggested that they would have their eyes on me.

That was when Charlie came into my life. I was going in to Santa Marta, and ordered a taxi from the Irotama Hotel, but it was so long coming that I decided to hitchhike. The lift was in a small truck, driven by the owner of a costume jewellery shop in Santa Marta. We talked about the Sierra as we drove, as he had just bought a farm on the lower slopes. I was uneasy about this; I supposed him to be part of the colono invasion that has been pushing the Kogi higher and higher, and deforesting the lower slopes, but he was not really a farmer at all. He did not want to cut down any trees – 'Oh no, they are beautiful' – and simply wanted to enjoy it. He was fascinated by the Indians, and ended up insisting that I should have his 'antique figure'.

We drove to his shop, a small barred cage in a narrow street, and he called to his partner, 'Bring out the antique figure!' His partner emerged with the object which I call Charlie, and they overrode my protests and insisted that I take him.

Charlie is a pot in the form of a squatting manikin, holding a snake-like appendage that grows out of his navel. The opening of the pot is in the form of a head-dress. His face has an oriental cast, with slanting eyes, typical of the Nariño pots made in south-western Colombia. The Nariños are an Andean people, whose territory was the most northern part of the Inca empire, and Charlie has no real place in the Sierra. But 'All Colombia was Elder Brother', and Charlie knew it. His lip curled in a delicate grimace of distaste.

I was very worried that I was now in possession of some ancient artifact, but later the same day I was introduced to Frankie Rey, who had once been one of the most celebrated tomb-robbers in the Sierra. Frankie was the man who had led the archaeologists to the Lost City. I showed him Charlie, and he assured me that this was no ancient treasure. Charlie was of recent manufacture. But he is no fake. He was made as such pots were always made, by a master craftsman who made offerings while he worked. There was no reason why I should not keep Charlie and take him with me. I found the strength of Charlie's personality disturbing, and wanted to be rid of him, but felt I could not dump him. By now I was convinced that everything that happened formed some sort of pattern, and I just had to accept it.

Frankie Rey was a wiry, gleeful man whose head was covered in tight grizzled curls. Like Carlos, he had grown up in Minca at the foot of the mountain, but he had learned about the Indians of the Sierra because he had gone in pursuit of the buried treasure of their ancestors. It was a pastime which seemed both adventurous and profitable, and which so far as he was aware was perfectly harmless. It had eventually become his career, and that was how he came to find the Lost City. It was he and his band of *guaqueros*, plunderers of the sacred sites, who termed it Hell. The ruins were close to the limits of a tomb-robber's endurance: he has, after all, to carry all his food on his back (even mules cannot cope with the rougher parts of the Sierra), and that fixes the distance he can range from civilisation. The incessant rain for most of the year made it impossible to light fires, and the density and hostility of the jungle made it a highly unpleasant place to be. Then came rivalries and killings at the site, and Frankie decided that it was time to get the place organised.

It probably did not occur to Frankie that the archaeologists would actually put a stop to the tomb-robbing. After he had brought them, he asked for a delay before guards were posted so that there would be time to loot the untouched sections, and was surprised when this was refused. In fact, for whatever reason, the archaeologists made no gold finds at all there.

They did find a tomb-robber, though. He was buried like a Tairona, in a pit in the centre of a house site. It was a very recent burial. There were no grave-goods.

Tomb-robbing was obviously an important part of the story of the Lost City; I had discussed this with the Mamas, and they too thought that it should be included in the film. For them, there is no distinction between the greed of a tomb-robber and the greed of an archaeologist, and they wanted to make it clear what it means to loot a sacred site. When I told Frankie what I was doing he was keen to cooperate. He offered to demonstrate how tombs are found, how they are robbed, and generally to provide an Open University course on the subject. I pointed out that this might not leave him smelling of roses in the eyes of the Colombian authorities, but Frankie brushed that aside.

I went back to the hotel with Charlie, whose expression had changed from contempt to rage. Over the next few days, as I continued making arrangements for the filming, his appearance softened. Of course, it was all in the imagination. I just wish that the change had not been noticed and remarked on by Javier and Felicity, separately.

The southern Sierra

The visit to Javier's community would begin at Valledupar, a city at the foot of the southern slopes, and we would travel by taxi. We began by going to the Casa Indígena to collect Amparo and Ramón. Ramón was there with his wife, and insisted that they would travel by bus. He would meet us in Valledupar. He seemed very distant, and I was worried that he might have been completely put off me by my dismal showing at Pueblito. I am not a good mountain walker, and good walking is a sign of inner quality.

As we drove along the inland base of the Sierra we passed through Aracataca, the home town of Gabriel García Márquez. It was just one more hot, tired little town. As we approached Valledupar the landscape turned ever browner. The Sierra here had been stripped bare, its easy slopes victims of the United Fruit Company and the peasant farmers it left behind. The Arhuacos, the dominant indigenous society on this face of the mountain, had much less chance than the Kogi to hide themselves away.

The next day, when we went to the Casa Indígena in Valledupar, Ramón had still not arrived. This place was very different from Amparo's compound in Santa Marta. There was an air of shifty uneasiness, and it did not seem particularly cut off from the life of the city. There was evidently a lot of drink circulating among the Indians there.

I was introduced to an Arhuaco chief, whose permit I would need to continue my journey. He was a fat man, with a beer gut protruding between his T-shirt and jeans. I had never seen a fat Kogi, or one who was not dressed in traditional costume. Obviously things were very different among the Arhuaco. He had also been drinking.

Alcohol has a devastating effect on Indians. Biologically, indigenous

Americans are distinct in a number of ways from people of European descent. One of the differences is that we have an enzyme which specialises in breaking down alcohol molecules, and they do not. The result is that they get hit much more dramatically by alcohol, becoming drunk more quickly and remaining drunk much longer. Within traditional societies this prolonged slightly ecstatic condition is treated with some respect as it is related to other forms of visionary state, but outside that protective structure it simply means that Indians who drink are more likely to be exploited, in debt, and regarded with contempt.

This man was the gate-keeper to an area of traditional society, but he had plainly chosen to operate in the world of the Younger Brother, and in his cups he alternately bullied and cringed. I felt very uncomfortable as he first tried to extort money from me, then gave up and wrote out a permit. In theory, we were free to take a four-wheel drive vehicle through Arhuaco territory to the Kogi who lived above.

I did not like this at all. Ramón's non-appearance meant that I had no translator, and I did not like the idea of having to set up a filming operation with the people here. In any case, this was not likely to prove the way in to the kind of isolated, traditionalist culture that I had encountered in the north. I decided to pull out, and go back to Bogota.

I did not know what had become of Ramón, and his cooperation was absolutely essential to the film. I wrote a long letter to him, which I left with Amparo, and returned to Santa Marta to pick up my gear.

The bus was superb: well-sprung, air-conditioned and fast. But any illusion that Colombia is a normal sort of place was cut dead as we approached Aracataca. Two days before a guerilla band had ambushed an army patrol here, killing two soldiers. Now the bus was stopped by a group of armed men in fatigues. Army or guerillas? Who could tell?

We were ordered off the bus and then, ominously, the men were separated from the women and children. I looked around. The only building was a roadside café, which the soldiers had appropriated. The road was slightly elevated: it was about 100 yards down the slope and through tall grass to the cover of the jungle. There were six soldiers; four of them had elderly weapons without ammunition clips. The other two, however, would make it unlikely that I could get to cover.

We were lined up against the bus, arms above our heads, and frisked. I was carrying all my money, several thousand dollars, in a body pouch, but the soldier patting me was more interested in my boots and did not notice it. And then it was all over. They were army after all – a very nervous group of young men, convinced that guerillas were lurking all round them. They were probably right. We got back on the bus.

Back at the hotel, Charlie seemed to be worried. So was I. And so was Andrés. The young medic from Pueblo Viejo, who I had expected would have returned to his post, had come to see me. He was superstitiously worried that Mama Valencia had put some sort of hex on him. He had been stunned by the Kogi, who he saw as magi, masters of the supernatural. He had sat at the feet of Mama Valencia and listened to him at length – an unrewarding activity, since Mama Valencia has very little Spanish and Andrés speaks no Kogi, but Andrés had been properly impressed. He had also accepted two gifts from the Mama, a *mochila* and an object which he took to be a charm against ill fortune. Apparently just before he boarded my helicopter, Mama Valencia had approached him and demanded a small payment for the *mochila*, five hundred pesos. A *mochila* is worth two or three thousand pesos in the Sierra, up to ten times that elsewhere. But Andrés could not afford anything, and brushed the Mama aside.

Mama Valencia glared at him with his glittering eyes, and Andrés was frightened. Now he had a telegram summoning him to see his family in Bogota: something was wrong. And he could not find the lucky charm – it had vanished. It was still holiday time, and Andrés did not have a flight booked, so he was waiting for a seat on a plane. I sympathised, but there was nothing I could do here. I caught the plane to Bogota and went to see Martín von Hildebrand with my own lucky charm, the filming agreement with the Kogi.

Martín von Hildebrand

Martín was the head of the Office of Indian Affairs. He was the man who had been running an Amazon field station for the Office when the Lost City excavations began, and whose station had been closed to help finance that. Now that he was in charge, the Kogi's claims to the Lost City and their detestation of archaeology had found a ready ear.

The Kogi see the whole of the Sierra as a single entity, a sacred world in the heart of the larger world. Indeed, they call it the Heart of the World. They have to maintain the harmony of the Heart of the World by making offerings, which they call 'payments', at a multitude of sites. If this is not done, then the harmony of the Heart of the World is upset and the larger world too becomes chaotic. Archaeology digs holes in sacred sites and removes the objects placed there, and that is no different from any other plundering. The consequences are just as devastating, whether the sacred gold ends up in a museum in Bogota or a private collection in Berlin.

The Kogi had sent a message to the President in Bogota spelling this out, and explaining that they could not maintain harmony in the world so long as archaeological plunder disrupted the Heart of the World. Martín had backed them up, arguing that the government was trying to establish a peace process with the guerillas, and to restore political harmony, and it might not be wise to assume that Western rationalism had a monopoly of wisdom. In fact to say to indigenous people, 'We know how to create harmony, you do not,' would not only be arrogant, and possibly create sympathy between those people and the guerillas, it might also look pretty silly. It is not as though Colombia has had a lot of success with promoting harmony.

So the archaeologists had been pulled out, and the Lost City was to be handed over to the Kogi. This fitted in well with Martín's overall approach to the indigenous people of Colombia. He has been responsible for the transfer of millions of acres of Amazonia to the control of the Indians who live there, and encouraged the government to recognise the Indians' stewardship of the rain forest. He has a profound and sympathetic understanding of the indigenous approach to nature, and at that time had the ear of the President. He treats the native people with respect, deference and an intelligence which they respect.

I needed Martín's permission for the film, but he simply took the line that if the Kogi, through Gonavindua Tairona, agreed to it, then that was fine. The task of his office was to ensure that we did nothing of which the Kogi disapproved, and that we did nothing to exploit or harm them. Everyone recognised the dangers of opening up this reserved area to a film crew, but Martín felt that as the five hundredth anniversary of Columbus approached, more and more film crews would be pushing their way in to these last standard-bearers of the world he split open. My film should be an excuse to keep the others out. Perhaps he could even offer them my off-cuts.

I did not think many film-makers would be content with that, but Martín quite correctly observed that this was not my problem.

The one part of the plan that he was uneasy about was that I was not coming back for nine months. In that time, a lot can change. I needed to have a constant presence there, perhaps an anthropologist who would keep talking about the film and ensure that problems were dealt with as they arose. I agreed to this, and Charlie, Felicity and I went back to England.

Charlie did not like travel, especially since his feet broke off on the journey and had to be glued back on. Back home, he glared fiercely at the family. It had occurred to me that not much had gone right since he was wished on me, and I wondered why the shopkeeper had been so determined to pass him on. However, I refused to fall into Andrés's superstitious mood, and regarded it as merely coincidental when, over the next few weeks, the dog was run over and lost a leg, and I fell from a window and broke my ankle. Anyway, once a couple of legs had been damaged and Charlie's healed, all that stopped. Now he just sits in the kitchen staring at the fishtank, watching the goldfish sicken and die, with a sat-upon expression.

Graham Townsley

The anthropologist I needed to send had to be male, so that he could participate in the life of the *nuhue*, the men's house, a fluent Spanish speaker, experienced in South America and with a good understanding of the demands of a film. There was just such a person to hand: Dr Graham Townsley. Graham had recently completed a thesis on the Yamanawa Indians of Amazonian Peru, where he had been studying shamanism, and was now working as advisor and researcher on a television film covering his own research. Graham is Canadian, and seems quite happy to spend his life in remote, isolated areas: he even lives like that in England, choosing to stay in Cambridge.

Graham arrived in Santa Marta in May, to find a very confused situation. Manuelito had stepped off a bus as it was slowing to a halt, tripped over and been killed outright. The Sierra was closed, in mourning, organising elaborate funerary rites. This was a blow to Gonavindua Tairona: one of its leading figures had been killed by becoming involved with the Younger Brother and his world. And there were deeper problems.

The nuns had been at work, spreading rumours against the film, perhaps more because Amparo was associated with it than for any other reason, but also because they had just been deeply humiliated. The Archbishop had made an Easter tour of the Sierra, struggling on mule and on foot through this arduous territory with its prodigious rainstorms to carry out baptisms and solemnise marriages among the Indians. Wherever he had gone in Kogi territory, there had been nothing. Not a single convert appeared. There were no baptisms, no marriages, no Christians. Four centuries of effort, 15 miles from the shore where South America was first discovered, had not produced a single living Kogi Christian for him to bless.

The vassals, however little they wanted to be Christians, were prepared to listen to the nuns' warnings against me. The Mamas had decided to open up and speak to the Younger Brother, but centuries of conditioning had shaped the vassals' minds, and they needed the security of secrecy. Now they were being told that the BBC was coming to steal gold, to steal land, to take over the Sierra. The nuns said that the BBC had forged the document of agreement with the Mamas. The BBC would take away their children, and turn them all into its vassals.

After a long wait, Graham was invited up to Pueblo Viejo, and walked. It is a stiff, difficult climb, impossible to find the right path without a guide, and all the harder during the ten months of rain, the long Sierra 'winter'. He attended a series of formal meetings, at which he identified himself and explained why he was there. He was listened to, his words about the film were apparently approved, and then he was told to go down again to wait. He should present himself at Mingeo in a week, and vassals would appear to guide him back up the mountain.

5

Testing Time

Profoundly impressed by the formality and grandeur of the Kogi world, Graham had gone back down to Santa Marta feeling exultant. One week later he was at Mingeo, as ordered, waiting for his guides. No one came.

There was obviously some mistake. He tried again the next day, and the next. Day after day he made the long trek out to Mingeo, but there was no one to meet him. He became frustrated and depressed as the days stretched into weeks, but he would obviously be making a grave mistake if he were to try to return unescorted. There was plainly a problem; the Kogi had cut themselves off.

Eventually Ramón, who was now in Santa Marta and solidly in favour of the film being made, sent a message giving his views and urging that Graham be allowed to go up. Marina, who works at the Casa Indígena, had to visit the Kogi on official business, and Ramón's message was recorded on Graham's pocket tape-recorder, along with a message from Graham. The Kogi made her replay it endlessly, and she came back saying that Graham could return, and was indeed invited to a festival in one of the major towns, San Miguel. So Graham climbed back into the Sierra, to live among the Kogi. He took up residence in a Kogi village close to Pueblo Viejo, and waited.

There is a floating population there, consisting mostly of families with farms close to the village. As usual, these families have a number of farms at different altitudes, and spend some time at each.

Shortly after dawn the village empties. Until the rain begins in the afternoon villages are deserted, except perhaps for a few women and children who have stayed behind. The doors of all the houses are locked, their massive and often antique padlocks emphasising how private these individual houses are. The ceremonial house is never locked.

The padlocks are not a precaution against crime. All Kogi houses contain much the same property: cooking utensils, needles and thread, animal skins and string hammocks, and some bags of fruit and vegetables. Theft is very rare and severely punished. The padlocks are symbols of family privacy, and they are often attached only to pieces of string, which pass through a hole in the door and around the door-post. When they are in town, the family generally eat together in their own house. They usually wash their hands before meals, taking a swig of water from a gourd and then pouring it over their hands from their mouth. The only communal cooking I have ever seen is when a cow is killed for a feast: then the women gather in the women's house, and food is carried through to the ceremonial house for the men to eat.

The nuclear family is the basis of Kogi society. There is no sexual licence; venereal disease is apparently unknown among them, and, although divorce is quite straightforward, the ideal is partnership for life. They are a puritanical and prudish people, and keep their bodies covered at all times in public. Even when they go to bathe in the river, the Kogi remain fully dressed. A Mama taking his bath is an extraordinary sight; he will walk steadily out into the middle of the river with his clothes on, sit down quite suddenly, wait a while, and then stand up and walk out again.

Women rule the house, the domestic arena; men have an exclusive domain in the public arena, the ceremonial house. That is not to say that women have no say in public affairs; there are many stories of lengthy debates in the ceremonial house, lasting several nights, at the end of which a decision is reached on how to deal with some community problem. Then the men go home, tell their wives what has been decided, and the following day they reconvene somewhat shame-faced and agree to a different solution. But in principle, it is the men who decide.

As life returns to the village in the afternoon doors are opened and fires lit. Smoke rises through the roofs. Men move between the ceremonial house and their private houses, constantly working their poporos. Women usually stay indoors, cooking and endlessly making bags.

All Kogi life is built around the complementarity of male and female. The Mother did not only create the physical world, but also shaped and peopled *aluna*, creating a Mother and Father for everything that exists. Life is meaningless without procreative energy, and whatever is alive must have a Mother and a Father – not only in physical fact, but also in *aluna*, in the metaphysical world. The Kogi perceive life in many things which are in our understanding inanimate; any object which has meaning and purpose in the world has a metaphysical form in *aluna*, and therefore must be sustained by a balance of sexual forces, by its own Mother and Father. They speak constantly about things in this way, and the complementarity of masculine and feminine is basic to their culture. In casual conversation, men talk about women as they do in any society – 'Do you have the same trouble with your women that we have with ours?' – but there is also an elaborate deference of men towards women.

The Mother told us that we should always be in agreement with women, that we should treat women well because it was women, the Mother, who gave us all things ... At first the Mother gave advice to men. She lectured them. That's why when women talk to us we have to look down at their feet. We shouldn't look at the Mother's face.

The speaker here was Mama Fiscal, who was demonstrating with his wife how to burn shells for use in the poporo. His wife is also a Mama, Mama Teresa Vacuna. They were educated together as children.

The Mother told that we should never give up poporos or the shells and the coca. We must never forget them. And we haven't. And the Mother gave us fire too. And we haven't forgotten how to make fire or to bless it. When Mama Valencia hears what I'm saying he'll agree and Mama Bernardo too. They'll say Fiscal spoke the truth. The Mother gave us all the plants and the birds and that's why I have to bless all these things. Just as the Mother wanted us to.

Mama Teresa listened to all this earnestly, and then joined in. The point she wanted to stress was that it is woman who gives men their manhood.

Yes, that's the way it is. I know how to give the poporo too. You put two coca leaves into the mouth of the boy and you bless them. And you also have to bless the poporo stick before you put it into his mouth. Just as the Mother first gave the poporo to men I also give it now. You have to be able to stay awake for four nights thinking of the Mothers and Fathers of coca and of the poporo stick and of the shells and of the poporo.

Rite of passage: the boy

The poporo is the mark of manhood, and is given when a boy is ready to be married. Although to my eye it looks like a penis, that is because our culture is particularly attuned to seeing phallic symbols. The only things which we see as womb symbols are those which cover, hide and protect us, like a cave. The Kogi have a much wider repertoire of female sexual symbols, and the poporo is actually an image of the womb and cervix. It is often called 'a woman'. The hole in the top is penetrated by the poporo stick. The powder of burned sea-shells inside is the essence of fertility, and for a boy to grow to manhood he must learn to feed on that. That, and the coca leaves, harvested only by women, will make him fit to father children and tend the land – to develop a relationship with a woman in the flesh, and with the Mother Earth.

This moment of maturity, and the whole of a Kogi's social and sexual life, must be carefully supervised by the Mamas. The life-force is fundamental: it is *aluna*, it is the intelligence of being. The Mamas must be told everything, so that they can arrange everything correctly – including marriage. Here is Mama Bernardo, helping a young man whose stomach rebelled when he was first given coca and the poporo. The problem, as the Mama sees it, must lie in the youth's mental attitude. He needs to learn how to put himself in the right frame of mind, and he needs to talk through his past behaviour, to find what has put him out of harmony with nature. It is a problem which must be solved if he is to become a man. He is nineteen years old. It is dawn, on a quiet hillside in open country, and the Mama is speaking quietly.

Go ahead now, eat your poporo but do it slowly, put the stick in slowly, then bring it out and suck it. And as you're doing this, think of the Mothers, you should be concentrating hard and not thinking about other things.

Think about where the Mothers are, think about the Mothers, the Mothers of the poporos, and think about the Mothers of the poporo sticks. Concentrate on this, don't think about anything else, think about the Mothers and eat your poporo slowly and quietly. You have to ask for your poporo in *aluna*, ask the Mothers to give you the poporo and the stick in *aluna*. Think of the Mother of the gourds, giving you this, and concentrate your spirit in Father Luawiko too, and ask him to give you the coca and the calc. Think hard, and if you ever give up the poporo again, I'll hit you with my poporo stick.

All this is being said in a calm, fatherly way; the boy has absolute trust in the Mama.

If you start to eat this poporo properly and go on then you'll be able to take a woman as your wife – careful – I'll hit you with my poporo stick! You mustn't give up using the poporo from now on, keep using it, otherwise you'll never receive a woman.

So now I'm blessing your poporo, its stick, the calc and the coca, so that you can go on using them. You should think about what the poporo means. This poporo is a woman; when you use it you can take a wife, but you've got to think carefully. When you have a wife you have to look after her, you have to work for her, make clothes for her, you have to care for her, you mustn't hit her ever or treat her badly. Now receiving this poporo you must think about these things.

If you want a woman you have to speak well too, you have to talk to her parents asking their permission, then you can talk to the girl, ask her to give you water, speak well to her. Yes, you have to care for her a lot. You should take her with you to bathe, collect firewood for her, and get food for her. You must look after a woman well.

This poporo I'm giving you is a *sewa* – a safeguard – you must find another one to use normally, you should store this one carefully in your house. And only use it when you go to confess to the Mamas, or if you go to a divination. And from today you must chew coca, you must never give it up. The Mother gave us coca and told us to chew it always. At night before you go to sleep you should chew coca, four times at least, and think carefully about the next day, what you're going to do and how you're going to do it.

And now that you're going to receive a woman you should build your own house separately, you can't go on living with the other boys. You'll live separately with your wife, work for her, bring food for her, so that she can cook, you've got to look after your woman, you really have to care for her, you must bring her food, bring her meat, buy her chickens and pigs so that she eats well. Give her animals, and when you go off to collect firewood come back quickly. Don't wander about looking for other women, other people's women. You've got your own woman and you have to look after her. When you've received your poporo, you have to act responsibly, you mustn't go on playing about with other children, you have to be responsible. Towards Mamas, *comisarios* and *cabos* you have to act respectfully.

Now that I have given you these things you must come to my farm and work for me. I'll work for you too, to make sure you get a woman. Here I'm giving you good advice and you've got to listen to it, you mustn't forget what I'm telling you, otherwise you'll never get a wife, you'll spend the rest of your life alone. So come to my farm and we can finish this properly, you must come and confess everything that you've thought and done, confess, confess, confess, confess everything. Then everything will be fine, I'll be able to get a wife for you.

And if your father-in-law has animals, if he has cows and goats, you must look after them as if they were your own. You must look after your father-in-law too. You must look after his animals, you must give them salt when they need it, look after them as if they were yours. And that way your father-in-law will like you and look after you as well. You have to be a good man so that your father-in-law likes you. You should never cheat your father-in-law or act badly towards him. You must behave well with him.

Mama Bernardo concludes, 'So are you taking in the advice that I'm giving you here, are you going to heed it?'

'Yes, I'm listening.'

'All right then it's done, put your poporo in your bag.'

Once the poporo is given, the young man must spend four days and nights sitting in public, in the *nuhue*, where the Mamas, *comisarios* and *cabos* will lecture him on his responsibilities. He is not permitted to fall asleep.

Rite of passage: the girl

The transition of a girl from childhood to womanhood is treated equally seriously. For a boy, the whole process is controlled by the Mamas: they decide when the young man is ready, and will divine to ascertain the correct moment and technical details, such as the wood from which his poporo stick should be made. But for a girl, of course, the transition is created by the Great Mother, which we call nature. Every female is the Mother, every female is Nature herself. The onset of menstrual bleeding is a demonstration that nature has the power of fertility, and it is the careful management of that power which makes the world of the Kogi an ordered garden, rather than a chaotic jungle at war with itself. They believe that if this powerful life-energy which drives the world is not properly tended, it will erupt in chaotic forms – sickness in plants, animals and people – and human society too will lose its balance.

When a young woman first menstruates, an old woman tells her, 'Daughter' or 'Granddaughter, when you get your period don't give me any lies, you have to tell me.' If the menstruation is not known about the world is put out of balance. Illnesses follow, many types of violence may appear, this is why we must not miss the menstruation. So the girl, when she sees that her period has started, goes straight away to her grandmother or mother and says, 'Mother, my period has started.' Then straight away they put her in a corner where no one can see her, covered up, kept there for seven days.

For seven days no eating meat, no eating fresh food, no looking at a dog, no looking at a man, no blowing out candles, kept there, only making *mochilas* and spinning thread, cotton to weave cloth. Why do they do this? They do this because once the earth was a woman, it was a woman, and when it began to bleed for the first time it was not red but something blue, something green, something dark; this is how such things as gold began to be formed. Then, finally, came the flow of blood.

So all the gem-stones that are blue or green are the menstrual blood of the Mother Earth. Now, gold is menstruation, the pure blood of Mother Earth. That is why the native people collected it, collected her period, her menstrual blood, and kept it in a jar, well protected in a temple, and there are precious stones from her bleeding that are blue or green, those too were kept; we respect Mother Earth.

So then, we know this, so even today we keep a young woman who has just had her first period in a corner, that woman cannot be touched. When she has had her second period, she has become a woman. When she is ready to love, then the Mama blesses the man, orders the man to confess. He orders the young woman to confess whether she committed any sin without the Mama's permission, without the permission of her mother, then she asks for forgiveness and the Mama makes a payment, purifies the person so that she will be cleansed, will have a clear mind, good heart, good soul and marries them.

The loom

The sexes are utterly different, each with its own realm. This gender division permeates every part of life. Take, for example, the loom.

A Kogi loom is a simple wooden cross, enclosed in four side-beams; it is about 4 feet square. The corners of the cross are the cardinal points of the world – not our north, south, east and west, but the points on the horizon touched by the rising and setting sun at the solstices. The loom is the fundamental structure of the world.

Every man weaves, for himself and his family. He weaves in the *nuhue*, while a Mama lectures him on the true meaning of his work. He sits at this simple structure, works slowly and thoughtfully, stopping frequently to meditate, working his poporo.

The Mother told us when you start to weave you should be concentrating and not thinking of other things. These are the clothes that we wear. They speak to the sons of the Mother, the Fathers of the world. They speak to Serankua and Luawiko and Sintana, so you have to weave them well thinking only of this. The loom is like a book, when you sit to weave it is like reading, you have to concentrate. That is why the elders say that only men can weave. Boys are not allowed to weave. It was hard for the ancestors, when they were first given weaving, but just as the Mother first gave it, I continue weaving now. That loom represents all the worlds, they must never be weakened.

A thread spun with a left-hand twist, with the hand moving downwards over the thigh, is female: this is the warp thread, the thread which spans the four corners of the loom, the link between the cardinal points. This marks out the nature of the cloth, defines it. It is passive, productive, timeless; it spells out shape and form. It is an aspect of the Mother.

A thread spun with a right-hand twist, with the hand brushing upwards across the thigh, is male. This is the weft, which travels between the cardinal points as the sun travels across the sky, moving in time, with a past and a future. The threads of the warp open to receive the shuttle, which penetrates it. And thus a cloth is made which is male and female, ordering and binding together the world.

The first loom belonged to the Mother, a small white brilliant star which was the cross-piece of all worlds. It was the essence of whiteness. This was before enlightenment: it was whiteness in blackness. The bar, *aldo*, which in English is called the sword, which compresses the weft between each pass of the shuttle to make the cloth fine and even, is black because it was born of blackness, preceding light itself. 'First she came with a little star, and rising, rising, the Mother . . . ' brought it up through the nine worlds, granting a shape to possibilities, making order thinkable, carrying the idea that maps the sky. The loom is a model for the frame of the universe, a basic concept of order, whose trace is seen in the four cardinal points of the sky, the limits of the sun's travel.

In that prehistoric time, before life had been defined, when the nature of maleness and femaleness was still shapeless, the Mother was the weaver, using the loom-bar herself; the Kogi joke about it as a male sexual organ. She kept the loom shut up in her house, in a private space – a space which would eventually be defined as female.

There were men, or the idea of men – for all this is in *aluna* – in the world of ideas. *Aluna* begins as the Mother alone, and then divides and branches into spirit beings with distinct personalities. And if men, at this stage of the story, are themselves *aluna*, then their thoughts are ideas in the minds of spirit beings. These men of *aluna* are thoughts that think, and they tried to grasp the principle of weaving.

Men wondered, how is this done, how is cloth made? Men thought about how the Mother made cloth, men thought, they thought. How they thought, those men! And then men wanted to see, but the Mother would not allow it; she was when she was, darkly, the Mother. Men were thinking, but were not allowed to see, everything was shut away.

And then the men went when the Mother was not weaving, when she had gone somewhere. Then the men made a little hole to see how she wove, they made a hole and they covered it up. Then they saw the Mother weaving, they opened it, where it was covered, to watch the Mother weaving. Then the men saw how it was. 'That's how it is,' they thought. Suddenly the weaving went badly. Then the Mother thought, 'What's going wrong? What is happening? Have they been here?' the Mother thought.

The spirit-men have penetrated the wall of thought behind which the Mother is concealed. Now the world is thrown off-balance, and the Mother's weaving goes wrong, develops a fault. She knows why. Now a new and better harmony must be found, so that weaving will go right.

Today, men have the loom; it is in a public place, the *nuhue*, the world-house. The man drives the shuttle: he is masculine, the maker of public events. Only the men may weave. Good weaving, careful weaving, makes the world well, and weaving is always conducted under the supervision of a Mama. But there is an uneasiness in the story: the men have appropriated too much, they have wrested a power that was not given freely. The Mother has been defined as more female, the men as more male, but the cloth – is it not her baby? In the heat of the day babies cry; will the Mother hear her baby?

All weaving stops before midday, in case the Mother hears the cry of the black bar pressing down the cloth, and comes to take back her baby. (Since cotton snaps when it is dry, it is in any case a bad idea to continue working when the sun reaches its zenith.) And yet permission must have been granted for men to weave. Humans had to weave. So there was an aspect of the Mother, a daughter of the Mother, Mother Navoba, who came and allowed at least this cautious morning weaving.

Mother Navoba told us this, she told us how we would be able to live. Then Mother Navoba went away, but Mother Navoba is still here. She knew how to weave the bag, to weave cloth, to weave everything. So Mother Navoba lived. 'I will give you that implement that you hold.' So Mother Navoba gave me the loom, that I could weave cloth, the bag, the customs that I cling to. Mother Navoba also showed the Younger Brother a way to live, and us too, she showed us how to live. Mother Navoba told me this, told me everything that we are going to do. So. We still know. We know how to hear things. We know how to make offerings to all the places where Mother Navoba is, we still know. Where is the Father of the loom? We still know. Where is the Father of the thread? We still know.

When we look at the Kogi world, we do not see what they see. Men and women are not simply people, they are the embodiment of principles. Marriages are not exactly made in heaven, but they are arranged by the Mamas, following divination, and they are part of the greater balance of masculine and feminine which drives the world and even shapes the syntax of their language, which clearly distinguishes masculine and feminine elements in words. Men and women both own land; it is usual for daughters to inherit from their mothers, and sons from their fathers. The harmony and balance of the world is constructed out of the partnership of masculine and feminine, the dynamic process of weaving on the loom of life.

All the sons and daughters are in agreement with this. Weaving is putting things in accord with each other. The crossed stakes of the loom hold the world.

Divorce

This is not to say that partnerships do not fail and break apart. If the woman leaves her husband, it will always be to enter into a new partnership – and men appear to have little trouble finding a new bride. But for an abandoned wife the problems are very serious. The balance has been destroyed, since neither sex can perform the other's work. A single mother is an anomaly: she has to become a dependant of her parents, part of their family once more. She may well be left with her own farm – indeed the Mamas will generally ensure in a divorce settlement that the woman has enough land to sustain herself and her children – but she cannot work it without the help of her family.

First you get married and the woman really likes the man perhaps. And then she gets pregnant, and then perhaps the man leaves her. Women think that men will look after them but then sometimes men leave them and they go off with other women. So a woman's there and she's got children and the man goes off. So she sits there and she thinks and she cries. I was left with five children and so I had to think 'What am I going to do now?' The little ones ask for meat so I have to go out looking for it. I have to go and ask for it from my brothers. You have to work but then who will look after the children? If you don't have a grandmother or a father who can do it you have to leave them alone. But the man, he's fine with his new woman. I also need clothes for myself but where am I going to find them? A single woman can hardly get any clothes. It's the father who has to make them for her. Women don't know how to build a house for instance.

When you're single and no one comes, no man comes to be interested in you, yes you have to be in the house with your parents. If someone does come, fine, you can go and get married again. But if not you have to be with your mother and father. You see women don't go looking for men. It's the men who have to look for us. But Kogi women when they've got five children no one is going to come and look for them, so then they know that they will have to stay single.

The paths

A farm used only to consist of plants; protein came mainly from fish from the sea, and from hunting. This was the case throughout the Americas before the conquest, and until recently this was how the Kogi lived. But the invasion of colonos in the lower part of the Sierra cut them off from the sea, and introduced more livestock. Now they keep pigs and cattle, and as they move from farm to farm the family procession may well consist of two or three men walking ahead with an ox or a donkey, women and children behind, spurring the beast on with sticks, and herding pigs along with it.

They are walking paved trackways. The Kogi walk, literally as well as figuratively, in the paths of their ancestors. As Graham moved from one community to another he was constantly passing people on the move, and the men usually stopped to greet him. Where was he coming from? Where was he going? When he asked the same of them, they replied, 'We are going to my farm,' 'I am going to collect a mule from the pasture,' 'I am going to look at some land of mine,' 'to visit my father,' 'to visit my brother ... ' He was impressed by a powerful sense of thousands of individual trajectories constantly crossing and recrossing the mountains, weaving an astonishingly dense web of relations between kin and places, and all these movements following well trodden paths paved by the ancestors.

Tairona stone-work, paving and terracing is everywhere, and there are many carved stones along the paths. Traces of the ancestors are scattered liberally around – and for the Kogi that includes mountains and large rocks as well as archaeological sites. These are places of communication with the spirit world, but they are dangerous to those who do not understand them. Only Mamas can use them and work with their power, and it is a full-time job for the Mamas to neutralise their danger and maintain the balance of things.

Frustration

Graham was kept constantly on the edge of this world, never quite admitted, never quite thrown out. One day, for example, he was sent to visit Mama Augustin at his farm. The Mama was not there. The young boy leading Graham, after questioning the Mama's wife, said the Mama was working and they must go to find him. They climbed down into a ravine. Graham became worried that this was no ordinary work, and proposed that they wait at the farm, but the boy insisted and they scrambled on, around a cliff-face. As they rounded a spur, there was the Mama, sitting with a young man under an overhanging rock. They were sitting inside a circle of stakes, in a swept clearing. There was a bundle in front of them, but Graham could not make it out. Obviously some ritual was in progress. Mama Augustin came over to Graham, beaming, and accepted the gifts he had brought. He smiled radiantly, and then said, 'Good, I greet you. I have done much work. Goodbye.' And that was that.

Events like this became commonplace. The Kogi are masters of tantalising concealment, and they were giving Graham the full treatment, watching his response. As the Mamas kept leading him on and then closing the door in his face, Graham was spending most of his time with the elder vassals, men who generally regarded the Mamas as a poor lot compared with the wonder-Mamas of their youth. The old Mamas could make huge rocks fly through the air, they could cure any disease. 'These young Mamas, they're more interested in their next meal and in their wives' vaginas than in learning wisdom. I know more than they do.'

In a society where all knowledge comes from the original revelation – 'The Mother showed us ... ' 'The Mother taught us ... ' – there is a constant awareness that the sum total of knowledge in the community can never grow, only diminish. At the back of this anxiety is the original trauma of the conquest, a holocaust in which so many died, so much was lost. The Sierra seems, from archaeological evidence, to have supported between 300,000 and half a million people when the Spanish arrived. Today the Kogi number around 11,000, and the total indigenous population of the Sierra is perhaps 20,000.

Sometimes Graham would raise the question of writing: if the knowledge was written down, would it not then be saved? It was a proposition which the Kogi always seriously considered, and always rejected. Knowledge is not words, it is understanding, experience, a mode of being. You cannot write it down. The Kogi keep no written records of any kind, and, though it seems strange to say so, that is by choice. Caesar recorded that the Druids rejected writing – they played a similar social role to the Kogi Mamas, and even had a comparable system of education (twenty years in a cave). He supposed that they disapproved of literacy because they felt that it would destroy their capacity to remember.* The Kogi say the same.

Eventually the time came for Graham to go up to San Miguel and see its annual secular festival. At last he was being allowed in through the door. One of these old men, Pedro, was his guide. Graham's notes say:

> This is the Rome of the Kogi world. Everything about it, and the way people talk about it, breathes tradition, respect, grandeur. As it comes into view, Pedro stops me and asks me to give him some coins. With coins in one hand, and the other holding me firmly so that I am facing the town, he intones a long incantation. He gives me back the coins. Afterwards I ask him what all that was about. He says this was a presentation, to put everything into agreement. Before arriving at the town we pass the Caciquial – the Cacique Mama's own village, with his ceremonial house in the centre and a collection of about ten houses around it. It is deserted. Half a mile further on the path descends into a stream and looking up one sees the huge gate: massive double doors in a sort of gate house. It is astonishingly imposing. Pushing through the doors and stepping over the threshold, it is impossible not to feel that one is entering a powerful and exclusive space. Beyond it the path leads through a carefully tended grove of trees and fique palms into the town (though by this time I feel like calling it a city).

At last, Graham felt he was getting somewhere. But this was not a solemn and sacred festival – it was a carnival, a Saturnalia. Once a year, each Kogi town has a few days of riotous gaiety in which all the

---

* *Gallic Wars* VI, 13–18

constraints are removed. Alcohol, which is normally regarded as dangerous and is not used at all in the higher cities, is suddenly freely available. Graham had been admitted to San Miguel at the one time in the year when it would be in a state of licensed chaos.

The festival is in full swing. Almost all the men, except the officials keeping control of things, and many of the women, are blind drunk. There is dancing and music. The instruments are long flutes and drums, played in shambolic processions of men and women which circle around the town. There is also a sort of tag game, in which women chase men all over the town. The overall effect is pandemonium rather than ritual.

People are obviously enjoying themselves. Fights occasionally break out, but the officials quickly intervene. I later learn that after festivals there are usually prolonged confessionals in front of the Mamas. Resentments come to a head and adultery is common. The Mamas are not usually too tough on them however, it being understood that festivals are importantly about letting off steam.

Three bulls are killed. The meat is cooked and eaten communally.

Pedro's diplomacy on my behalf continues. All the Mamas are drunk and it takes twelve hours to get them all together in one place. He takes my presents to them individually, talks on my behalf and arranges the meeting. They are very drunk and say yes to everything. One is trying to do a divination but keeps spilling the water and dropping the bead. He gives up, grabs my arm and holds it saying blearily, 'Everything is very good, everything is good,' grinning manically into my face.

The Cacique Mama, Mama Valencia, arrives late and has not been drinking. He immediately becomes the centre of a small crowd. As people talk drunkenly to him they hold on to his hands, gently hug his head and treat him with extraordinary displays of adoration. He is absolutely impassive and acts as if this happens to him all the time. He looks like a saint.

Not long afterwards, Konchakalla [a Kogi from the southern slopes who had been the cause of trouble before] begins hectoring him aggressively, and he tells me to go. There is a crowd of young men, and real hostility is brewing. It is immediately past the point where reasoning or discussion is possible. I am just beginning to get seriously alarmed when Jacinto, the Jefe Mayor, arrives and, beside himself with drunken fury, starts screaming in a weird falsetto voice, shaking his head and throwing his arms about in a completely uncoordinated way. 'I am the leader here! I have invited him! He stays!' He looks totally demented. Mama Valencia and the young men leave very fast. Jacinto grabs me, smiles and sinks to the floor mumbling, 'I am the leader. Me. Only me.' The *cabos* throw Konchakalla out of the town. Five minutes later Jacinto is unconscious.

That was as close as Graham came to the inner heartland of the Kogi. He was never allowed back. By late July, he was becoming increasingly depressed at the feeling that he was getting nowhere.

I have a strong sense that things are going against the film and the very frustrating sense that there is not a great deal I can do to counter the tide of opinion. I have by now put the case for the film to almost everybody to whom I have access — a number of times. Each discussion or speech has been met with a resounding 'yes' and followed not long after by a wave of doubts and/or a resounding 'no'. Everybody by now knows the arguments for and against; it has become a question of confidence. The nuns are making dramatic moves to convince the Kogi that I am a con-man, thief and a potential killer, and that I should be thrown out. In Pueblo Viejo hostility grows and nobody wants to discuss the film further. The atmosphere is terrible. More protestations that in fact I and the BBC are very nice people and not out to rape and pillage at all, are now all quite beside the point.

The Kogi were also becoming angry at the way in which the Younger Brother in Bogota responded to their basic message, that ecological catastrophe was looming. Carlos came up from the Casa Indígena in Santa Marta with the message that the government too was alarmed, and its ecologists wanted to reforest eroded land in the Sierra with guayaba trees. The reaction was hostile: the Younger Brother does not know anything and does not listen to wisdom. These trees, which seem an effective barrier to erosion near rivers, have wider effects which, the Kogi say, are disastrous in this ecological zone.

If the Great Mother had wanted guayaba in this part of the Sierra she would have put them there. Why do you come here and tell us these things? You know nothing about it. You come and tell us we need a bridge [a reference to a government project lower down in the foothills]. You send machines to dig huge holes in the ground. You don't know what you are doing. You are digging into the flesh of our Mother. You are taking her blood.

The bridge project has been going on for years, and has been steadily milked of funds by a group of corrupt politicians and contractors.

At the same time, the complaints of the nuns had been passed on to the National Organisation of Colombian Indians (ONIC), a lobby which claimed to represent all the indigenous people of Colombia. In fact there was virtually no contact between ONIC and the Kogi, but the story as they heard it was that there was a plot between Amparo and the BBC to sell Kogi culture for cash, and they protested vehemently to the government.

Martín's visit

The film was now a political issue, and Martín von Hildebrand, the head of the Office of Indian Affairs, had to sort it out. The Kogi invited him to attend a ceremonial offering, and he took the opportunity to travel into the Sierra on a State Visit.

This was Martín's first journey to the Kogi. The Kogi themselves treated it very seriously. He was asked to come to one of their higher towns, close to the inner heartland which is shut to all outsiders. There, as in all Kogi towns, there is a square building erected as a church by missionaries, a building which is never used and is permanently locked.

The church was opened and battered leather armchairs were dragged out and placed in a row in front of it. Martín, Amparo and Graham were told to sit and were given oranges, and the men of the town were gathered. Eventually the Younger Brothers were summoned to a hillside meeting.

A few nights before, at a lower town, a group of Mamas had assembled for a meeting and four hours of divination. When the

divination was ended, after sunset, Jacinto, the Jefe Mayor, called
Graham and Carlos to speak to him outside the village. He said that
they wanted to make the film, though they would not allow filming
above a certain point. Carlos asked wryly when he would change his
mind again, and the Jefe Mayor smiled and said that Mamas do not
change their minds easily.

The following morning Martín had arrived, on his way to the
hillside conference. He asked Jefe Mayor what he thought of the film.
Jacinto, without batting an eye, and with Graham looking on, said,
'The Mamas do not want it.'

At the meeting, the nuns were invited to state their objections. One
complained that it was wrong to film Indians, because then the outside
world would believe that all Colombians were like this, primitive,
pagan.

They took a sufficiently arrogant tone for Martín to feel obliged to
make his own position clear. He was the head of the Office of the Indian
Affairs. The indigenous people were his responsibility, and the nuns
were present by his permission. If he wanted, he would close their
mission immediately.

He went on to say that a clear decision should be made about the
film, and once made it should be stuck to. But it was not for him to
decide. The Mamas must decide. And the nuns must respect their
decision, as the government would.

The Mamas listened in silence and did not reply.

It was time for Graham to go back to Bogota. He paid a farewell
visit to one of the friendliest Mamas, Mama Bernardo, who presented
him with a token which, he said, would guard him from harm on the
journey. On the way down the steep hill from Mama Bernardo's
home, in a drenching downpour, Graham slipped, fell, and cracked the
base of his spine on a stone. He lay unconscious in the mud.

He came round, got up and left the Sierra in a state of deep
depression. Walking the tough, steep path down, he passed a stone
which is a shrine to the Mother of the Younger Brother. A gesture of
respect should be made here, a token act of laying a certain kind of
palm-leaf on the stone. This would regulate his coming and going. It is
an act with meaning in the spirit world, in *aluna*. When the harmony of
aluna is disrupted, the Kogi say, this shows in things, people, animals
becoming sick. A seed planted in the wrong frame of mind may rot in

the ground. A pot made without the right attitude of thoughtfulness may crack. Weaving carried out without the correct mental framework may go wrong. A man who does not show proper respect to the spirit world will become ill.

Graham stopped at the stone, and stared at it. He was sodden and cold and very tired. The Kogi had led him a terrible dance, and in the end he had got nowhere. He thought about the palm-leaf, and decided not to bother.

He arrived in Bogota with a streaming nose and influenza.

The drugs war

It was September, and I was coming on my promised journey to finalise filming plans with the Mamas. The omens were not good.

Colombia itself was then something of a mess. The presidential elections were to be in a year's time, which up to now had only had one significance for me: the film had to be made before the elections, when all the contacts I had established in government agencies would probably be swept away. But for Colombians campaigning was in full swing, and one candidate led the field – Galán. Galán's popularity was linked to his image as an honest man, and his public proclamations against the drug barons.

That was why they shot him dead.

At that moment, Colombia changed. Half a million people followed Galan's funeral cortège. Suddenly there was a national revulsion at the power and arrogance of the criminal cartels.

Colombia had tolerated the drug barons for many reasons. The two largest cartels operate out of Cali and Medellin, and these are the two most prosperous cities in the country. A small fraction of the billions of dollars from cocaine were used to look after the cartels' own constituents, to provide public housing projects and hospitals and public transport. The drug barons appear to be genuinely loved by many of the poor. There is some necessary connection between organised crime and charity – it is not only in Colombia that these things happen. The Big Man is usually open-handed, especially if he comes from a deprived background.

But in Colombia it went further, especially in Medellin. The Cali bosses are more like modern businessmen, perhaps colder, more discreet than their Medellin rivals. They are also better educated. They are, as it were, the Old Money of organised crime, at least in the popular mind. The Medellin bosses also ran their operations through computers and financial offices, but they had started out as petty criminals – some of them got their initial stake through tomb-robbing in the Sierra, and through the marijuana boom there of the 1970s. They wanted money, unlimited money, but they also wanted respect. They wanted to be recognised and deferred to. It was the same impulse that had prompted the tomb-robbers to demand recognition as a syndicate.

The top men, Escobar, Gacha, Abello and their associates, were public figures. They wanted people to know who they were, and to accept them and admire them. This, together with the public works side of their activities, was taking them into politics. There was (and remains) a real possibility that Colombia could be controlled by them. They were backing candidates in every election, and winning control of towns and provinces. Escobar was in the Senate.

Anyone who spoke against them was liable to be gunned down, not simply because he was a threat, but because of the disrespect. The judiciary and police were virtually completely cowed by the simple alternative they were offered whenever a *mafioso* was arrested: lead or gold. Faced with the choice between a substantial fortune and a burst from an automatic rifle, the abstractions of the law lose their meaning for most people. However, it should never be forgotten that a large number of Colombian officials and journalists chose lead. They still do.

The murder of Galán was not just one more step in the process by which the Medellin cartel was taking power. It was an insult to Colombia. The cartel had treated the country with contempt, and the nation and the government chose lead. They declared war on the drug barons. Nobody doubted that this was suicidal. In the red corner, The Colombian State. A plucky challenger, but impoverished and ramshackle. Its army and police include some courageous and honest men, but in general are disorganised and deeply corrupt. It offers to judges who have received death threats official cars which turn out to be broken down jeeps. Senior government officials in dangerous zones have bodyguards who knock off at five o'clock. In the blue corner, The Champion – sleek, well managed, with unlimited funds, armed to the teeth with sophisticated weapons and with private armies trained by Israeli, British and North American mercenaries.

Every state official and family, every journalist, everyone who went into a government office, as well as the whole of the judiciary, knew that they were being sent into a war to the death on the losing side. But the insult they had been offered was intolerable. They chose lead. Almost at once, the offices of the liberal, campaigning newspaper *El Espectador* were blown to pieces.

At this moment of national heroic suicide, I was supposed to go to Bogota? All United States citizens were warned to leave Colombia. I am not a citizen of the United States. All foreign journalists were warned they would be shot. I really do not think I am a journalist. The Colombian Embassy informed me that all helicopters had been grounded, but Helicol, the company that provides my helicopter, assured me that there was no problem. In desperation I called the British Foreign Office, trusting that they would advise me not to go. 'We are not actually giving out any advice not to go. I wouldn't go myself, but it's your job, isn't it?'

I went home and stared at Charlie. He stared back. No help there. I did have a broken ankle (I had stepped out of an office window to have a cigar. No, it was on the ground floor. How was I to know about the basement? The BBC should never have banned smoking on the premises. It was a Hamlet. I dropped like a stone, lit up, heard the music and passed out. Smoking Can Damage Your Health). But I could walk with a stick. And my wife, Sarah, would come to prop me up. She made it perfectly clear that if I was prepared to go, she would be there too. The BBC, instead of rejecting this idiocy out of hand, gave her a temporary contract to look after me on the trip. There really was nothing to do except make our wills and get on the plane.

Bogota dangers

Bogota was tense. The government had swooped down on a number of big houses, and confiscated cars, light aircraft, high-powered boats and helicopters, but always too late to actually catch anyone important. The cartel bosses were all in hiding, but were organising daily bombings and assassinations. Some of the nicest houses around the Charleston Hotel were under police occupation, and every shop and apartment block was defended by a worried man with a gun. The Colombian journalists I met were particularly nervous. They had stopped receiving death threats. The drums had stopped beating. Bad trouble very soon.

I wanted to involve Colombian television in the project, and on my last visit I had discussed this with the Minister of Communications, who had been very keen. But now he had been reshuffled. I went to see Inravision, the State television company (which is a kind of public service channel alongside commercial television). They were very polite, and provided me with an armed escort for the journey across Bogota, but they were evidently unlikely to do anything more without political instructions.

The new Minister of Communications was Lemos Simons, one of Columbia's most experienced politicians. In the last few critical weeks he had been Acting Prime Minister and Minister for Justice, both jobs which carry automatic death sentences from the cartel. Now a new Minister for Justice had been appointed, a young lady of thirty-one who was on an extended and ever-extending visit to the United States, and who announced that her ambition was to make it to thirty-two. Simmons had a few minutes free, and agreed to see me.

Coming from a country like Britain, where bureaucratic suspicion and inertia dominate, and where there is rarely any need for genuine courage in government, only posturing, I find Colombia very impressive. Simons lived with sub-machine-guns at the office door. He was a key part of a government literally fighting for its life against an insurrectionary criminal conspiracy. Yet he found time to listen to me, to understand what I was talking about, and to set up a meeting within twenty-four hours to commit Inravision, Focine (the national film board) and Audiovisuales, the State production house, to backing the film.

Actually turning the wheels of these three organisations would, of course, be a slow and cumbersome process. But it was impressive.

The next stop was Reichel-Dolmatoff, who was now in his apartment in Bogota. I had written to the Grand Old Man earlier in the year, telling him that the Kogi had said they wanted to make a film and asking for his help and advice. He wrote back saying that he disapproved of the project and wanted nothing to do with it. What the Kogi really wanted, apart from medical help, was to be left alone.

I hoped it would not end there, as Reichel was the only anthropologist with a serious knowledge of these people and I needed all the help I could get. I was peered at suspiciously through the spy-hole in the door, and then a great number of locks, bolts and chains were undone to admit me.

Reichel and Alicia complimented me on my *ruana*, the woollen blanket-like garment worn in the Andes.

'I bought it in your beautiful town of Villa de Leyva.'

'Not our town. Not our town at all. We were driven out. I sold everything and fled. Everything, just as it stood. The books, the furniture, everything.'

Reichel felt that he was in danger there. I was shocked. What a terrible thing, to flee from one's library, to lose everything.

'No, we are used to it. It has happened before. Right from Russia, in 1905.'

I stared at the erect, white-haired man in his high arm-chair, with his rotund, well-elocuted English. How large was his library in 1905, eighty-four years ago?

'Geraldo, how old are you?'

Well no, he had not actually personally fled from Russia in 1905. But his family. And he was persecuted, threatened, here in Bogota. The war of the drug barons seemed a minor diversion from the war of the anthropologists. His enemies had seized the University.

'There are those who call me an Indian-lover, who would kill me because they think I help the Indians. And others accuse me of being paternalistic.' Both accusations seem reasonable enough. 'They accuse me of TAKING TEA!' That too seemed accurate. 'I am called an agent of American Imperialism.' I felt that his enemies were on dodgy ground here. 'And they say I am a LEVI-STRAUSSIST!' He slammed the arm of his chair with his fist. I could understand why the last accusation would annoy him. Reichel is not a follower, he is a figure on his own, a monument in his own right. And I was puzzled.

'Surely being a Levi-Straussist is not a capital offence?'

The Great Man looked at me kindly. 'You do not know Colombia.'

I was abashed at my innocence. The accusation was fair.

'I never go to the University now. They are all my enemies. They held a commemoration, the twenty-fifth anniversary of the Department of Anthropology. I founded it. I started it. They invited me to give the keynote address.' He handed me the printed programme, with his lecture at the top. 'I did not go. They had to play Hamlet without the Prince!'

Rational standards do not apply in Colombia. Outside, men were planting bombs. One person in ten on the street was a privately-hired guard with a rifle. And in the context of Colombian anthropology, Reichel was not just the Prince, he was the King.

All Europeans who achieve a position of prominence in Colombia are made acutely aware of that country's defensive and insecure feelings of nationalism. Colombia is trying to assert its national academic credentials, to show that it is not simply an outpost of Europe and North America, and there are people who feel that this demands hostility to *émigré* scholars. Reichel was virtually the creator of Colombian anthropology, and so is used to seeing himself as a lonely bastion of European rationalism. In Colombia, where to identify a public figure as a foreigner can be to put him literally in deadly danger, a lonely man can become terribly afraid.

But what about the film? When I had last seen him, Reichel had given me a copy of an article he had published in the *Journal of Latin American Lore*. Its peroration was stirring:

> What I am really concerned about is this: What does the Kogi world view teach us about ourselves? ... I truly believe that the Kogi ... can greatly contribute to a better understanding and handling of some of our modern dilemmas, and that we should consider ourselves fortunate to be the contemporaries of a people who, perhaps, can teach us to achieve a measure of 'balance' ... My appeal is to humanists, to psychologists and philosophers, to historians and to the community of international planning experts who, I am afraid, are far removed from the Magna Mater of the Sierra Nevada de Santa Marta.

To follow this through, surely he should help me to ensure that the film was accurately and properly made? We talked at length, and Reichel said that he had come round to the view that it should be done, and that he was prepared to assist. He would have to do so from a distance, as he had decided to abandon Colombia and work in Japan. There he would be safe, and appreciated. He was leaving in a few days.

I urged him to meet Graham, and talk to him. Yes, he agreed. Then he looked at me.

'You say he studied at Cambridge?'

'That's where he did his PhD, yes.'

He asked who had supervised Graham's thesis. In fact he had already guessed, and the knowledge made him suddenly back away.

'I cannot see your anthropologist. It is a question of territory.'

I was baffled, but here was a stone wall which could not be moved. What did he have against Graham's education?

'He is of a different school. Your anthropologist is of a different school from myself. His approach is different.'

'Of course his approach is different! He is of a different generation from you. You would not want everyone to hold the same views, to ask the same questions over and over again, to think in the same way, would you? He should be different.'

Yes, this was true. But I must understand territory. Reichel would not want to conflict with another anthropologist and his mentor. There was evidently some long-standing grievance at the back of this, another feeling of betrayal. At the end of it all, we reached an agreement. Reichel would correspond with me, would advise me privately, but no one should suppose that what I produced was his work, or produced under his tutelage. Fair enough. It isn't. But I wanted his views on it, and the benefit of his work.

I left bemused. There were no taxis, it was dark and was pouring with rain. I hobbled back to my hotel, the longest walk I had undertaken since breaking my ankle, over the chaos of paving slabs. Bogota had changed: with so many guards, the level of street crime had dropped significantly. The streets were less dangerous than usual, unless you were marked as a target.

Back at the hotel I was interviewed for Colombian radio. I was relaxed, had plenty to say, until the interviewer asked, 'Doesn't it worry you, coming here? Don't you feel that it is dangerous?' I explained my impression, that it was really only dangerous if someone had a reason to want to get rid of you. As I spoke, I hoped that no one would see this as a challenge, or decide to make a point. I had enough trouble, without that. I tried to avoid sounding like a Levi-Straussist.

The Mamas speak

Graham was, not surprisingly, worried about what would happen when we got to the Sierra. In his view everything should be taken very slowly, the Kogi needed more time to come around to the idea of the film. I felt that this was unlikely. I had not had to endure the trials he had been put through, and I was sure that was what they were. He was being tested. The Mamas had made up their minds when I had seen them. Obviously there were problems with the vassals, but that was only to be expected. Centuries of suspicion and secrecy are not easily laid aside. But in the last analysis, that was a problem for the Mamas, not for us.

Santa Marta airport was littered with small aircraft whose tyres had been let down. They all had papers fixed to their cockpits, stating that they had been impounded. These were the planes of the drug industry. The offensive was in full swing.

Ramón greeted me warmly, but warned me that things would be difficult. I was unperturbed. I would not put any arguments in favour of the film. If the Mamas want to speak to the Younger Brother, I would like to help. If they do not, if they think that the dangers outweigh the benefits, they are probably right.

With Ramón, Adalberto and Amparo, Graham, Sarah and I took the helicopter up to Pueblo Viejo. Two ladies accompanied us, from the office of the President. This was becoming serious.

The town was almost deserted. We went to the medical post where some of us would sleep. The calor-gas stove had no gas, the water pipe was broken. There was no medical student here any more, and Arregoce was no longer on hand to set things right. He had now become Manuelito's successor, an official of Gonavindua Tairona. As the arguments had flared, Arregoce had been caught in the middle of them, and the Mamas were not pleased with his performance. He had much to learn, and Arregoce was not having an easy life. He looked cowed and unhappy.

Amparo, who was there to ensure that we behaved properly towards the Kogi, asked me if we could not postpone filming for another year. No, we could not. If the Mamas wanted to make a film, good, we were here to help. If not, I would go away. This was their film, their project, not simply mine or the BBC's.

I do not think I had any doubt what would happen. The Mamas had impressed me too deeply with their terror at what was happening to the world.

We are the Elder Brothers.
We have not forgotten the old ways.
How could I say that I do not know how to dance?
We still know how to dance.
We have forgotten nothing.
We know how to call the rain.
If it rains too hard we know how to stop it.
We call the summer.
We know how to bless the world and make it flourish.

But now they are killing the Mother.
The Younger Brother, all he thinks about is plunder.

The Mother looks after him too, but he does not think.

He is cutting into her flesh.
He is cutting into her arms.
He is cutting off her breasts.
He takes out her heart.
He is killing the heart of the world.

When the final darkness falls everything will stop.
The fires, the benches, the stones, everything.
All the world will suffer.

When they kill all the Elder Brothers then they too will be
    finished.
We will all be finished.

What would they think if all the Mamas died?
Would they think, well? so what? or what would they think?

If that happened and all we Mamas died, and there was no one
    doing our work,
well, the rain wouldn't fall from the sky.

It would get hotter and hotter from the sky,
and the trees wouldn't grow,
and the crops wouldn't grow.

Or am I wrong, and they would grow anyway?

The Mamas know that this process has begun. I still did not know how they knew, or what precisely had so frightened them, but the constant mention of water was obviously significant. Over and over again they warned of heat and drought, and the end of life. This is not a game: it is the most important thing in the world, for them and for us.

That night a group of Mamas came to see me. They spoke gravely, and very briefly.

'Our yes is yes. The Mamas do not speak with two tongues.'

6

History

The first word the Kogi taught me was *aluna*. The mind.

> In the beginning, there was blackness.
> Only the sea.
> In the beginning there was no sun, no moon, no people.
> In the beginning there were no animals, no plants.
> Only the sea.
>
> The sea was the Mother.
> The Mother was not people, she was not anything.
> Nothing at all.
> She was when she was, darkly.
> She was memory and potential.
> She was *aluna*.

'Tell me about the creation of the world.'

'You do not need to know that. The Younger Brother cannot understand and has no need to understand. We will tell you what you need to know.'

I agreed that I did not need to know the whole story. The chapter headings alone take nine nights, and then for nine times nine nights the great epic of creation is spelled out in detail. Translated into our way of thinking, shaped by our linguistic ideas, the story loses its meaning. And anyway, as they knew very well, I had neither the grasp nor the stamina to take it in.

But I needed to understand *aluna*, because without that I would never understand anything.

Aluna contains everything which is past and everything that may become. *Aluna* is intelligence; it is the concentrated thought and memory which forms a bridge between the human 'spirit' and the universe, but it is also the hidden world of forces which govern the world's fertility. *Aluna* makes possible growth, birth and sexuality; it is the spiritual energy that makes things happen. If it did not, the world would be sterile. It would never have begun.

Aluna was and is the Mother. The whole of Kogi life returns again and again to this fundamental principle of reality, the life-force which is intelligent thought, which has personality and gives birth to personality, which shapes the world and makes it flower. Through concentrated thought and meditation, the Kogi enter the world of *aluna* and act there.

In the beginning there was only *aluna*, the amniotic sea, the cosmic principle: the Mother. The Mother concentrated, the nothingness which was the original sea of thought, spirit and fertility pondered and conceived the idea of the world. It began with a womb, a world-house, which was a cosmos. This was the great egg of the universe.

In *aluna*, she then conceived nine levels, nine worlds, within this womb. They were her daughters. Each world has its own character, its own colour, its own soil: her children had their own personalities. The mysteries of creation and fertility are to be understood as a process of *aluna* dividing, by an effort of concentration, into separate spiritual bodies. She also conceived of sons, among them Serankua. The Dawning began with the definition of these powerful beings, whose existence defines the Mother as a being too.

The concept of femininity begins here; by embodying sons, by conceiving masculinity and separating it from herself, the Mother is also defined as female. *Aluna* constantly requires balance, harmony, and give and take of parts which are distinct, but which have to be in accord with one another. Sexuality and gender are part of that.

She and her sons then addressed themselves to the problem of fertility. 'How will we create a living thing?' Through eight of the nine worlds the soil was infertile; eight of her nine daughters could not conceive. Life could not begin there. It had not been properly thought through. Only in the ninth world, the world of black earth, had the Mother conceived a daughter capable of fecundity.

Here her son Serankua fertilised the world. The details are, I was told, unimportant. What matters is how hard the Mother had to think – hardest of all to make the first man. How does an eye work? How should it be made? The foot, what should it be like? Creatures were conceived with eyes and feet wrongly made, then finally success, and a history began, an epic sweep of rising and falling peoples of different kinds and different colours, until finally the nature of mankind was settled, stabilised.

And then the punch line.

>   There were still no people.
>   There were no plants, no animals, no sun, no moon.
>   Only the Mother.
>   Only *aluna*.

The Mother had conceived the world in *aluna*, shaping possibilities. There were nine worlds, and life and history existed only in *aluna*. Now it could be made flesh.

Now the Mother made the physical world, the world we inhabit. This is the place of the second word I was taught, 'Gonavindua'.

Go means 'something being born' or 'birth'. *Na* means 'something coming' (it is the word for the first light before dawn) and *vi* means 'something moving in the stomach', like something moves in the stomach when a woman is four months pregnant. *Du* means 'all things that have life'; *duas* means sperm.

It is the word for the quickening of the world.

It also means 'the mountain where the world began, the law-bringer'.

The mountain where the world began is, of course, the Sierra, and the Sierra is the Heart of the World. Here the Mother stuck her spindle and spun it, turning the world on its axis, spinning out the thread which is time as well as space, and which heaps up in the cone of the Sierra, and which then develops, in an ever-widening spiral, into the whole of the world.

All things have a hidden connection, linking traces deriving from their common creation at the time of the Dawning, Gonavindua. The cosmos is a womb, a *nuhue*, a world-house, with worlds at different levels. The mountains are world-houses; the Sierra contains the cosmos within it. The links have to be constantly reaffirmed. Maintaining reality is a difficult balancing act; ensuring stability in the dynamic flux of *aluna* requires deep thought, profound understanding. I had to learn this, I was told.

The first people

The Sierra, as I heard about it and experienced it in the company of the Mamas, appeared to be a garden of Eden, a heart of the world containing the whole of the world. And here, I was told, the Mother's offspring, her male child Serankua, created humans. They were made to look after the world, to care for everything in it. Animals and plants were placed not under their dominion but in their care.

The Kogi word for themselves, *Kaggaba*, means 'people'. I believe that it comes from *kaggi*, meaning 'earth'. Similarly, our word 'Adam', which in Hebrew means 'mankind', comes from *adamah*, also meaning 'earth'. But the Kogi do not simply mean that people were created from clay; they mean that humanity shares in the nature of the earth, and is part of it. The second half of *Kaggaba*, *aba*, means 'mother'.

Everything that could be, everything that will be, already was known to the Mother. If she had not thought it, if it had not been shaped in *aluna*, then it did not have the possibility of being conceived. And if it cannot be conceived, it cannot be made. Helicopters, television cameras, all our inventions, are not ours alone I was told. These things already were, from the time before time.

Much later, Serankua created another kind of human being, a Younger Brother to the original people. This was a creature with a butterfly mind, which paid no attention to the Mother's teaching; the Kogi say 'he changed colour, from red to green and other colours'. His descendants, ourselves, are called *Kasaoggi*. This Younger Brother was not to remain in the Sierra: he was ejected. He was given a different way of knowing things, a can-do, technological knowledge, and exiled to lands designated for him across the sea. The Elder Brothers, caring for everything spiritual and material, would take care of the heart of the world, and leave him to his own devices.

That is the story as I was told it, and it awakened many different kinds of echo in my head.

There can hardly be any human societies which do not regard themselves as the original creation, the real people, and in their origin myths place the centre of the universe in their territory. 'Elder' and 'Younger' is not all that unusual in the Andes: Felicity had encountered it as the distinction between highland and lowland communities, and it would be natural for the Kogi then to see the indigenous people of their mountain as 'Elder' and us, who came from below, as 'Younger'.

But the Sierra is a strange world. Its form, this natural pyramid, reaching from the sea to the sky, an island outcrop, does make it unique. Its range of habitats and environments, the incredible diversity of plant and animal life, does truly make it a model of the larger world. Its placing, between northern and southern continents, with day and night twelve hours each all year round, without seasonal changes of temperature, seems almost unnatural to a northerner like myself. The expression 'The Heart of the World' is not simply a conceit.

The story of creation is reminiscent of the biblical myth. The world of the Kogi will do very well as the Garden of Eden. I had often wondered what sort of physical environment human beings were designed for. Not England, obviously: man arrived late there, already knowing how to protect himself from the elements. The Sierra seems more like it. Above the rain forest, on the far side of 'El Infierno', the Kogi live on open savannah, neither too hot nor too cold, where fruits abound, corn and vegetables grow fast, and there is constant cool fresh water in the fast-flowing rivers. The Sierra, taken as a whole, is a completely self-sufficient system, and if it was designed as a home for humanity the architect could hardly have done a better job.

From that perspective, the Younger Brothers are the descendants of Adam and Eve, expelled from the Garden. Is all this some reworking of a tale heard from missionaries, in which the Indians have decided that, since this is white man's history, they must belong to a pre-Adamite creation? It may be, but the changes are interesting.

Adam and Eve, in the biblical story, are expelled as a punishment for doing wrong, before they can know what it is to do wrong. Only after eating the forbidden fruit do they know the difference between Good and Evil, but by then it is too late. In the Kogi story, the Younger Brother is exiled because he pays no attention to the teaching of the Mother, and having no moral understanding he meddles with things. He will make machines. That is why he is dangerous. His exile is not a punishment, but a defence for the world. The sea exists as a barrier, to keep the Heart of the World safe.

Perhaps it is a thoughtful corruption of a Bible story. But what about *aluna*, this insistence that the world is made of ideas, essences, and all existence is a reflection of that? Kogi religion – and it is a religion, comparable in its profundity and insight with any of the major religions – has to be taken on its own terms. If there are elements which seem to be related to Christian myth, they should be seen as parts of a shared understanding, not as something borrowed and corrupted. Kogi theology must have had its own historical development, but we have no way of knowing what that was.

Many of the Kogi's beliefs are echoed in other of the world's great religions. *Aluna* is startlingly similar, for example, to the Buddhist concept of *Tao*, the changeless reality which sustains heaven and earth:

> There was something formless yet complete,
> That existed before heaven and earth;
> Without sound, without substance,
> Depending on nothing, unchanging.
> All-pervading, unfailing.
> One may think of it as the mother of all things under heaven.
> Its true name we do not know:
> *Tao* is the name that we give it.*

Like *aluna*, *Tao* contains within itself the generative energy of masculine and feminine, which are called *Yin* and *Yang*. Kogi religion combines this concept of a metaphysical living reality with a particularly thoughtful and beautiful version of a creation story shared by the high religions of the world.

Where have these people come from? What is their 'knowledge'?

---

* Tao Te Ching, XXV, trans. by A. Waley, *The Way and its Power*, London 1934, p. 74

Tairona society

The so-called Tairona civilisation was not one society but many, living in a highly compressed space. We have a slight knowledge of them from Spanish accounts, but these are naturally sketchy. The Spaniard who wrote most knowledgeably about them was Juan de Castellanos, an adventurer who accompanied Jiménez de Quesada on his epic search for El Dorado, which resulted in the founding of Bogota. Around the middle of the sixteenth century he explored Tairona territory searching for wealth and adventure. His major work, the *Elegías de Varones Ilustres de Indias*, lay unpublished for three hundred years. Castellanos wrote in verse, to give his observations greater stature.

He mentions the way the Indians worked to ensure health and fertility. He connects this with fasting and with 'los alunos', a word which he did not explain, and which has probably only come down to us because he was stuck for a rhyme.

> At great and tedious length they fast
> For their children or for what they sow,
> The *alunos* only then, at last,
> When things have to be done, will go.*

Apart from that, and references to Naomas (who are the Mamas of today) and caciques who obey them, the Spanish chronicles have little to say about the structure and beliefs of the indigenous community. 'They held their festivals and dances [which were] of a strange grandeur, cleanness and curiosity, on paved courtyards of huge polished stones',† and when they fasted 'the Devil speaks to them telling them a thousand lies ... with such a great wind and hurricane that it seemed it would uproot the hut'.‡ The Devil was very real to the Spanish.

The chroniclers were vividly struck by the high quality of Tairona

---

* '... tienen prolijísimos ayunos
  Por sus hijos o por su sementera;
  Y entonces solamente los alunos
  A cosas necesarias salen fuera.' (8, 258)
† Simón, V, 191
‡ Simón, V, 217

agriculture. 'There is a lot of beautiful corn to be found in the countryside along with yucca and many trees of guayaba, guanabanas and other fruits and a lot of pineapple.'* 'What were most pleasing to the sight were the many crops of roots and corn, batatas, yuccas, names, ahuyamas, perrers, cotton and the fruit trees, of apples, guamos, guaimaros, mamones, guayabois, cherries, curos, pinones and many others bearing fruit.'†

Irrigation systems were impressive: 'They found cultivated orchards and the fields were watered by ditches excavated in admirable fashion, in manner no different from that in which the people of Lombardy and the Etruscans cultivated and irrigated theirs.'‡ And of course they were impressed by the scale and variety of Tairona jewellery. But to understand how this society functioned, we have to turn to another source.

The Mamas have an account of their own past which, so far as I am aware, fits perfectly both with the archaeological record and with what is known of other mountain societies in the Andes. Since they have to rely on an oral teaching, and are highly competitive in their knowledge, few errors are likely to creep in to their story.

The Sierra consists of numerous ecological platforms. At the northern base is the sea. Here were sea-side cities, which gathered salt and fish. One such city, right on the shore, has been discovered at Chenge; it specialised in the extraction of sea-salt. These cities also drew on the products of the dry forest that comes down to the white sand, with its tall palms, cashew, almond and gourd trees, and cactus fruits.

A little higher, in places such as Pueblito, were cities specialising in the crops of the hot jungle. Pueblito is at the bottom of this jungle, where god-trees, zambo-cedars and tagua palms grow 100 feet high, and in their shade carob trees, avocados, rubber trees and laurels are strewn with lianas. This jungle also provided meat from monkeys, iguana, alligators, macaws and large rodents.

At a slightly higher level, where it is cooler and wetter, the jungle is rich in fruit and larger game animals. Here, too, fields could be cleared for cotton and maize. Yet higher, at the level of the current frontier between the Kogi and the outside world, is the wooded savannah, rich in plantains and sugar cane, root crops and maize.

* Oviedo, 8, 255
† Simón, V, 191
‡ Oviedo, 8, 245

Each city also developed specialist crafts: stone-working at Pueblito, metal-work at Bondigua, and so on. Each city had its own tribal identity (Pueblito, for example, was called Tayko, home of the Tayko people), its own mode of dress and probably its own language or dialect. The Lost City was Teijuna, home of the Teijuna people, whose name became in Spanish 'Tairona'. The word itself represents a masculine symbol, the penetrating beak of the hummingbird: it also means place of origin, seed-bed, related to a word meaning testicle, and is the name of the founder of the Teijuna people.

Each city was distinct, adapted to its local situation. But none of them could survive alone. They were interdependent, exchanging goods along the dense network of paths and stairways that cover the Sierra like a web.

Stone-work was the key to it all, the remodelling of the landscape to build flat agricultural terraces and well drained paths that could be used in all weather. This required a supervising hand whose authority extended over the whole Sierra. This was no Inca, no great King. It was the hand of the Naomas, the Mamas.

Mamas were in every town, giving their guidance and blessing to the work of daily life. But their real abodes were up above. It may be that the towns had a large mobile population, as they do now, with people moving between farms and only attending in town when required for ceremonies and communal work. The Mamas were certainly mobile, with their ritual centres and places of meditation high above the urban population. The upper part of the Sierra was always a closed world, with the vassals living below 6,000 feet.

They supervised the large-scale public works which this society needed. And they also supervised agriculture and trade. They were the experts on which crops to grow where, on which terraces to use, and on what exchanges were required. The Spanish described this exchange as trade, and spoke of Tairona merchants, but that was because they had no other way of understanding it. They were actually looking at a highly-regulated society which had no concept of trade or private ownership, because it did not know the idea that an individual can do whatever he likes with land or with anything else.

In the beginning the Mother taught us how to live together like brothers. And we lived together like brothers. We the Elder Brother lived right down to the sea, we lived at Mingeo, we lived everywhere around here, and we didn't destroy or do harm to anything. We lived in peace and we didn't sell or buy anything. The Mother taught us how to live and make our fields in peace. But the others started to sell everything. If we make a field and plant it and then sell it it's like cutting one of the Mother's breasts or her legs or her arms. We lived peacefully but when Columbus came it changed. They knew how to read and write. They started to say to us, 'This land here is mine, that land there is mine, this over here that's mine.' We didn't know anything about measures or acres. We worked our fields and then we moved on to another one. But when Columbus came he started to say, 'This here is mine, that there is mine, it's mine, it's mine.' But the Mother never said anything like that. And so we've never said anything like that. But then we did learn to say, to talk like that, and say, 'That piece there is mine, that field is mine, I'll sell it or I'll buy it.' The Mother told us only that we should live together in peace. Columbus taught something different. So we've learned too to think this piece is mine, that over there is mine. But to us Kogi the Mother never taught us anything like that. She didn't teach us to buy or to sell or anything about receipts.

The system of exchange was neither barter nor gift: it was a system of balance, of necessary regulation to stabilise the world. The Mamas saw the Sierra as an organic whole, functioning through the exchange of food and other goods. What we see as trade, in this society was a moral necessity. It was an outward expression of the inner nature of reality, and a response to the demands of that reality.

The making of a Mama

The world was an expression of a cosmic intelligence which gave order and meaning to reality: reality was intelligible. The Mother was both the physical world and the intelligence which shaped it. Life was sustained by maintaining harmony between its various parts. The Mamas also learned that they could never consider any act in isolation. It had to be understood in relation to the totality, in its effect on the whole balance. Partly this could be handled through mnemonics, through spells and technical devices, but only partly. There really did have to be a deep understanding of the effects of any changes to this complex structure, and there really did have to be profound thought.

If we look in a crude way at the Kogi's ideas on cause and effect, they appear naïve and superstitious. That is the Younger Brother's attitude, for example, if he is told that when things are out of balance, sickness follows. Especially when the diagnosis is specifically stated: 'If the water is not blessed, you will get warts.' But these are crude simplifications of a serious idea. If work is undertaken thoughtlessly, and its full significance and effect is not considered, there is a strong probability that it will have unforeseen consequences. The health of the world will be disturbed.

We, who know about nuclear power, about intensive farming, about aerosol sprays, already know what this means. It is not a very strange idea. It seems to be the truth.

It is beyond human understanding to grasp the full significance of all things, or of anything. But since the world is a single living harmony, a single Mother, the question can be put and answered. Divination becomes the key to everything.

The idea of a society based on divination runs deeply counter to our own values. It demands submission to the unknowable, while we value critical intelligence and demand the right to make our own decisions. We are secular, rational, individualists; the Kogi world is at its heart religious, mystical and authoritarian. But we do not have to share or admire these values to recognise that the Sierra sustained a very large population in a highly organised society for at least one and a half thousand years on the basis of decisions made by divination. Our own civilisation has yet to demonstrate that degree of success.

Divination is not simply an easy way to shuffle off problems on to the Great Mother. It requires prolonged mental effort, to consider the full portent of the question, to define it properly, and to interpret the reply. The diviner's own mind is *aluna*, and thus with proper concentration it is possible to pass beyond the material world and work in the world of *aluna* which binds all things together. To make this possible, to achieve this transcendental condition, the upbringing of a Mama is of the utmost importance. That was true at the time the

Spanish chronicles were written, and it seems that education then followed the same pattern that it does today.

> The priests, before taking possession of that office, had to ... fast, for ten or sixteen or twenty years, without eating in that time more than a ball of corn meal every day, and so withdrawn in the depths of the forest, or in caves, that they must not see other men, other than those who brought them their food, and if by chance they saw some woman, they discounted as nothing the fast they had held until then and started it over again.*

The student Mama, or *moro*, is raised, ideally from birth, as a different kind of being from the rest of the human race. The mind has to be attuned to the spirit world, to *aluna*, and contact with the material world is kept to the absolute minimum required for survival, and for the physical senses not to atrophy. Mama Bernardo described what this means.

> To pass on the teaching well you have to choose a new-born child, and keep it in a ceremonial house. To make a really good Mama, you have to take the child right at the moment it is born, and then you keep it shut away. You bathe it in a stone mortar. And you move the water around in the stone mortar, so that it is purified, and then you bathe the baby in it. And then you have to shut away the child where there is no fire and no light. It should be kept where it sees nothing, no light, and is not seen by anybody. It is in a small ceremonial house, which has had partitions made inside it, so that there is a small room for the baby. It is alone with its mother, who lives in a house near by and takes care of it. A *cabo* looks after the baby all the time. He only brings it out in the middle of the night. Whenever the baby cries, the *cabo* calls the mother to come and feed it. At night, the mother comes and bathes it and dries it outside, she breast-feeds it, then the *cabo* takes it inside again.
>   The mother must not eat any food that has blood in it; no chicken, no pigs, no beef, nothing that has blood. She can only eat white beans, white potatoes and snails (a type of white grub called *Moi hoi*

* Simón, V, 218

hoi), which have fat to make her milk. And she must not wander about or bathe in the river. She has to be in her house all the time.

To make its bed they use only *watta*, a type of soft white palm fibre. It sleeps on a bed of *watta* which is hard underneath and soft on top. Its clothes are also made from *watta*. So that hard part of the *watta* is like the baby's bench and there it lies. The bag that it is carried in is also made of *watta*, the soft fibre of the *watta*. But even the *cabo* doesn't stay inside the room with it, he stays outside and he should not sleep, he should never sleep. He is always awake, looking after the *moro*.

And then the baby starts to grow and at five months it starts to crawl. So then the *cabo* has to be constantly alert so that it does not go out and leave the house. The mother still stays near the house looking after the baby, still eating only *Moi hoi hoi*. She feeds the baby and then leaves it alone, so that it stays there in the quiet. So then the child grows and gets older, one year, two years, and the *cabo* and the mother are still looking after it, making sure nothing happens to it. The *cabo* is always thinking about it, looking out for it in case it gets ill. And so is the mother, always thinking about how to protect it.

And the *cabo* is there, always eating his poporo so that he does not sleep, he is always on the look out, always sitting there awake. But the mother can sleep. They feed the *moro* on flour ground from potatoes and bakata. Sometimes they put a little bit of a small coconut in it. The mother can only drink warm water, she must not drink cold water. Otherwise she could make the little boy cold – there are no fires remember, so she must not drink cold water. She cannot drink sugar water, but she can drink a sort of sweetened water, water that contains a plant from the paramo, high in the Sierra. That is good for her, it fills her breasts so that she can go on breastfeeding. They bring out the baby and she feeds it, first from the right breast and then from the left, and after it is fed it is taken back in again.

When the baby is four years old it is taken off its mother's milk, the mother is blessed, and once she has been blessed she can go and bathe in the river again. When the child has been weaned the mother can go about again. But still the child cannot go out, he has to be shut away inside all the time.

One night the mother comes and she bathes him throughout the night in warm water: four times, every two hours through the night. And once she has done that then they can begin to bathe the child in cold water. After that his water doesn't have to be warmed any more. And then she gives the child over to the *cabos* completely. They bathe it in water in stone mortars, they move the water about, they move it about, they're swilling it about and they bathe the child in the cold water. And from then on the child grows up with the *cabos*.

It grows and then it begins to sing. All by itself, it begins to sing. When it is older they begin to take it out at night, always with a straw head-shade on.

This head-shade is a woven straw mat, a square whose side is almost as large as the child. Laid over the top of the head, it ensures that the *moro* can see neither moon nor stars. All that he knows is the world he sees with his mind's eye. And then this child that has been reared in the spirit world begins to hear the inner music of the universe, and he begins to act in accordance with what he hears. He begins to dance.

They take him out, to teach him, so that he can do offerings and he talks in *aluna* to the fathers and the masters of the world. Sometimes his mother still comes to the door of the house, and then the child dances, he dances, dances, dances, playing. He's dancing and dancing and the mother sings to him and then he is shut in again.

So a *moro* doesn't know about anything. He's never seen a chicken and he's never seen a pig, he's never seen trees or birds, he doesn't know anything about the world outside the house. And the Mamas are always praying to Serankua and asking him for food in *aluna*, for meat, all the foods, but in *aluna*. And they give these to the *moro*. They bless him and they give him food in *aluna*. And to make him grow strong, they rub him, they massage him, they massage him, massage him, massage him, with a sort of a cloth which is also made from *watta*. The mother also rubs him with this so that he'll grow up to be strong. She rubs him, she rubs him, she rubs him. They bring him out only for that and then he has to go back inside again. So he's massaged and massaged, and massaged and massaged.

He is also given a type of potato from the paramo to eat. That potato was planted there by Serankua. So he can eat white potatoes, he can eat the potato from the paramo and he can eat white corn. These are all cooked in a very small white pot that is special to the *moro*. They are cooked and then carried to the ceremonial house and given to the *cabo*. The *cabo* takes it inside and gives the *moro* his food. When they are cooking for him they have to count the things they cook. They put four white beans into the pot, then they put four white potatoes, and then on top they put a single white grub. They cook them together and then they give them to him. Sometimes they'll give him one of the grubs having baked it on a piece of pottery from a broken pot over a fire. The grub has its own fat so it cooks in its own fat, until it is really brown and toasted all over. Then they give that to the *moro* to eat. But he only drinks purified water from the stone mortars, water that has been blessed. Every time he eats, they give him water to drink. But only water that has been blessed.

The child asks for water, he asks for it. And then perhaps he looks in the water and notices the bubbles and likes them. He goes on asking for water because he likes it, he learns by himself, the Mamas don't really teach him anything, he learns from listening, listening spiritually. Knowledge comes to him in *aluna*, the Mamas themselves don't teach him directly.

Moros are chosen by divination. At adolescence, a decision is made whether to continue with this education. In some cases the *moro* does not have the qualities required to develop further; in others, the child simply cannot bear the privations involved. But some, like Mama Bernardo, have grown up with an other-worldly simplicity which will lead them to mature into true Mamas. Mama Bernardo was not taken as a baby; his confinement as a *moro* began when he was a small child, and that made it harder to bear. It lasted for nine years.

When you want to be a Mama you have to concentrate, you can't wander about thinking about girls, thinking about this and about that. You have to concentrate and really listen to what the Mamas say to you. And when you start to be a *moro* you can't just do whatever you want, everything is controlled. When the Mamas take you out to make an offering you have to fast, you go without eating, and when you come back they also don't give you anything to eat.

Perhaps in the middle of the night they'll give you something to eat. So there you are, hungry, you want to sleep and you do not understand what the Mamas are saying – you want food, you want to be with your mother and father, you want a drink of water, but you are not allowed anything. It's really hard learning to be a Mama. But in the end you get used to it. You get used to being hungry, to only eating in the middle of the night. When you're older you get used to it.

So when you've grown up, when you are a man, they give you your poporo, they give you the beads and they give you the bowl for divining. When you receive these things, the beads and so on, then you learn and are taught by the elders. You take your knowledge from the Mamas. You are able to work alone, divining and helping people. You can do all this. I was taught by my elders.

The elders used to lecture me, they told me not to steal, not to take other women, how to act properly. They also told me that one day the Younger Brother would come and ask us about how the world was, and how it started. And I thought, no that's impossible, why would Younger Brother ever come up here asking about all this? But now that you have come, I remember what the old Mamas told me. So we're not going to say here that we don't know how to dance – when we do know how to dance. Our mothers teach us to dance from the time we're young children. We know how to dance, we know how to dance the dance of the drums, the dance of the flutes, and the dance of the staves. We know the dance of the sea-shells too. So we're not going to say we don't know how to dance, we do know how to dance. We have forgotten nothing.

The Mama with the most profound understanding is the Mama who speaks with the greatest simplicity. There is a kind of state of grace, which the whole community recognises, which some truly great Mamas achieve. It is seen sometimes fleetingly in drink, or in ecstatic understanding produced when the Mamas fast and go without sleep for days and nights on end, but in some special individuals it becomes the way they are. These people have, as it were, stepped through the limitations of human understanding. They become like children, the world is ever fresh to them. They understand their own ignorance. These are, to the Kogi, the wisest people.

'Does everything live in *aluna*?' I asked Ramón.

'When the Mama looks, he sees the spirit world. He sees that rock, but he also sees the spirit rock. He sees that river, but he also sees the spirit river. And they are not in the same place.' Ramón looked at me, helplessly.

'And can the Younger Brother work in *aluna*?'

'Oh, he does. He thinks, he makes things, he has ideas. But he does not understand, so he makes things wrongly. They may not look wrong if you cannot see the spirit, but they are wrong. He works in *aluna*, badly.'

The shape and nature of the physical world, its processes of birth, growth and decay, are dependent on a complex ordering in *aluna*, and the function of humanity is to sustain the harmony of that ordering. At one moment the Mamas appear to be speaking of ethical gods (the Mother, Serankua), supernatural persons who have laid down prescriptions for living; at another, when they make statements such as 'I know how to call the rain', they appear to be working with spells. In fact the Mamas neither submit humbly to gods nor cast spells to control them; they work in *aluna*, interacting with the ocean of spirit that is all life. The Mamas do not see themselves as magicians, obliging nature to perform at their bidding, nor as priests acting as supplicants to and intermediaries with a god or gods. They have simply been detached, by their upbringing, from complete immersion in the material world, and believe that they are therefore able to work with a clearer understanding in *aluna*.

I think that the way the Kogi understand *aluna* helps to make sense of the beliefs of other early American people. Throughout North America, from the Tlingit of Alaska to the Calusa of Florida, there was a general belief that man, plants and animals shared a common spirit-life. That same idea evidently informed both the high cultures and the forest Indians of South America. This perception often led to descriptions of the earth as something living, capable of being wounded and injured. Different societies tried to work in different ways in the spirit world, some by using hallucinogens, some by divinations through sacrifice, some by entering into the character of some other creature. All seemed to recognise dancing as being particularly significant. The distinctive feature of the Kogi is the emphasis they place on the mind and on consciousness as the doorway between the physical and metaphysical worlds. To work in *aluna*, a Mama does not take drugs or dress up as a bird or sacrifice an animal or chant ritual words. He concentrates.

Sixteenth-century Christianity, of course, did not have any trouble categorising this kind of belief. Christianity had confronted pagans in Europe by inverting their values: their gods were devils. What the Spanish saw, when they looked at the Tairona, was a society of devil-worshippers in a state of untamed nature. And what the Tairona saw when they looked at the Spanish were savage barbarians with outlandish weapons of extraordinary power.

Conquistadors

The Spanish crown had already authorised the enslavement of the Caribbean Indians on the grounds that they were barbarians, imperfectly human; they were 'not as savage as the Turks,' but could not live independent lives as 'true men'. The evidence against them was that:

> they went naked and had no shame; they were like idiotic asses, mad and insensate ... they were inconstant; they did not recognise advice; they were very ungrateful and lovers of novelties; they valued drunkards, and had wine of various fruits, roots and grains; they became drunk with smoke ... they were bestial ... traitorous, cruel and vengeful ... sluggards, thieves, liars and of low judgment ... witches, quacks and necromancers.

Thus far, the accusation was not very impressive. In fact it would have justified the enslavement of the whole of Europe. But there was more compelling matter to come.

> They were cowardly as hares, dirty as pigs, they ate fleas, spiders and raw grubs ... they had no art, nor manners of Men ... they had no beards, and if some began to grow they pulled them out.*

* Herrera, V, 32

When the Spanish first landed, in 1514, they followed up their initial
seizure of the beach with a foray inland. They found only empty
villages. The Indians had fled in haste, and the Spanish soldiers found
hammocks and clothes, 'and even gold was found in sculpted pieces,
hidden among the clothes.' Later the soldiers were attacked:

> Coming up the wide and beautiful road, lined by many trees on its
> side, planted there for its adornment, were more than a thousand
> Indian bowmen, with much shouting and blowing of their huge
> conches ... and they came in great concert, formed in squadrons,
> with their head-dresses and all painted with that ochre that they use.*

Dávila ordered that there should be a combined response: gunfire, a
charge, and the release of man-hunting dogs. The result was chaos. The
shots missed, the dogs attacked each other, and in the general mêlée the
Indians vanished. The troops pursued them but found only more
deserted villages. However, they picked up seven thousand pesos of
gold before returning to their ships.

Eleven years later, in 1525, having scoured the Caribbean for fifty
families who would come with him on this great adventure, Don
Rodrigo de Bastidas began to construct a town at Santa Marta.

There are many lost cities in the Sierra. The chronicles speak of more
than a hundred and fifty towns and cities. Some, like Irotama and
Gairaca, are remembered in modern place names. Others, such as the
city of 'Taybo' which Bastidas discovered, have disappeared from the
map and the white man's memory.

> In this place Taybo it seemed that there was much gold, and the
> governor commanded the Christians, with the threat of heavy
> penalties, that they should not take it from the Indians, because he
> said that from the start he wanted to pacify the land. They should
> understand that this was in their own interest; but the soldiers had
> other ideas, and became restive under this restraint ...†

Mama Valencia referred to the people of Pueblito as Tayko. He has
never read or heard of the Spanish chronicles. It is his task to remember.

* Oviedo, VII, 121–34
† Oviedo, VI, 106

Mama Valencia sat on a stairway at Pueblito, and remembered. He remembered the first settlers, and their acceptance by the Indians.

Long ago the Younger Brother and the Elder Brother used to communicate with each other in *aluna*. They were fine, they were at peace and there was no problem. They lived well and between the Elder Brother and the Younger Brother there were no problems, no problems at all. And then came the fighting. Christopher Columbus started to kill the Elder Brother. The native people lived here, they lived everywhere here, and they lived in Bogota, in Cukatoo, in other places, other places, other places. The Elder Brother lived everywhere, but then Younger Brother came and made war on us and we fled in fear, and we went up into the mountains. We became frightened and we fled. And so we ran, and as we ran we left behind all the things that were ours. Here there were native people, they lived in their way, with their own hats, their belts and their clothes. But they ran leaving everything behind them. Here they set dogs on us. The dogs gave tongue, and we fled and some fell over, some were killed, and the soldiers were chasing us from behind, the conquistadors, the soldiers of the Conquest were at our backs. Aaii. All the finest things we left behind, they took them and they hid them away. And so when the Elder Brother finally stopped running and looked for his gold pieces, and his other things, his bag, they weren't there, they'd fallen, they'd been dropped, all gone, all gone.

Of course, the only purpose of this settlement was the seizure of the Indian's wealth, but Bastidas and his successors intended to achieve this through the imposition of formal tribute backed by armed force, rather than freebooting.

This was not easy: Bastidas was soon murdered by his own men when he tried to take away their loot. But a stable system was gradually established around Santa Marta, based on *economiendas*, large estates. The idea was that the Indians should work these estates and supply the Spanish with provisions.

The Indians did not take too well to this, and a desultory war began. The first Spanish expeditions of reprisal were defeated, but between 1530 and 1536 a number of Tairona towns were burned and the Indian economy was brought to the brink of collapse. It was sustained by the efforts of the Mamas, who tried to maintain the stability of the Sierra and prevent its disintegration into anarchy. The Spanish gradually became aware that the coastal cities were only continuing to function because the Mamas insisted on it. In 1558, for example,

the natives of the towns of Dursino, the Ciénaga and Gaira, which were afflicted and oppressed by the ill treatment of the said Captain Manjarrés, and had nothing with which to pay the excessive fines and tributes which were laid on them, left and went into the Sierra where the native Indians who lived there assisted them and gave them gold to pay the fines and tributes which were laid on them so that afterwards they would go back to live in their homes and seats, because having gone away they could not supply the Indians of the Sierra who all depend on the salt and fish collected by the Indians of the said towns of Gaira, the Ciénaga and Dursino.*

Throughout the sixteenth century the world of the Sierra was gradually being undermined. Individual expeditions from the growing Spanish settlements were met with sporadic but determined resistance; then a brief peace would follow and more trouble. Cooperation always ended at the point where the Spanish tried to evangelise. When, for example, a Spanish commander brought troops to Pocigueica, the Tairona helped them to build houses and brought them food, but when he started to talk to them about conversion to Christianity and obedience to the Spanish crown, they declared at once that they did not intend to become enslaved and would defend themselves. The Spanish had to fight their way out, and on the way captured an Indian who they impaled on a stake in front of Pocigueica as a warning. The Indians attacked and put the Spanish to flight. They also captured the governor's nephew, who they immediately impaled on the same stake.

Inevitably, the Indians' poisoned arrows were only partially effective against armoured men. Slowly, steadily, the world of the Elder Brother was shrinking.

Nevertheless, the civilisation of the Sierra Nevada continued to function for seventy-five years. The Spanish extended their colonis-

* Juan de Espeleta, *Accusation presented against Captain Luis de Manjarrés*, MS 1558, National Historical Archive, Bogota, Caciques e Indios T. XXXI fol. 568 v

ation around the base of the mountain, but, though the Incas and the Aztecs had been broken, the densely-woven integration of this mountain had survived. It was overthrown not by plunder but by a crusade.

The Spanish could not endure the Indians' relationship between the sexes. It was so fundamentally different from their own as to be an outrage. The men did not dominate the women.

The slaughter

The conquerors from Spain were devoutly sexually repressed. They were surrounded and embraced by all-male societies – the ship, the army, the church – and came from a country which was totally immersed in a crusade for moral purity. One quarter of the adult population of Castile had joined a religious order by 1570, and their sexual behaviour was subject to the supervision of the Inquisition. The counter-reformation cultivated a detestation of the flesh, and the human body had to be kept covered at all times. Women of high status had to learn to walk with tiny steps so that they appeared to glide; they were not to be seen to have legs.

Since the Spanish spent so much time in single-sex societies, the temptations of the flesh were very likely to be homosexual. This was, therefore, the most terrifying vice of all. It seemed self-evident to them that without rigid controls and a stern morality, men would naturally enjoy each other's bodies. They therefore believed that it was very important to emphasise manly virtues, which included sporting beards and moustaches. Their own women had to behave as though they were constantly at risk from these virile fellows, and were encouraged to behave with a submissive modesty. It was not unknown in Madrid for a husband to stab his wife if she was immodest enough to show a glimpse of her feet in public.

They expected to find all manner of physical abominations in the New World, where nature was evidently untamed and savage. European speculations had included images of people without heads, the Blemmyae, whose torsos had eyes and mouths, and others, the Monocoli, with only one enormous foot, which they used as a sun-shade. They had not found much evidence of these people, but moral abominations were just as likely. Anthropophagi, cannibals, were originally reported as being found all over the Caribbean, but this fear gradually faded when there was a steady failure to produce a single eye-witness to a cannibal feast. The one horror left, and the one most readily observed, was sexual licentiousness.

The Indians clearly did not share the Spanish terror of the flesh, and, so far as the Spanish were concerned, it was quite clear that the men of the New World must be addicted to homosexuality. You just had to look at them. There was the lack of body-hair, for a start. Men who grew no beards were obviously effeminate. Then there was the fact that they were often submissive towards women. The Kogi still are.

At first the Mother gave advice to men. She lectured them. That's why when women talk to us we have to look down at their feet. We should not look at the Mother's face.

The Spanish were also quite unable to recognise the forms of social control that existed among the Indians. Sexuality was managed very differently in Castile. Among the Kogi, for instance, sexual initiation is an important part of the rite of passage to adulthood, and the complex control and correct usage of ejaculation, semen and menstrual blood is, in their view, a vital part of the control of life – not just human life, but all life. Since *aluna* is generative energy, sexual emission needs to be integrated into the interaction between the physical and spirit worlds.

For the Spanish, all this was simply licentiousness. Oviedo, in his massive account of the New World, stressed the 'perversity of sodomy' common in both sexes there.* Balboa had forty Indians thrown to the dogs for the offence.† Fray Pedro Simón was utterly convinced that the Taironas were 'so immured in this vice, that in order to incite themselves to commit it more, they had their temples full of a thousand abominations and horrendous figures.'‡ Homosexuality was an idea which obsessed the Spanish conquerors of America; they were terrified by it. It was an inner terror, a fear of their own nature. And so they set out to eliminate sodomy among the Indians.

---

* Oviedo, VI, 140
† For a fuller discussion of European beliefs about unnatural behaviour among the indigenous Americans, see Peter Mason, *Deconstructing America*, London 1990
‡ Simón, IV, 356

The Kogi still do not see homosexuality as unnatural, only as slightly unusual. The subject once came up over a meal with Ramón, when we were talking about what it means to balance masculine and feminine. For example, could there be a lesbian household?

Yes there could. Ramón knew of an example, where two women had decided that they wanted to live as man and wife. They talked it over with a Mama, who agreed that if that was the way they were made, that was the way they should live. There is even a story of two women among the ancestors who lived together in that way. In the story, sex between the two women was said to be far superior to any other sex they had ever experienced. He went on to mention that male homosexuality was sometimes encountered, but it was rather odd and he himself had never tried it.

Of course, Kogi society is not the same as Tairona society. The Kogi exercise a close control over sexual behaviour, and licentiousness is regarded as a serious crime. The Tairona may not have been so rigid, but the claims by some Spaniards that they had witnessed homosexual orgies seem to be quite fantastic. They seem, however, to have deeply influenced a new governor of Santa Marta, Juan Guiral Velón, at the end of the sixteenth century. It was to be expected that savage society was in a state of moral confusion, and sexual abominations would be the most alarming form of that confusion. It was to be expected that a Spanish governor would attempt to introduce moral order in his dominions. But all the suppressed demons of the flesh seem to have been working exceptionally fiercely in Velón. In 1599 he called a meeting of the native chieftains at a town called Jeriboca, at the base of the north face of the Sierra. He told them that he intended to put a stop to their 'wicked sinfulness'.

It is not clear whether they understood in detail what he meant. But they fully understood the implications. The coexistence, however awkward and uneasy it had been, between Spanish and indigenous people had come to an end. The Younger Brother now intended to destroy the Elder, by imposing his own law in place of the Law of the Mother. Missionaries were already setting up chapels in their towns, erecting crosses, teaching that the *nuhue*, the world-house, was the house of the Devil. Now it was plain that the laws of the missionaries, ignorant men who did not know how to make crops grow or the rains fall, were to be imposed by force. The Heart of the World was threatened and had to be defended.

The word went out from Jeriboca. And now the full strength of the 'Tairona' proto-state became plain. The Spanish identified many different communities ranged against them: Masinga, Masinguilla, Zaca, Mamazaca, Rotama, Mendiguaca, Tairama, Buritaca, Tairona, Maroma, Guachaca, Chonea, Nahuanje, Cinto, Gairaca, Mamatoco, Ciénaga, Dursino, Durama, Origua, Dibocaca, Daona, Masaca, Chengue, Sacasa, Daodama, Guarinea, Cominca, Choquenca, Masanga and Mauracataca. There were more. They raised a force of thousands of warriors, and planned a coordinated strategy.

Extra seed was planted throughout the Sierra to ensure enough surplus food to sustain a war. The Mother was consulted, in divinations and dances, and Mamas worked in *aluna* to ensure the success of this crop which itself was an unbalancing of the world.

Santa Marta was blockaded, and plans were prepared for its destruction. But when the attack came, Santa Marta had been forewarned. A missionary, Tomás de Morales, had erected a cross in the central square of Masinga; when he had come back to the town, the cross had disappeared. The Indians had told him that they had destroyed it. He had also seen that the 'House of the Devil' was full of bows and arrows. Another missionary had actually been directly told of the plan of attack in Jeriboca. Both had passed their information on.

The uprising erupted on the planned date, 29 July, all over the Sierra. Nearly forty Spaniards were killed, chapels in the Indian towns were burned down, and Santa Marta came under a hail of flaming arrows. But Santa Marta had prepared. Since the Spanish had control of the sea (at least when there were no pirates) they were able to send out for help, and by this date there was a fully developed military presence in Colombia. Relief forces were dispatched immediately.

It took seven weeks for reinforcements to gather in Santa Marta, and there was nothing the Indians could do to stop it. They tried to prevent the Spanish from breaking out, digging man-traps with poisoned stakes on the roads, but two hundred men with armour and firearms were more than a match for the two thousand warriors who tried to block them with envenomed arrows.

The Spanish advance was inexorable. Slowly they moved along the coast, sacking and burning each town in turn, until they arrived at one of the communities adjoining Bonda. It took eleven bloody days to destroy Bonda and establish total military supremacy. By then most of the chieftains had been captured. They wore gold pieces in their ears, noses and lips. Their ears, noses and lips were sliced off. The overall commander of the warriors, Cuchacique, was pursued into the Sierra and captured.

For three months the Spanish occupied one community after another, burning, looting, hanging, destroying crops and houses and taking prisoner all the leading Indians with their families. Then governor Juan Guiral Velón pronounced sentence. The leading Indians were, of course, condemned to death, Cuchacique being dragged by two horses and then quartered, the parts of his body and his head being distributed on public display. And now the real meat of the matter could begin.

And if any other Indian is found to have committed or to practise the wicked and unnatural sin of sodomy he is condemned so that in the part and place that I shall specify he shall be garrotted in the customary manner and next he shall be burned alive and utterly consumed to dust so that he shall have no memorial and it is to be understood by the Indians that this punishment shall be extended to all who commit this offence.

And they shall be condemned, any and each of them, and their houses shall be demolished and burned in which they lived when they committed the crime, and no person whatsoever of whatever estate or condition shall dare to return to rebuild or populate it without permission of the magistrates under sentence of death.

From now on, it was declared, Indians would live in designated sites and in the open parts of the valleys, and were forbidden under pain of death to retire into the Sierra Nevada. Their towns were turned over whole to the soldiers for them to sack as they wanted for their services and 'those Indians who they wish to live' were condemned in addition to pay a fine of 'pacification' amounting to 1,500 pounds of gold.

> When Columbus came
> they took away the things that were ours.
> They took away our gold.
> They took away all our sacred gold.

They set dogs on us and we had to flee,
we ran in fear,
and as we ran we left everything behind us.
We had sacred gold pieces when they set dogs on us.
We lost them.
They took our soul.
They took everything.

A good man-hunting dog would hold military rank and be paid a salary. It was an affectionate gesture that cost nothing: soldiers hardly ever received their salaries. For the Kogi, the dog-soldiers have become the strongest, most hated memory of all.

When Columbus came he set dogs on us, and he made us run, and we had to leave behind our sacred things, so they took them, they set dogs on us and took everything. Everything.
Everything.
And to steal those things they had to set dogs on us. Because of the dogs we lost those things. To get them they had to set dogs on us. When the dogs attacked us, we ran, we were afraid and we left our things behind.
Before then, everyone knew how to dance, all of them, all of them, all of them. Every Indian knew how to dance.

The Kogi survivors

The shattered remnants of this society, the lowest-ranking people, the unnoticed survivors, fled through the jungle and up the mountain. They went to the Mamas, the keepers of the flame. The Kogi memory is of thousands and thousands of refugees, a great mass of humanity from all the many tribes of the Sierra, desperate for food and succour. There was little enough for them.

Many thousands died of starvation. There was also the decimation from European diseases, which everywhere destroyed 80 or 90 per cent of the native population of America. But there were survivors. Over and over again I was told the story by old men, one as the narrator, the other as his chorus, rattling their poporos in the dark, thick smoke of the *nuhue*.

When Columbus came, they took all our sacred things and they're still doing it to this day, and Columbus's people came right up here to rob as well. So when these people came, we fled, we ran, we were afraid, and that's why we live up here now. Isn't that the way it is? Isn't it true that they stole everything?

And the chorus responds, 'Yes, that is how it is.'

When Columbus came we fled and came up here, and they chased us right up to here too. They followed us, so we had to come up here. Only four groups of Indians were left and they came up here.

The Mama says: I stayed without gold,
I remained without anything,
but with thought strong, profound,
still esteemed.
A system.
'Let us keep these customs.
Keep the tradition.
Let us keep it.'
We respect the Mother Earth.

Here the Mamas eventually pieced together a society that could survive. Their own work, the work of sustaining the world, had to continue. The possibility of surrender did not exist. It would have meant quite literally the end of everything. And although the Spanish had destroyed everything down below, they never colonised the mountain. It remained, for them, impenetrable.

There were now only four recognisable peoples surviving (one of them has since vanished). There would never again be overlord chiefs, caciques who ruled individual cities. The structure of specialists, with different forms of agriculture and different forms of manufacture in the hands of different people, could not be restored. This would have to be a subsistence society, in which each family would have to make do with the minimum.

The Mamas pieced together a new social order, based on simplicity and material equality. Each family had to have farms in different locations; there could no longer be the large-scale exchange of produce which sustained the Sierra in the past. But in *aluna* that exchange would still continue. The Mamas would carry on making offerings, carrying tokens from one part of the Sierra to another, adjusting and regulating the world in spirit. The material life of the Sierra had been devastated. But its metaphysical life carried on, and the work of the vassals was now to sustain that metaphysical life, by sustaining the Mamas.

It is not clear when the Kogi became private, individual owners of land; by their own account, this was something that they were compelled to learn from the Younger Brother. This has, inevitably, created a difference between richer and poorer Kogi, and some Kogi have become very wealthy by any standards, with hundreds of cattle. Others can be very poor: Pedro, for example, the illegitimate son of a divorced woman, grew up in poverty and inherited nothing. But all Kogi, rich and poor, live in identical houses with the same few utensils. And all Kogi submit to the authority of the Mamas in every aspect of their lives, so as to sustain the harmonising of man and nature. Without that, they believe, rich and poor alike would perish.

To the Kogi, it has always been clear what will happen when the world ends. The Last Trump, the signal for final destruction, will be heard at the moment when the Younger Brother reoccupies the heart of the world where he was born. That moment, when Columbus reaches his final goal, will be the death of the Mamas and the descent of the world into chaos. The snow will melt on the peaks, the waters will dry up. The balance of nature will be overthrown.

In the nineteenth century, missionaries and peasants began to work their way into the north face of the Sierra, and a school and a representative of the Colombian government were installed in San Antonio by 1875. It was generally assumed that the Kogi were on the verge of extinction, but there are no records of any penetration, by officials or peasants, into the higher and more sacred parts of the northern Sierra.

It is only now that the Heart of the World is being seriously threatened – not by penetration, but by the effects of what is taking place lower down. Our society presses them ever harder, and has cut them off from the sea. At the same moment, we heat up the world. They say we are doing this by cutting down the trees and by digging out the minerals in the earth.

That is why they have to warn us. That is why they have to speak on television.

Being accepted

After that clear pronouncement – 'Our yes is yes. The Mamas do not speak with two tongues' – I was summoned to the *nuhue*. It was dark, and the rain was pelting down. The path to Pueblo Viejo was a torrent of water, and with my broken ankle I could not stand up in the flood. I had to walk down half-carried by Graham. The building was full. Mama Valencia rose to speak.

When you first came, I was in favour of this film. I thought it would be good. But I have been visited by two men from the Indian Council. They say you are bad people, that you have come to steal from us. If that is true then we must not make the film. If that is true then you must go away. So tell me. Is it true?

I sat on my stool, and leaned on my walking stick. What could I say?

When I came here nine months ago, you said that you wished to speak to the Younger Brother. You said that you wanted to warn him to change his ways. Otherwise the heart of the world will die, and everything will end. I said that I would help you. I promised to come back and I have come back when I said I would. While I have been away, I have been arranging for the work to be done. I have been arranging for the world to hear your words. If you had said no then, I would have stayed away. If you say no now, I will go away. The Mamas must decide.

How can you show that you are to be trusted? The Mamas had looked at me, they had watched Sarah and Graham, they had listened and decided, and the whole community assented. They would make a film with us. The only exception was the town of San Antonio, which had been convinced by the nuns and was not represented at this meeting. San Antonio was always at odds with everyone else, and had been quarrelsome long before its dispute with Ramón began.

When Amparo had first come into the Sierra, she had approached the Mamas and explained that the government in Bogota wished to help them, and she represented that government. What could the government do for the Kogi?

The Mamas had listened, and wondered what kind of trick Columbus was now thinking of. So somebody made a wryly humorous request, testing Amparo, to see whether she was offering a new way to destroy them.

We have heard that you have atomic bombs. For many years we have had trouble with San Antonio. Please give us a bomb to blow up San Antonio. That would help us.

I was told not to worry too much about San Antonio.

The following day the mood was very cheerful and relaxed, and I distributed presents. I had brought fish from Santa Marta, and shells. The shells had been a problem; after much hunting in England, I had found a shell importer in Devon who brought them in from the Pacific. I had heaved an enormous sackful half-way round the world.

They had been a considerable stumbling-block at El Dorado airport in Bogota. The idea that I was bringing shells into a country as gifts for the Indians was obviously so preposterous that I must be hiding some more sinister purpose. But what? Was I perhaps the first man to try to smuggle drugs into Colombia?

A more serious question was whether the Kogi would accept the shells. They take a firm line on gifts. Those which seem to them to have a proper place in the Sierra are accepted gravely and without gratitude. 'These things should be here, and you did right to bring them' seems to be the attitude. Those which have no place in the Sierra are curtly rejected, or so I had been told. What would they make of these Pacific shells?

I offered them tentatively, explaining that I did not know if they were of any use for the poporo. The Mamas pored over the sack, taking out samples and passing them around. Every different sort of shell had a name, and no, these were not to be used in the poporo. They were sacred shells, as used by the ancestors. Some of these ancestral shells, which must be centuries old, are still used today as offerings and in rituals. Later I was to see identical shells in Santa Marta museum. They had been discovered as grave goods in Tairona burials.

It seems that before 1600 the Sierra had been receiving shells from the Pacific. I had brought a great treasure. The Mamas were delighted, but the vassals, having looked forward to receiving a good supply of poporo shells, were less enthusiastic. They gave me samples of exactly what kind of shell I was to bring next time.

The other present I had brought, on Reichel's advice, was a pack of needles for bag-making. Every Kogi woman is always making a *mochila*. They teach the looped stitch to their daughters as soon as they can toddle about.

The bag is a spiralling loop-stitch, beginning at the centre of the bottom and rotating outwards and upwards, with plain stripes building up as it grows. It is the universe, the bag that holds everything, and the rings around it are the layered worlds of the universe. Whatever must be carried – wood, fruit, coca – must be carried in these bags. If it is heavy, the strap will be passed around the forehead, with the bag resting on the top of the back. That is how babies are carried, and the bag is as much a womb-image as is the *nuhue*. Every baby is the first human, the original Elder Brother. The woman who carries it on her back is the Mother. She shaped the bag of the world, and she placed life in it.

Kogi women are very reticent indeed, and up to this point no woman had spoken more than a few words to me. With such a strong division drawn between the sexes, I was not sure how the needles would be received. I had to give them to the men – I could not give gifts to women – and I was not sure whether the men would be interested.

They were very interested indeed. Jefe Mayor took charge of the distribution, making sure that each vassal received a fair share, and as soon as they were given out the men rushed away. I was used to a much more stoic approach to presents, and could not understand the excitement. I could see all the men vigorously discussing something outside Arregoce's house, and after about half an hour they returned beaming.

It seemed as though I had done the right thing.

The atmosphere was now relaxed and contented, with everyone sprawled around the medical post. Mama Bernardo, lying in Amparo's hammock, became intrigued with Adalberto's superb woven helmet, and put it on his own head. 'How do I look?' Mama Augustin fell around laughing. 'You look so handsome! Really good-looking!' Mama Bernardo grinned broadly, showing a row of stumpy teeth blackened with tobacco and greened with coca. 'All the girls will be after you now,' declared Mama Augustin. 'They will ruin you as a Mama!'

As the laughter subsided, one old man sitting in the window leaned back and spoke, smiling broadly.

Now we have said yes, you will tie us up with string, take us away and make sausages out of us. And the only people left will be the people from San Antonio.

7

Filming Begins

Graham came back to London with us, and then returned to Colombia ahead of me to sort out the logistics of filming. I suggested that when he went back to the Kogi he should take the catalogue of the Museo del Oro. If there was some piece in the museum of special interest to the Mamas, we could make a replica and bring it for them to explain.

Graham went back into the Sierra as a welcome guest, and was treated with a warmth and courtesy which he had not experienced before. When he wandered out of his little house to talk to people, they spoke freely, and he had streams of visitors, male and female, dropping in for a cup of coffee and a chat.

He saw many people being given tokens like the one Mama Bernardo had given him just before he slid down the hill and cracked his spine. The Kogi take them very seriously, as visible signs of the work done by the Mamas to protect them; when Graham recounted his own experience everyone thought it was hysterically funny. Obviously Mama Bernardo had been over-reaching himself in trying to protect such an impure specimen of humanity. Graham had other views, and told Mama Bernardo on no account ever to give him another charm. The Mama roared with laughter.

Up on the mountain everything was obviously fine, but down below the situation in Colombia deteriorated rapidly as the date for filming approached. I was on the phone to our cargo agent in Bogota when news came through that a plane had been blown up on an internal flight. The bombs were getting bigger and more daring. The headquarters of DAS, the security police, were demolished by a massive car-bomb in mid-morning. The explosion killed dozens and injured hundreds more, including many foreigners who were standing in line to have their visas renewed.

Ramón heard that the guerillas wanted to talk to him, so he went into hiding, posting sentries around his home. A hotel in Cartagena was bombed, killing two American journalists. Perhaps not surprisingly my sound recordist, who had filmed many adventure trips, called the BBC a week before departure to say that he had decided to stay at home.

In fact we had a degree of protection from the drugs war, or at least Graham did. He was sitting eating in a bar in Rodadero when he was suddenly surrounded by expensively-dressed, bejewelled men with gleaming Rolex watches and Ray-Bans, who began exclaiming and even weeping. They were deeply moved by the sight of him. These were relatives of 'El Mono' Abello, the local drug baron, who had been captured and extradited to the United States. Apparently Graham was his double.

We subsequently studied photos of El Mono, trying to spot the similarity and not really succeeding. Anyway, it was not just a question of looks. The way Graham smiled, the way he turned his head, the way he used a knife and fork to eat his food – all this was just as El Mono did it.

So long as no one tried to arrest him, Graham would be safe. All the rest of us had to do was stick close to him.

Gold making

The filming began with gold. Gold was obviously important as well as spectacular, and the Museo del Oro at Bogota was the natural place to begin work. But I did not fully grasp the significance of gold until it emerged in the course of filming.

Mama Valencia made the selection. He chose one of the most impressive pieces, which the museum describes as a 'pendant'. It is a free-standing squat figure about 4 inches high. Its legs are stumpy, with knees slightly bent. Its hands are on its broad hips, with thick elbows sticking out from the sides of its body. This posture, together with the snarling mouth on its feline head, gives it an aggressive appearance. A number of similar pieces have been found, with different faces. They are often called 'warriors'.

The figure is naked below the shoulders, apart from armbands at the elbow. It holds a bar across its stomach, from which two small spirals extend on either side. It is the pose of a weightlifter.

A collar runs across the shoulders. But the dominant feature is the head, disproportionately large and surmounted by an effervescent, boiling explosion of whorls. A large, broad flap extends from either side of the head, a pair of birds with huge beaks sit on the headband, and, behind, eight spirals, each with a ball in the centre, are thrown out like whirling fireworks.

Its date is vague, 'prehistoric', which means simply pre-Columbian. Like all Tairona gold, it is not pure gold at all, but *tumbaga*, a mixture of gold and copper.

It was made by a master craftsman. He probably carved the original figure in a mixture of clay and powdered charcoal: fragments of this mix have been found inside many of the gold pieces. This would have dried in the sun for a couple of days, to prevent it being cracked by steam during casting.

The next stage was to prepare a thin sheet of beeswax, melting the wax, straining it to remove impurities, and rolling it out until it was paper-thin. This was pressed over the model, and the detail shaped on the wax. The more delicate parts of the figure, such as the spirals of the head-dress, were constructed in wax from the start, held in place by tiny drops of molten wax that acted as rivets. The whole thing was then painted with a solution containing fine-ground charcoal to make the casting sharper.

The craftsman then dried the figure once more, encased it in a wet clay-and-charcoal plaster, and baked it. The charcoal granules in this plaster were quite coarse, so that gases could escape through it harmlessly. There would have been a hole at the base of this plaster mould for the wax to run out as it melted, and another at the top. Delicate waxen bars must have run down the sides of the figure; as their wax melted, these would have left channels in the mould for the rest to drain away. Pins extending from the model into the plaster would have prevented it dropping a fraction as the wax ran out.

So the craftsmen now had a baked plaster cast, containing a clay and carbon figure pinned in a void. While it was still hot, the molten gold/copper alloy would be poured in through the hole in the top. The alloy had to be at exactly the right temperature, poured evenly, so that it would flow into the void without trapping any air. When the metal was cold, the mould was smashed open. If he had not carried out the whole process perfectly, he would have to begin again. Both the carving and the plaster mould had been destroyed.

What emerged was a hollow coppery figure. The inner core was scraped away, leaving the thin skin of red metal. Then the final magic. Some strong acid was prepared, distilled, according to the chronicles, from the juice of a herb. The figure was dipped in this and reheated. The copper on the surface turned to copper oxide and dissolved in the acid, the gold did not. The creature glowed and shone. Nothing could corrode or change it except a return to the furnace. Its surface would never dull. It had come alive.

The origin of this particular figure was unknown, as was its meaning and purpose. But it belonged to the great collection that Cano the tomb-robber had amassed and given to the museum, and Cano had taken a mould from it. Now his son agreed to replicate the process of making it.

As the piece was made, I learned how delicate was the original workmanship, and how economical of metal. No one now is able to make the wax as thin as it was originally made, so the replica weighs more than the original. The temperature control is so tricky that even modern electric kilns do not always produce good results.

I asked Cano the Younger how he felt about the plundering of tombs. He answered that these treasures made Colombians aware of their past and gave them a sense of history – and after all, these objects belong to no one. The civilisations that produced them, the Quimbaya, the Muiscas and so on, disappeared centuries ago. But the Tairona did not disappear, I pointed out; the Kogi still lay claim to these sites. He looked uneasy, and said that he did not approve of robbing Tairona graves. 'If the Mamas want what we are making, you should let them keep it. As a present. I do not know if they will want it.'

Ricardo

We sent the few rolls of film we had shot back to the labs in London, so that we could be assured that our equipment was all right, and set off for the Sierra.

At Santa Marta, everything was fine in principle, if not in practice. Argument over the film had died right down, but Ramón had not been seen for some time and would not be coming on the first part of the filming.

Graham had solved the translation problem by arranging for Mama Bernardo's son Juancho to work with us. Juancho had been taken out of the Sierra for a few years by missionaries when he was a child. Mama Bernardo had evidently felt that it was useful for his son to know something of the outside world, and had no doubts that his son would come back. That judgment had been correct; Juancho now lived with his father.

Graham had also hired a Guajira Indian, Ricardo Núñez, to look after us. Ricardo is immensely tall and thin, with a pot-belly like a beach-ball. He has the dark skin of the mestizos – people of mixed indigenous and African genes – common on the coast. His long machete, worn on a special belt in a highly decorated scabbard like a sword, indicates that Ricardo is closer to the world of the conquest than to mine. He carries himself gravely, his speech, laden with proverbs of bizarre meaninglessness, uttered in a thick, sing-song accent. We rarely knew what he was talking about.

The people of the Guajira know no law except that of the vendetta and personal loyalty. The State is meaningless to them, because it has nothing to offer them. Ricardo was born into a typically large family, and he and his siblings were left to grow up, in his own words, 'wild'. His father was an agricultural worker who lost both his legs in an accident with a reaping machine. Ricardo and his brothers told the hospital that when he came round and saw that he had no legs he would kill himself, and they were right. The family was given no support of any kind, and when Ricardo's mother fell ill her sons supported her until they had nothing left. 'When we had no more money for medicines, she died.'

He now has a place of his own, a small farm in the Sierra, which he was given by a man who he found sick at the roadside and took to hospital. But without money he cannot afford to work it.

Ricardo is a respected man, and mothers often ask him to intercede with the police on behalf of their sons. There had been a case recently where a boy was being hunted as a bandit, and his mother came weeping to Ricardo and asked him to help her son give himself up. The problem was that without an intermediary the boy might be shot as soon as he revealed himself. Ricardo arranged for the boy to surrender, and he was given bail, partly on Ricardo's assurance that he would keep out of trouble.

Within a fortnight the boy's mother was back begging Ricardo to help her son surrender again. 'They say he's a bandit and they are going to shoot him. Oh the police are such liars! Please help him.' Ricardo felt that his own integrity had been compromised enough, and told the mother that of course her boy was a bandit, everyone for miles around knew that he had been holding up buses and robbing the passengers, and the police were absolutely right.

Ricardo values personal dignity and family honour. In the families of the Guajira everything is shared, and whenever Ricardo has any money he has to spend it all on presents. He is particularly proud of his military record, as a driver for a general, and of his nephews.

Those are good boys. If I go out drinking and I say to them, 'I must be back at ten o'clock,' then at ten o'clock they come to find me. No matter what I am doing, they tie me up and carry me home. Those are good boys.

He was based now in Santa Marta, but had grown up in Dibulla and had seen the invasion of colonos into the lower part of the northern Sierra. It began in the 1960s, when the rain forest was being cleared by loggers, and then the marijuana farmers moved in.

At that time there was a lot of violence, many murders, many hold-ups. They would seize people; kill them to steal their money and their shopping. And they would kill anyone who did not hand over his goods. It was done very brutally, with a lot of bloodshed. That was until the heads of the area of the villages decided to put an end to these crimes. They made everyone get out.

The effect of this vigilante movement was not to improve conditions but to clear peasants off the land for the big men. Now large areas near to the coast are closed to most people because they have been sealed off by millionaire ranchers with private armies.

Ricardo would keep us safe: equipment which needed to travel overland, by mule, in the lower part of the Sierra would not be touched by bandits if he was with it. Nor would we, which was just as well. Vehicles travelling out of Santa Marta, especially buses, were now regularly stopped by armed gangs. Christmas was approaching, and they were collecting presents for their families.

Ricardo was not only a useful guardian: he was also known and liked by the Kogi of Pueblo Viejo. Since Ricardo is almost twice their height, he moves among them like a kindly giant. He has developed an attachment to the Kogi as passionate as Amparo's and does everything possible to help them. Having a farm in the Sierra makes him, I suppose, a colono, but Ricardo does not think like a colono. While the government is trying to establish reforestation programmes of which the Kogi do not approve, he has used government money from the project to establish a nursery to grow the saplings which the Mamas want.

Ricardo had been Graham's constant companion in the Sierra, and his support, along with Carlos's, had helped Graham get through the difficult months when he seemed to be getting nowhere. Now he was going to ensure that the Mamas would cooperate fully with the filming. 'I will cook them a very special meal.'

Ricardo did not need to cook a very special meal. When we arrived at Pueblo Viejo, everyone was ready to work. Our only problem was that the film we had dispatched from Bogota had not yet arrived in London, so we could not be absolutely certain that the camera was all right. There was not much we could do about that.

Blood

The first thing that had to be done was for a cow to be killed for a feast. We filmed the killing, which seemed an unnecessarily cruel and prolonged affair. Instead of dying immediately from the knife thrust into its neck, the poor creature's death agonies lasted about five minutes. I found this quite sickening, and was baffled at what I took to be incompetence by the butcher. Later, when we translated the conversations that were going on, the reasons became clear. The Kogi were determined to ensure that the Younger Brother pays attention, and so turned the event into a spectacle. It seemed as though their mental preparation for filming had included an analysis of television ratings. It was a great surprise to find that they were saying to each other, 'This will come out nicely in the film.'

There is a broader significance for anyone tempted to over-romanticise the Kogi's attitude to nature. While the Mamas seem quite able to empathise with the Great Mother, and the suffering caused to her by a broken rock or a hole in the ground, the vassals were quite unperturbed by the distress of the cow they slaughtered.

They were particularly anxious that we should get pictures of the blood draining from the knife-wound in the animal's neck.

Bring me a bowl for the blood. This little one is no good ... We need a spoon for the blood. Well, are they taking pictures or not?

We were obviously in the hands of people who had thought through what they were doing.

It was inevitable that our first problem would be a minor demarcation dispute between two towns in which we were to film. Each town belongs to a political and clan alliance. These two towns are actually 200 yards apart; if they had been discovered as archaeological sites, no one could have guessed that they were separate communities at all. But they are, and their allegiances are quite distinct. Each regards itself as guardian of the wisest, most profound heart of the knowledge of the Elder Brother, and the other as distinctly second-rate. It was finally agreed that the main address to the Younger Brothers would have to be split between the *nuhues* of the two towns. Each community felt sure that we would recognise the profundity of its own contribution, and the shallowness of the statements made by the other.

When night came, it was time to begin filming the first major statements in the *nuhue*. By now it was clear that the Kogi were operating in an efficient and professional manner, and our own professionalism was on the line. The first problem was where to site the

generator to light the building. It was impossible to get it far enough
away to avoid recording its sound, so we built an enclosure for it.
Unfortunately it immediately overheated in there and cut out.

Plan B involved large gas lanterns, fed from big cylinders, placed
outside the entrance. The Mamas sat patiently in the *nuhue* watching us
assemble the equipment and turn on the gas. They remained stoic when
the rubber tube carrying the gas broke free from the lanterns and
blasted a 6-foot jet of flame directly at the wood and thatch structure.

That was the nearest we came to bringing about the end of the
world. A foot or two closer, and the Kogi Mamas would have been
incinerated where they sat.

Eventually we had a safe rig, and began. The Mamas started to
expound their message.

Father Serankua made the world for it to be left in peace. When will
the world end? If we behave well, if we think well and we go on
making offerings the world will not end. The Elder Brother has not
forgotten his ways but if the world ends we will all die. The Elder
Brother and the Younger Brother will all die. All living things here,
everything, they could all die.

They explained that the world is a living being – a creature. And like
all living creatures, its life depends on blood and water.

It is blood that gives us strength. It is the same with the earth. We are
not harming the earth. We are not harming the Mother but the
Younger Brother is. He is taking out all its gold and its water. From
the conquest right up to the present they have been doing it.

This was not quite what I had expected. What was the blood of the
earth? And why this association between blood and gold? Had the
cow-killing sequence been intended as some sort of lesson?

All right, cut its throat now so that the blood comes out fast!

The earth has its blood and it has its water. When we bleed we die.
When they dig things out of the earth, when they take stones out
they are bleeding this world and it could die. Taking the gold out of
the earth like this it can die.

Pot making

In the days that followed, the real meaning of gold grew clearer. It is the key to the work of the Mamas in ensuring the fertility of the Sierra. Gold was formed, they believe, when the earth first became fertile. And just as a woman's fertility is evidenced by her monthly flow of blood, so gold is evidence of the fecundity of the earth.

The making of a golden object was not simply a technical exercise, and the object itself was not simply attractive or decorative. To make something out of gold was to work with the very stuff of fertility, the most direct interaction possible with the fundamental principles of life.

Today, the Kogi do not work in gold. But they do work with another secretion of the earth, clay, and from the way they make clay pots we can gain some insight into the way in which gold-work was approached.

A clay pot is, of course, the earth itself. In a world in which all things are contained within all other things – which is how the Kogi perceive the universe – an earthenware jar is one more aspect of the womb-mother. It is the male equivalent of the *mochila*, the all-containing bag made by women. The roofs of houses are crowned with small jars; the house is inside the pot, contained within the embrace of the Mother. Food is cooked in earthenware pots, which ensure its healthiness.

Women do not need a great effort of spiritual preparation to make a *mochila* because every woman is in a sense the Mother. But pots are made by men. Men must approach the making of a pot with as much care and seriousness as they approach the coming of manhood. A pot which is badly made, without knowledge and preparation, will be corrupted and its power will be void. A pot is not thought of as being man-made, but as being granted to the potter.

The Mother gave us pots. To receive these properly one has to be like one who is going to govern, to have strength to defend the weak, to help the sick.

A young man, if he wants to make a pot, or would like to make a pot, goes to the Mama and says, 'I want to make the container.' The next day, the Mama climbs a hill, sits down with his divining bowl and asks the oracle if it approves or disapproves. The oracle may say no. Then the pot is not given to him because at that time he does not have the power. He does not have power to receive it. If the Law says, the oracle says, yes, then the Mama hands him a white stone from the sea. He hands it over as a surety, as a token; as woman gave it, so he gives the surety to the man. And the Mama says, 'From today you must not look at a woman,' and he keeps him in a ceremonial house. There he sits.

The white stone is a '*sewa*', a guarantee that the work has been regulated in *aluna*. It is a token of the balance that has been established between man and nature so that the work may be done. Such tokens are given for all the work that the Mamas authorise, from cutting down a tree to building a house. Since the potter must dig out clay from the earth, it is essential that this balance, this adjustment of forces, must be established.

In Colombia all the land was sacred; you could not dig out oil, you could not build a highway, cut open a hillside, you could not do that. Serankua said, in Colombia, take care of the Sierra Nevada. So we remained like this; and that is why today when the Mama begins to have a pot made, he gives tribute in *aluna* so that no illness will appear.

The clay of the earth was woman. That is why when a Mama is going to have a pot made he has to make a payment.* The Mama has to talk with Serankua so that when he digs out the pots or digs out the clay no suffering or illness should appear, to men or women, no violence or problems of any kind; so the Mama makes a payment.

It takes the potter four days to dig the clay. He takes it out, he goes to the river to pile it up, to grind the clay, so that it is like dust, and the Mama says to him, 'You have to be perfectly obedient. No eating salt, no looking at a woman, no going into the house of a woman, that is forbidden.'

Then the young man has to obey those rules until he finishes all the

---

* This seems to suggest that the balancing payment is thought of as a dowry – a bride-price – for the clay.

jars. He makes about thirty jars. It takes nearly a month, without touching a woman, without seeing a woman, he only goes to bathe at night – at eight o'clock at night he is sent to bathe.

The potter's work requires the constant presence of the Mama, working in *aluna* while he works in clay. The potter sits at a flat stone which has been used for this purpose for centuries, and he begins by making an offering: a leaf, a small stone and a piece of cotton are held firmly, meditated on, and then placed beneath the potting slab. Then the work can start.

He is making a very simple object, a coil pot, which begins with a spiral that grows upwards and outwards. Exactly as a *mochila* grows in cotton or palm-fibre, a pot grows in clay.

And once the pot has been made you have to know how to bake it properly, you have to bless it properly. If you don't bless it properly smoke from your fire will spread everywhere, it will not cook well, so it must be made by one who knows how to bless properly, who knows how to bless well so that the smoke should go up vertically.

And then when the pot has been baked you let it cook, then you have to bless it again, and if you don't the person who eats out of it could get ill. So it must be made by one who blesses it well, well, well.

The old ones taught me how to do this, the great Mamas taught me everything. All types of food are cooked in these pots, potatoes, cauliflower, meat, everything. So to protect those things you have to bless the pots well.

After a month, the Mama says to the potter, 'Call your woman,' and he says to Serankua, 'This young man obeyed and received the pots, so protect him so that he has no problems, nor illnesses, nor pain.' Then the Mama asks permission from Serankua and prays for or blesses the man and the woman and then sends him to sleep with the woman. Now it has been received.

So the Mamas taught potters how to make the earthenware pots, here in the town. This pot that they make here is not taken to Huamaca, it stays in this town. The pot that is in Huamaca belongs only in Huamaca. The pot that is here, stays here, only in this village, only this village. That then was ordained.

A pot which has been properly made is itself a balancing of forces, a point of harmony in the world. Such focal points of harmony are linked to concentrations of power which are referred to as 'Mothers'. The ordinary pots are called *canyayimacu*, and their existence creates a balancing-point between the material and spirit worlds, the place of Mother Canyayimacu.

So when diarrhoea comes one has to protect the children against it, asking the Mother Canyayimacu; one has to concentrate on the Mother Canyayimacu, to cure the child and stop it vomiting and end its illness. You concentrate on the place where Mother Canyayimacu lives.

And when one has received the pots, one can bless the earth. One can bless the places where people are buried.

And you can bless the earth where crops are planted, I know how it is. If you have not received the pot, this cannot be done. The Mamas have the pots.

And the gold figures go inside the pots. Also the gold serpents go into the pots. And now they are destroying them all. Why?

So when you receive the pots you receive strength, you are like one who governs.

In earlier times, the old Mamas made their earthenware pots with figures, figures of birds, of pigs, of deer, of snakes, of all sorts. And they also made earthenware containers to bury us in; when a chief died – a Mama – they would make him a large earthenware container, and bury him in it. Why did they do this? Because we know that the land is our Mother Earth.

But once Younger Brother had come from another country he said whoever made these pots with those drawings was a sorcerer, and had to be annihilated, and Younger Brother, who came from somewhere else, sent a patrol to annihilate the indigenous people, with dogs. Some began to fight, they fought but they couldn't win, as they had only arrows. Younger Brother was always winning.

The decorated pots are no longer made, not because the Kogi do not know how to make them but because the blessings and prayers, the divinations and oracles connected with their making, have been lost. In the great flight from the cities destroyed by the Spanish, the specialists were destroyed. And although the craft could be relearned, there is no point in mastering an empty physical process. Without the correct work in *aluna*, such work would only create discord, disrupt the harmony and balance of life, and so inevitably produce sickness and violence.

The same process of reverence, control, prayer, meditation and work in *aluna* went into the making of Tairona gold. This too was working with the very essence of life, and it had to be done correctly on every level, spiritual as well as technical. Once more, such objects were not thought of as being made but as being granted. The real maker, of a simple pot or a golden figure, is the force which shapes reality. Reality is the Mother, the shaping force is Serankua.

The power contained in an earthenware pot provides a clue to the power in a golden object. If a simple pot may, because of its perfect harmony, be a healing power, then a magnificent golden figure, made under the supervision of a Naoma, a Tairona Mama, in a period of fasting, abstinence and meditation, a figure granted by Serankua to the goldsmith, has a far greater power.

These objects are specific; their power is directed to some particular aspect of the world, such as the health of the plantain, the yucca, or the macaw. They have their own life, and dwell in clay pots in the earth.

Philosophers' gold

Before going any further into the significance of these golden objects for the Kogi, it is worth reflecting on the meaning of gold in our own world. Virtually all human societies have considered gold to be quite different from other materials. Its incorruptibility and beauty are aspects of this, but they do not really explain the sense of awe with which we face a piece of gold. We hardly think of it as a metal. It represents some kind of ultimate perfection: an 'Age of Gold' signifies a time of purity and splendour; a 'golden boy' is a youth of superhuman perfection. There are many substances which, ounce for ounce, are more valuable than gold, but gold has an aura which we see as the essence of value.

Perhaps its meaning is most clearly expressed in the Museo del Oro in Bogota. Here our own gold-worship is stated by placing the grave-goods of the indigenous Americans in our own version of a holy place – a temple constructed as a bank vault. We do not have any architectural expression which states more forcefully 'This is what is most precious to us'. A cathedral is, by comparison, a mere conceit. An impregnable safe is meant seriously. Just as the Kogi would not allow me to film their most intimate secrets, so the Museum would not allow me to film the doors of the room where the gold is displayed. Any visitor can see those doors; this was religious awe masquerading as security. When we speak of gold, we pass beyond superstition to some atavistic conviction that we are speaking of something which has value beyond price.

Our own attitude to gold is incoherent. We perceive this sense of awe and value without having any framework that helps us understand it. At the time of the conquest, the dominant enterprise of the savants of Europe was alchemy, the effort to convert so-called 'base metal' into gold. There was no rational explanation for this; as a pursuit of wealth it was as unproductive as any work imaginable. But what was being sought was not simply wealth, it was 'philosophical gold', which transcended corruptible mortality in every way. 'The gold engendered by this Art, excelleth all naturall gold in all properties, both medicinall and others.'[*] Somehow this sense of a transcendental quality in gold, which real gold may lack and so disappoint us, seems to persist.

The Mothers

The Taironas and their attackers shared this understanding of gold. For the Taironas of the sixteenth century, and for the Kogi of today, the golden artifacts are 'philosophical gold', gold engendered by an art that works in the world of *aluna* as well as the material world, and so concentrates the life of the metal into a material which has the property to enable the world to transcend its own corruptibility. These objects ensure the continuity of life itself.

[*] *Mirror of Alchimy*, attributed to Roger Bacon, London 1597, p. 19

If we plant an orange tree or any type of tree and then pull it up by the roots it will die. Digging out the earth's gold is the same thing. It could die. We've all heard many stories that the world is dying. Why is it dying? It is because they have robbed so many tombs. The world is like a person. Robbing tombs, stealing its gold, it will die. We don't take out the earth's gold. We know that it is there but we do not take it. We know from our divinations that the advice of the Mother is not to take the gold. We know where it is but we decide only to make offerings to it.

A golden object is a focal point in which is concentrated the spiritual power for which it was shaped; the power to nurture a specific aspect of life. It is the resting-place of the Mother of that aspect – the Mother of yucca, or the plantain, or of the Younger Brother. It is vital to the life of the Great Mother.

How is it that we are able to live? Without blood we cannot live and without bones we cannot walk. Here all the Mamas are in agreement about what it is we are going to say and how to speak. If I cut my foot off I cannot walk. When they dig into the earth and take its gold it is the same thing. Down below by the sea there was a lake and there were many Mothers there. They have drained the lake and they have dug into it to take petrol. One day the river itself will catch fire. Gold has its own thought and it can speak. It is a living being. They must stop stealing it.

If they take all the gold the world will end. The Mothers of the banana trees, of all the trees and of all the birds, they have all been stolen. They are cutting off the flesh of the Mother's body. They have taken everything. They have stolen the spirits of all things from the Mother. They are stealing the very spirit and thought of the Mother.

As the Mothers are dug out of the ground and taken from their pots, so the forces which they represent are dissipated and the world slides further towards chaos. The harmony contained within them is shattered, and that is shown by the plants and creatures of the Sierra failing to breed and disappearing. The Kogi have no reason to doubt their understanding of the world, because that disappearance is taking place before their eyes.

Down below by the sea there were the Mothers of yucca and sugar cane, of bananas, of trees, all the trees, and all the birds. Younger Brother started to dig them out. Younger Brother learned how to rob tombs and they started to dig all the Mothers out. That gold down below – it was like seeds in a field. Serankua planted it there but the Younger Brother started to steal it.

It was Serankua who brought all the birds here, the macaws and the parakeets. They used to fly right past here up to see their Mothers in the sacred lakes on the paramo, but they don't any more. With so much damage that's been done, they don't come up here any more.

Yes, the Sierra has changed, the grass has changed, the straw grass for making our roofs is disappearing. The hills are changing, and bushes and creepers are growing that we don't know anything about, that we've never seen before. They have destroyed the Mothers of the grass, they go on destroying and destroying and destroying. So now it has stopped growing, and other grasses are disappearing.

On one occasion I went with Mama Valencia to the site called Pueblito. He had come with offerings for the golden Mothers, tokens which carried food and drink in *aluna*, part of the endless round of tribute which the Mamas must carry from place to place in the Sierra to harmonise the world. Among the Christmas tourists in their gaily-coloured clothes, picnicking on the stones, Mama Valencia wandered like an elderly Jew who has been brought to look at the site of Auschwitz. His infinite sadness was not only a response to the tragedy of the place, but to what it represents. He tried to explain in the simplest terms to me, knowing that he was speaking to a culture which has no conception of the rent which it has made in the fabric of life.

All our gold pieces and stone beads should live in pots, but now they are scattered. Imagine if you were thrown out of your home and had to sleep outside, it's just like that. Serankua said that all things should have their houses. We see them as pots but Serankua made them as houses; the Great Mother created all things in their pots. She created the Younger Brother too in a pot, but the Younger Brother does not think about that any more, he only destroys. The Mother made everything, she made the Mothers of all things, and now they have been taken and destroyed. The Mothers of the trees, of the birds, of the animals, of the people, everything has been destroyed. The Mother of the birds was a little bird in gold kept in a jar, the Mother of the jaguar was a little jaguar. And all of them lived in their pots, all of them have been taken.

So I come here bringing offerings to the Mothers, but what do I do? I leave them by the empty holes where they used to live. Perhaps they can still receive them, perhaps they can't. But what else can I do? What else can be done? And I want to know what the Younger Brother thinks of this. Does he think it is good, what he has done?'

When I presented Mama Valencia with the gold figure which Cano had made, he sat silently holding it for a long time. It had tiny golden leaves suspended from the points of the shapes around its head. He stared at it intently, shaking it gently so that the leaves quivered in the sun. He knew exactly what it was.

This is what was lost. This is one of our secret objects that they took. It looks just like one of the secret objects we had before. It looks like it but is not the same.

The Elder Brothers had these objects but the Younger Brother came and he set dogs on us and as we ran in terror we dropped them and the dogs got hold of them. It is like the objects they took but it is not the same.

The Elder Brother had seven of these but they took them all. They set dogs on us and we were terrified and as we ran we didn't think and since they followed us we left our bags behind. Where did they get this?

Now this is making me sad. It hurts me because it reminds me of what we have lost. Down below they have robbed so much. That is how it is that in Bogota there are so many gold pieces in the Museum. It was Serankua who made this gold. It is Namsiko. It belongs to Sintana.

He explained that the figure represents one of the world-creating sons of the Mother, and that the spirals above the head are eight of the nine worlds in *aluna*. The spirals of the worlds, each with its central ball-like knot, are images that call to mind immediately the bottom of a *mochila* or the base of a pot, when the making has just begun. The figure itself, or elements of its dress, signifies the ninth world. The birds on its head are condors.

Namsiko is a chief. The birds, the snakes, the jaguars, they're all like the vassals of Namsiko. He was chief of all the animals and all the birds. He was their chief. First came the earth, then came Namsiko, and then he was in charge of everything. When they first started to make gold, Namsiko was there, making the pots to house the gold.

But the object itself was as dead, as inert as a photograph. It had not been made in the right way, it was merely a technically faithful copy. It had not been granted, not shaped in *aluna*. It was not made of 'philosophical gold'.

We had special things, objects, and when we fled like that in terror they took our things and started to use them to rob tombs. And then they even started to come up here and rob tombs. On the paths there were sentinels of gold and they dug them out and took them. When we lived here before only adult men could go down to the sea. They knew that the gold pieces were dangerous for children and women, but now everybody goes down. The ancestors thought, well since they've taken all the gold nobody will be in danger. But since then we've all started to get ill. Now some Mamas say, 'Well, even though they have taken the gold it is still worth making offerings,' but others say, 'Why bother?' Some say it is still worth it. But it's not worth it.

   We are suffering, we are suffering from many sicknesses and from injuries. The Younger Brother could help us. I am an Older Brother. I look after the sun, I look after the mountains and the birds.

I've done whatever I could
but before long I am probably going to die.
I am suffering from a cough.
Younger Brother could help me. He could save me.

If all the Kogi die, do you, Younger Brother,
think that you will also go on living?

Many stories have been heard
that the sun will go out,
the world will come to an end.
But if we all act well and think well it will not end.
That is why we are still looking after
the sun and the moon and the land.

We always make offerings to the sun
and to the mountains
and to the stars.
That is why we live here.
If I go on doing it nothing will happen
to the Younger Brother either.

Tomb-robbing

Towards the end of our filming trip, we were invited to film tomb-robbers at work. Some of Frankie Rey's friends were excavating some tombs right down at the water's edge. The spot was actually inside the 'Tairona National Park', an area under national government protection, and we had to buy an entrance ticket. Presumably the tomb-robbers did the same.

Just behind the beach there was a lunar landscape of craters. Dozens of burial chambers had been crudely excavated, leaving a dense pattern of open pits. The team of robbers were a jovial bunch. Their leader, a powerfully-built mestizo, claimed to have been one of the people who set Mono Abello up in business in the early days of the drug trade.

What they were doing was illegal and, from the point of view of both archaeologists and the Kogi, very destructive. But the *guaqueros* think of themselves as honest citizens hampered by the law. They are not generally much involved in the narcotics trade, they seldom have enough land to be able to survive easily, they do not usually have a trade that will enable them to buy a house and enough to eat. If there is gold in the ground, and they are bringing Colombia's heritage to light, then surely, in their view, they are serving both themselves and the nation by digging it up.

The ordinary Colombian does not generally have an encouraging experience of the law. At a personal level it means the police, who tend to use their position for petty extortion – people are helpless in the face of fines and confiscations that are simple robbery. At a slightly more abstract level, the law is perceived as the tool of corrupt factions. The *violencia* of the 1950s was brought to an end by a pact between Liberals and Conservatives which excluded any other parties from power. The result was to confirm political power in the hands of local and national oligarchies, and authenticate a deep-rooted structure of patronage and corruption. Few Colombians equate honesty with law; they think more in terms of behaving honourably than conforming to statutes.

The *guaqueros* are bound by the same obligations of hospitality and friendship that made Ricardo such a useful guarantor of our safety. We were their guests, and whatever we wanted to film we would be allowed to film. A couple of nights later, when some of the crew decided to have a celebratory night out in Santa Marta, the robbers accompanied them to make sure that they came to no harm. They even drove out to the airport when filming was over to make sure that we got away safely.

They do not think of themselves as enemies of the indigenous people. Quite by chance I had first met one of them before in the street at Santa Marta, where he was accosting passers-by and selling grave-goods. I invited him to bring a selection to the Casa Indígena, where some Kogi would be able to look at what he had. He came with two others, one of whom was the robbers' leader. They spread out their wares before a group which included Ramón and Mama Valencia.

I felt deeply uncomfortable, as though I had asked concentration camp guards to show the gold teeth extracted from their victims to relatives of the dead. I did not know what would come of this confrontation, I was simply interested to see this meeting of two mutually uncomprehending moralities across objects which had great value to both sides.

I asked the Kogi, who were shocked by what they saw, which object they valued most highly. It was the one I had been offered in the street, a braid on to which had been sewn a collection of *sewa* stones which would have been used as offerings, given by a Mama to someone who had been granted permission to undertake some piece of work. *Sewas* are circular, the size and shape of coat-buttons, cut from translucent semi-precious stone. The Kogi speak of them as 'seeds', and say that without seeds all plants must die. I bought the braid and presented it to them.

There was, then, no question in the *guaqueros'* minds about my own position: I was closely involved with the Kogi, who laid claim to these tombs. But they do not see themselves as the Kogi see them, as barbaric looters and desecrators. They are proud of their role in bringing Colombia's heritage to light, and, though of course they are doing it for profit, they also have great respect for what they find. I have met archaeologists who were taught by tomb-robbers how to look at and read the landscape, and to interpret their finds, and certainly these men had considerable knowledge about the tombs they were digging. They pointed out, for example, the trail of crushed, burned shells in the soil which lead from the grave-goods to the body, in the grave they were excavating.

They do not, on the other hand, have the slightest notion of the mystic significance of their finds. That particular tomb contained a huge pot. It was pre-Tairona, but I have no doubt that its function was exactly that which the Kogi described, of creating a point of balance, harmony and health. For the tomb-robbers, of course, its value was purely financial. When they tried to lift this great and splendid object from the ground it shattered into a cloud of dust, leaving two of the band holding the empty rim above their heads and roaring with laughter in the powder-filled air of the grave. As an image of the Younger Brother, thoughtless destroyer of the harmony that holds the world together, it was a spectacular and powerful moment.

It was a profitable day for them. Golden objects, 'left there like seeds', were coming out of the ground in extraordinary numbers. One boy, working quietly in a grave away from the rest, pulled out some $14,000 worth of gold in half an hour – more money than he could expect to earn honestly in years.

We had, by chance, been filming at exactly the right moment. A robber might make a find of this order perhaps once a year. Some of them have begun making replicas, *à la* Cano, and one of the robbers we were filming was now much better known as a faker. In fact he had once seeded a grave with his own pieces and led archaeologists to it. According to his own account, they were completely fooled 'until they found the gold elephant'.

It did seem very likely to me that we were being set up by people who had now become quite expert fakers – so expert that they even knew that they should not include elephants in the find. In fact I was quite convinced that these were fakes, planted to be sold to us, and my conviction was strengthened when I was told quietly, 'Buy them from the boy. You'll get a good price. He's only a peasant, he'll be happy to take what he can get.'

Later I discovered that his finds were sold to El Mono's wife, which has led me to revise my opinion. You do not sell fakes to the wives of drug barons.

Museum gold

In the early days all the gold taken was melted down. That does not happen now. It goes into museums or private collections. The objects sit there, mute, to be stared at by people who perceive their power as gold but who do not understand their function or significance. Graham was once in the Museo del Oro when he saw an Arhuaco Mama moving from case to case, singing to the golden Mothers. When I took Mama Valencia to Santa Marta, we went to the little museum there to look at the display. We began with the body decorations, breastplates and wrist bands.

These are *haga*. They wore them to dance with, they wore them around their necks and wrists, when they danced to call the rains and to bless the trees and the rivers. When you want to speak to the ancestors you wear these *haga*.

He moved on to the images of figures, including one of Namsiko, similar to the replica which Cano had made. And there were more, golden Mothers taken from their pots in the ground.

That over there is the Mother of all the Younger Brothers, look they've got them all, ahh.

If I could speak their language I'd ask Younger Brother how are they looking after them? How are they feeding them, how are they bringing them firewood? They're sad in there, shut away like that. That's why so many sicknesses have come. How are they looking after them here? If I could speak their language, I'd ask them that. The Mother left them in their proper place, and now they've taken them and shut them in here like prisoners with no food, to be looked at.

The food and firewood of which Mama Valencia was speaking is, of course, the offering in *aluna* which must be made for the Mothers to function. Their power ebbs, and the world slides into chaos.

The Elder Brothers do not expect us to become Kogi, to make these offerings. We do not work in *aluna* or understand it. But they are utterly convinced that the robbery of the tombs strikes at the foundation of the world, and unless it stops, whatever else we may do is meaningless. Not all the science in the world can restore the broken harmony. And now there are very few Mothers left untouched in their pots. The last threads of the world are being cut. The last drops of blood are being stolen.

We do not know in which month the world will end or on what day the world will end; we do not know yet. Why is the earth falling? Because they have plundered so much, petrol, oil, coal, and have torn out the minerals, ripped out the Mothers, that is why it will fall.

Because of all this pillaging the sun itself will go out. When the earth ends everything will stop, the fires, the benches, the stones, everything. It will all end.

8

The Heartland

That first filming trip, which began by nearly destroying the *nuhue* and all who sat in it, started just before the midwinter solstice and ended at New Year. Up in the mountains above us, Mamas were dancing the nine-day ritual which turns the sun around from its southward journey, and which ends when it starts to weave northwards across the sky.

We were not permitted to witness this ritual; it was not considered to be a necessary part of the message which the Kogi want to convey. *Cabos* were posted on the roads and ridges around them to prevent any intrusion. But Mamas would come from many towns to spend a few days with the film, and to make their contribution to it. And all the time we had the supervising presence of a group of Mamas, including Mama Valencia, the Cacique Mama, and Juan Jacinto, the Jefe Mayor.

In the evenings, we celebrated our own rituals. The crew had brought fragments of Christmas, including a tiny inflatable snowman of surpassing beauty and a small supply of alcohol. Ricardo would supplement this from time to time, disappearing into the jungle at night and returning later with a flagon of *chirinche*. *Chirinche* is home-brewed rum made from sugar cane, and is nominally illicit. The colonos believe that this is because it is such a magnificent drink that the rum manufacturers have bribed the government to keep it off the market. I have come across similar fantasies among home distillers in Ireland. In both cases, there may be some truth in the belief that large manufacturers have conspired against smaller ones, but I am able to assure you that the simple jungle-dwellers of Colombia are mistaken in their belief that the world would flock to *chirinche* if it was given the chance.

The best you can say about *chirinche* is that the further down the bottle you go, the better it tastes. The last third is actually quite drinkable.

My own seasonal ritual is Chanukah, and one of my office colleagues had thoughtfully given Felicity a supply of Chanukah candles for me. So every night at sunset I would light my candles, one more in the cluster each night, until reaching the full set of nine. More and more Kogi would drop by to watch this little ceremony, but I have no idea what they made of it.

The Kogi's curiosity about the outside world is limited, but I was frequently asked to explain where I come from, and sometimes to say a little about how we live. The most rewarding conversations along these lines were about the position of Britain on the globe. The idea that as you go north the climate grows colder was not hard to grasp, and the general consensus among the Kogi was that Britain is a land close to the paramo, comparable to the higher reaches of the Sierra. I think they tended to pitch it a bit too high, but they certainly felt that the plants and trees I described belonged to highlands. The concept of seasons seemed interesting to them, too. The only technical question I was asked concerned our clothing: what was the fibre, and what were the dyes we used?

These last questions were put by Mama Fiscal, when he came down with his wife from one of the most sacred centres to demonstrate the ritual burning of sea-shells for the poporo. I had brought a sack of the right shells this time, together with a small supply of highly-valued offering-shells for the Mamas. I was a little worried because the shells were pre-washed, but I discovered that poporo shells have to be washed, and everything that is on them swept downstream back to the sea. Once more I had been lucky in my choice of gift.

Shells

Mama Fiscal taught a group of children how to build the fire for shell-burning, with a fixed number of sticks laid at right-angles between two posts, the '*cabos*' of the fire. It is an image of the loom, of the floor of the ceremonial house; it is the cross which marks out the universe. As he counted out the seven layers of sticks, which are seven worlds, and sandwiched two layers of nine shells between them, he gently ribbed Juancho – the mission boy come home – who was translating.

> You have to think well. When you are burning shells you must think in *aluna* of the Mother Methusa. You don't just go and burn them carelessly. If you did that, using that calc would give you chills. That is why we wash the shells carefully. All right, I have to speak straight to the Younger Brother here. At first the Mother counted out nine shells which meant her nine sons and then she counted out nine shells again, which meant her nine daughters. Juancho, you're becoming like the Younger Brother. Do you think we should leave all these ways?

Juancho, rather embarrassed, said no, he did not think that would be a good idea.

Once burned, the shells were crumbled into a gourd and water added. I watched steam rising from the gourd, and remembered a school chemistry lesson. The shells are chalk. Burning chalk adds oxygen, making calcium carbonate (quicklime). Quicklime plus water produces calcium bicarbonate (slaked lime) in an exothermic reaction. The chemistry teacher, I recalled, concentrated on proving that hydrogen gas was released. He never explained why anybody would want slaked lime. He had probably never thought of eating it with coca leaves. But why, then, did he want us to know about it? Life is full of mysteries.

Mama Fiscal was having a splendid time. Once filming ended he was filled with inspiration, possibly gently topped up with *chirinche*, and began to dance. Bill Broomfield, the cameraman, infected with the same pleasure in being alive, was playing with small children and swung one up over his head. Mama Fiscal skipped up to him, crying, 'Me too! My turn!'

One of the most delightful memories I have of the Sierra is of Bill Broomfield, a huge man with a bushy red beard, holding aloft the tiny beaming figure of Mama Fiscal.

The nuns

The only slight unpleasantness was the flow of rumour coming out of San Antonio. The direct opposition of the nuns had been squashed, and the church had sent a young priest up to the mission for a few days to ensure that they did not cause any trouble. He had very little patience with the nuns, plainly regarding them as backward even by the standards of the sixteenth century. 'Who cares what they think?' he asked. 'It's what the Kogi want that matters.'

This excellent man one day confided in Graham that the nuns' school was capable of holding one thousand pupils, but had only twenty-three, 'and they would not have those if it was not for one intelligent nun'. Every time a child fell sick, the Intelligent Nun told its parents that it had to be kept in the mission until it was cured, and the cures went very slowly indeed.

Although the nuns had been silenced, the waves of anxiety which they had generated were still rippling around San Antonio, and stories were emerging that we were stealing gold, stealing children and turning the Kogi into vassals of the BBC. However, it seemed that no one in our immediate vicinity was concerned about this.

The ceremonial house explained

I had told the Mamas that if the Younger Brother was to take them seriously they would have to authenticate themselves – to explain how they know what they know. They fully appreciated this, and set out to explain as much as possible of the background to their knowledge.

The transmission of knowledge is, of course, fundamental to them. Among the men, it takes two forms. One is the education of the *moros*, the student Mamas; the other is the life of the *nuhue*, the ceremonial house.

The *nuhue* is a multi-purpose building, part court-house, part council chamber, part school-room, and part dormitory. A large proportion of the time spent in there by vassals is passed listening to lectures by

Mamas, which are called 'giving advice'. These may often become extremely vehement. On several occasions Graham had sat uncomprehending in a crowded *nuhue* while Mamas, *cabos* and *comisarios* raged and stormed hysterically at the vassals. Half of them would be listening attentively, the other half would just sleep through it. Eventually one of the Mamas would go outside for a breath of air. 'What on earth is going on?' Graham would ask. 'Oh, nothing special. We have to remind the vassals of the Law. It's better if you shout at them, that way perhaps they will listen. But they are all lazy and forget.'

Now the Mamas were giving advice to the Younger Brother. It was an activity they were well used to, and it is interesting to analyse the form of one of these speeches. Take, for example, Mama Bernardo's explanation of the *nuhue* itself.

His speech was in four parts, which, as he explained, is the way anything should be analysed. Part one concerned the nature of the *nuhue* as a living thing. He began by talking about the presence of water in the structure of the *nuhue*. It is there in two ways: firstly in the wood of the structure, and secondly in the image of the *nuhue* as a mountain, for all mountains have water. The significance of this was so obvious that he did not trouble to explain it, because, in the language he was speaking, 'water' automatically refers to the primeval waters of creation. In the beginning all was water, and the water was the Mother. It was *aluna*. Where there is water, the essence of life, there is memory and potential. The earth, too, is the Mother. So he began by explaining that water is the link to the life-force, and what is dry is dead.

Why is it that we now say 'the earth'? Why do we say 'water'? We can only do this because they existed from the beginning. This is why we still say 'water'. In the beginning we were formed in the water. The Mother formed us there. And all the trees, that tree, another tree, another tree, another tree, all of them had water. When the trees are dried out they can be cut and used for firewood. All types of tree can be used for fire.

We all need water. We cannot live without it. We wash our shells in water. We cook in water. Many things. And all the mountains we see have water.

The first ceremonial houses were very small. They were made in *aluna*. But these ones that we have today are large. The Mother told us to look after all mountains. They are ceremonial houses. We know that all the mountains we see are alive.

So the first point that we are asked to understand is that water is not just a liquid: it is the original spirit-ocean from which we come, and whatever contains water partakes of the life of *aluna*. The ceremonial house, like the trees and the mountains, has water and a spirit-life.

The creation of the world was an ordering and shaping of *aluna*. The resulting shape takes the fundamental form of a cross – a separation of opposing and complementary forces, differentiated out of chaos. Their definition and separation was the foundation of world-building. That is the content of the second part of the lesson, which teaches the division of the world into pairs of opposites, into fours.

To speak about a single mountain it would take four nights. The Mother told us that about everything she made there were four important ideas. That is why they put four fires in the first cere-monial house. There are two posts in the house which divide it into a left-hand side and a right-hand side. (The posts have stone beds around the base. These are their benches.) So you have to speak of four things. The Mother said this. When speaking of a sacred mountain the Mamas always speak of four things. Every mountain has its thunder-men which live there. There are also thunder-women in every mountain. And from bottom to top it was they who made the mountains and lived there.

When the Kogi speak of a 'bench', it signifies a place where one is well seated, in harmony with the world. The posts which mark the clear division between right-hand and left-hand are in a state of rest, well balanced.

The thunder-men and thunder-women are the Fathers and Mothers of thunder, forces in *aluna*, and like everything else which shares the water they have life.

Having established the life-force of the ceremonial house, established that it is comparable to the life-force in the mountains, and made plain its ordering into opposites, Mama Bernardo introduces *Homo sapiens*. Humanity too, he explains, is part of this world; humanity too is shaped in the waters of *aluna*, and has its place in nature.

First we were formed in water and that is why we now have tears and saliva. When she first made a man the Mother began by forming the eyes and they are round like everything else which she first made. Younger Brother thinks we are forgetting but we are not. We still know. We still know how hard the Mother worked to form that first man. And now the Younger Brother is asking us how it was that first man was made and we have to tell him.

The Mother formed us way, way down below and we came up earth upon earth. Earth, another earth, another earth, nine of them in all until we reached here. But we are still only in the middle. There are nine worlds above for the spirit too. The Mothers and the Fathers went further, further up. They went up into the sky beyond, and when they die the spirits of all people also go up into the sky. So from the bottom up to Kurian it was seven earths, and that was where the Mother rested and then she went further up and came to here, our earth. And then she went still further up, and we will follow her, too, up into the sky when we die.

It is good that we tell Younger Brother how it was in the beginning so that he understands. Perhaps Younger Brother thinks that we cannot tell him how it was, how it was that we were all first formed.

This progression through the nine worlds below, and the existence of nine higher worlds, must be explained for the next passage, on the structure of the house, to make sense. The significance of the seventh world, Kurian, is something which I do not understand. Mama Valencia would sometimes tell me that I am a man of the seventh world, while he is a man of the ninth. This was always said in terms of affection and regard, but was also clearly meant to indicate that he was more complete, wiser, more fully formed. There may be some association between this and the Kogi's perception of a premature birth as a seven-month pregnancy, a birth which produces a baby whose bones have yet to harden.

The final stage of the lesson is that the *nuhue* is not built to an arbitrary plan, but to one learned from the Mother herself. It is a home of the Law of the Mother.

It was the Mother who taught us how to live and she taught the Younger Brother too. Look at the *cantoto* [inclined posts supporting a ledge over the inside of the door]. Those are the *cabos* and vassals guarding the Mamas and the *comisarios*.

We take four poles and we put them at the top of the roof so that they hold up the two horns of the roof and that tiny circle of vine up there is the bench for those horns. The mother gave us grass so that we could make these roofs but that we'll talk about when we're outside.

To put the thatch on properly we alternate the directions of the straw, one pointing upwards, the next pointing downwards, the next pointing upwards and so on. We lay on nine layers of straw like this. So going up to the top of the roof it's like the nine worlds that we came up in order to arrive here on our earth.

Perfect harmony depends on a balance of the forces at work in the world, and that includes a balance of gender. The *nuhue* is a men's house, women have separate houses, but there must also be a balance of gender within each house, in *aluna*.

You've seen that there are four fires, two on the left and two on the right. There are stones around these fires and those stones are women. In every women's house there are three stones who are men. And when the fires are lit and burning there should be two logs on each side. And on top of those logs, sticks are put. These are to warm the Mamas, the *cabos* and the vassals and the *comisarios*. In the *nuhue* the stones are near the fire. In the women's house the stones and the fire are far inside the house.

In order to bless the fire we have to concentrate on the Mothers of fire and on the Mothers of logs. We ask the Mother permission so that she gives us fires to put in our ceremonial houses. And Serankua told us to put a *dumuna* [a plant] in each ceremonial house and to burn it. We do this in order to get rid of the bad spirits. We burn *dumuna* in every house, both ceremonial houses and women's houses, in order to clean them out. There is good *dumuna* and bad *dumuna*. There is left *dumuna* and right *dumuna*. We put big *dumuna* on the left of the *nuhue* and the smaller one we put on the right.

Finally, the Mama summarised his explanation and demonstrated how the *nuhue* works as a centre for the continuity of Kogi tradition and knowledge, an inner heart in the Heart of the World.

So there are four fires in the ceremonial house. These are the cardinal points which sustain the world, and support it, and they support the ceremonial house too. When we bring a boy to confess and give him advice we stand him in the middle of the house. Mamas always say this: to give him advice properly you have to bring him and put him in the centre of the ceremonial house. It was the Mother who first gave us advice. She taught us. And we now know how to go on giving advice to our children.

A trial

The actual pattern of advice-giving can, as I have said, be pretty vigorous. Whenever we were filming inside a ceremonial house things were fairly restrained, but one night we managed to eavesdrop on some serious advice-giving. (Juancho would translate our recordings and keep the Mamas informed of what we were doing, so there was no secrecy involved.) A young man was arraigned before the community for trying to seduce a married woman. He was sat in the centre of the house, while the woman, stripped to the waist (a deep embarrassment), was kept at the door. It was around midnight, and cold outside.

The session began with the *cabo* bringing the guilty parties, and challenging the young man to take the woman as his wife.

'Why do you young men follow women around who aren't yours? You should respect other women. If you want her then take her. You spent a whole night boasting you were going to take her so now what? Take her.'

'No I'm not going to take her.'

'Hurry up, take her, take her.'

Then a junior *comisario* joined in. 'Well are you going to take her or not?'

'No I'm not going to take her.'

'Well are you going to take her? Are you?'

'No I'm not going to.'

The challenge had been seriously meant; it was quite possible for the young man to take the woman as his wife and make an offering of compensation to her divorced husband. But since he was not willing to go through with that, he was now being humiliated. The *comisario* launched into his attack. 'How many times have I lectured you all about treating women properly? Many, many times and still you go on this way. The Mamas too are always telling us that we shouldn't take women who are not ours. But we don't listen, do we? This problem will never stop. No matter how many times the young men are lectured they go on. You have to call them back, over and over again. Then they run away and hide themselves in the bushes, and do whatever they like, but it shouldn't be like that.'

The Kogis view all wrong behaviour – and licentiousness is definitely wrong behaviour – as being out of harmony with the world. It follows that it must be part of a pattern, and to correct it the Mama must help the wrongdoer trace back his actions and find the key to the pattern. This is the process which the Kogi translate as 'confession'.. The acts are merely a symptom of a deeper problem. The wrongdoer has gone wrong in *aluna*, in the relationship between thought and action, otherwise he would not be behaving in this way. Mama Santos's advice was therefore, 'You should go to the Mamas and confess. Confess well so that you stop acting like this.'

At this point the less alert members of the community began stirring in their hammocks.

'So has he agreed to take her yet, has he?'

'No, he's said that he's not going to.'

'All the young men have been lectured many times about this but they never listen.'

'And that woman out there, she should go to the Mamas and confess.'

'Yes, the woman too.'

'Go on, take the woman, we're tired of talking about it, we've been here all night and we're hungry and tired and our coca's running out.'

'Why don't we send somebody off to get some new coca?'

It was plainly time to return to the matter in hand, and the *comisario* began to restore some order to the situation.

'They all go off to confess, but here we divine and we know that they haven't confessed everything; that's why they go on and go on and do it again. If they confess – but they don't confess everything and, divining here, we know it. If they confess everything, we also know that too. I know that this one hasn't confessed everything so he should be made to confess again. Ask the senior *comisario* what he thinks. Wake him up, we need to know what he thinks. Come on, all of you out there, come back in.

'Is everybody inside? If they're not, go and look for them round the village, bring them. Everybody should be here. Now, take him outside and face them with each other. We'll see if they're telling the truth.'

By now the senior *comisario*, Clemente, had been woken up. Clemente, a wood-carver and flautist, having missed the start of the proceedings, decided to wind back to the beginning.

'Well have you taken the woman yet?'

'No.'

'Well do it and hurry up about it, I'm sleepy.'

Mama Santos rubbed salt into the wounds of the young man's pride. 'If you're going to take her, do it. Tell her husband you'll find another woman for him and take her.'

By now the boy had had as much as he could take. 'I've acted badly. Why did I do it? We're always doing this, but we shouldn't, we shouldn't do this.'

Now that he had broken, the *cabos* and *comisarios* laid into him with force. 'Tell the husband that you're going to take his woman. Tell him, go on tell him.'

'Take her. Tell the husband and take her right now. Find him another woman and take her.'

'Tell the husband that I'm not going to take his woman. He should take her. I won't.'

'It's you the man who is to blame. It's the men who go and look for the women. It's not the women who go looking. You went out last night and all the *cabos* were looking for you. You were hiding, so now tell us where you were hiding.'

This promising line of attack was interrupted by a report from the door, where the woman had been speaking to a *cabo*. 'She says that she was sleeping and that when she woke up the door had opened and he was inside the house. She says that he ran out immediately, nothing happened. She says she thought it was a *cabo*. But it wasn't.'

Why should she think it was a *cabo*? Was she suggesting that one of the *cabos* was in the habit of visiting married women in the night? Was she trying to protect her lover? Clemente was convinced she was lying.

Obviously, the whole of Kogi society depends on truthfulness, and the penalty for lying in this situation is very severe. It involves being forced to kneel on broken potsherds, with a heavy stone held at shoulder level in each hand, while being 'lectured' by *cabos*, *comisarios* and Mamas. If the stone is lowered, the victim is beaten with a poporo-stick until the correct posture is resumed. Graham had seen one man punished this way for stealing an ox and lying about it. The poporo-sticks were used quite violently, even being jabbed into his ear. At the end of the night, he was in a very bad way. His head and ears were lacerated, his knees swollen and raw, he was totally unable to move and was delirious from pain and exhaustion. This punishment is called, simply, 'being knelt'. Clemente thought that it might be needed here.

'Ask the *cabo* if this is true. If it's true, that's fine. If she's lying then she will have to be knelt here in the house. If it's true he has to say so; what I don't like is people lying. If it's true and he wants to take the woman, he can take her. That's fine. If it was a *cabo* and he was going after women, we'll kneel him here in the house. So which is it, what's the truth? What's the truth? If you're going to take the woman take her now. She's getting cold out there. Go on take her, take her. Are you going to take her or not?'

'No I'm not going to take her. And nothing happened.'

'We're all tired of this and we're sleepy and it's your fault. Make up your mind fast.'

There was a long pause. The young man considered the options. Somehow his girlfriend's attempt to get him off the hook had turned into a false charge against a *cabo*. The consequences of that could be very unpleasant indeed. Perhaps the best thing was to throw himself on the mercy of Clemente.

'Listen, I'll give her back to her husband, he should keep her, and I'll give him two beads for all the trouble. Yes I took her, but now take her back. I'm not going to take her away.'

Clemente rose from his hammock and spoke the ancient words of doom:

'The legs are for walking, the head is for thinking, ears are for listening – now KNEEL!'

The punishment seems barbaric. Once it is over, the matter is finished. There is no lasting shame. Kogi men are physically very tough and proud of it, and 'being knelt' appears to leave no lasting mark, physically or socially. The nuns of Pueblo Viejo told Graham that they wished the Kogi would use some less barbarous punishment, such as shaving the culprit's head. An enduring stigma of that sort would, in Kogi eyes, be truly savage – better to make the punishment very nasty, and have done with it fast.

The world outside

It was a strange experience to live in this isolated mountain state, totally cut off from the outside world. The only law here was the Law of the Mother, as enacted in the *nuhue*. Although the Kogi have allowed certain goods to enter their territory from the outside, the whole pattern of life and thought has been unchanged for centuries. One of the most extraordinary sights was the morning work-detail being assembled to clear paths and public spaces. The men of the whole community would be kept talking most of the night, returning to their wives' houses shortly before dawn. Then at first light the *cabos* would go round the houses, yelling and barking, occasionally pulling people out physically, and assembling the work-team.

The Mamas would stand to one side, working their poporos and working in *aluna*, concentrating on the Fathers and Mothers who preside over such works – an activity which they translate as 'blessing' it. Meanwhile the *cabos* and *comisarios* ensured that everyone took their turn at labouring. It is likely that the form of the Kogi's costume was modified in the eighteenth century to include pantaloons, and it is certain that the tools they used before the conquest were of stone and bone rather than metal, but apart from that nothing has changed.

Meanwhile every day we were tuning in to the BBC World Service, listening to accounts of the revolution taking place in Romania and the collapse of the Berlin Wall. Our world was being transformed; the thermo-nuclear sword of Damocles which had been suspended over it all our lives was apparently being winched down and disassembled.

The Kogi are not wholly ignorant of the threat of nuclear destruction, and sometimes, because of the system of 'confession', can be remarkably well informed. I know one archaeologist who was working in the Sierra when a Kogi emerged from the jungle and spoke to him in Spanish. 'I know that you have made a new kind of bomb. This bomb will kill people and not destroy your houses. Why have you done this? Who will you kill?' The archaeologist did not know what the Kogi was talking about. When he returned home some weeks later, he read about the 'neutron bomb', news of which had only just been released. Stories like this tend to reinforce the idea that the Kogi have mysterious telepathic powers, but I believe that news of this sort spreads extremely fast among Indian communities, who take it very seriously.

Martin von Hildebrand once told me of an Amazonian shaman who got hold of a transistor radio and began listening to the news. The poor man was profoundly disturbed by what he heard, and told other shamans who began to work with him. The problem, as they explained to Martin, was that there were two very powerful men called USA and USSR. These powerful men were competing for the favours of a whore, whose name was Israel. This whore crouched with her legs open, giving birth to a stream of bombs, which were very hot and had the power to destroy the world. The shamans were therefore working to lock the bombs inside a spirit-mountain where they could cool down. Fortunately they succeeded and the world was saved.

The Kogi are not so certain that they understand our world – in fact they are quite certain that they do not. Our occasional attempts to explain the news we were hearing were regarded as both baffling and irrelevant. What difference does it make if we do not destroy the world in one way, when we are about to destroy it in another?

The Mother put a solid beam here, and they are undermining it with all the things they are taking from it. The earth is collapsing. If we cut our leg with a machete we could bleed to death. It is the same with the earth. If they keep on taking from the earth it will come to an end. If the world comes to an end we will all die. Older Brother, Younger Brother, all that lives on this earth will die.

More immediately relevant was the news from Panama. The United States' contribution to the drugs war was a full-scale military invasion of Colombia's northern neighbour. Invasion is something on which the Kogi have strong views, and we were asked a number of times whether the United States was planning to move into Colombia. We hoped not. Colombia was enough of a problem to work in, without having a war going on round us.

Not being shot

Just before New Year's Eve, the helicopter came to give us a few days' break. The first shuttle flight down to Mingeo nearly ended in disaster, because the army personnel there had been changed and the new commander did not know who we were.

The pilot, rather foolishly in my opinion, having seen that guns were aimed at him, flew around in a circle to give the military a chance to identify him. Helicol had been faced with a problem supplying this helicopter because they were one machine short, and I think it is a shame that no one had told the full details of that loss to our pilot.

It had been an incident on the south side of the Sierra, in November. A helicopter carrying out work for an oil company had been surrounded and seized by guerillas. The pilot meekly handed over the pistol he was carrying and asked for mercy. The guerillas told him to fly them over a nearby police station. He did, and they circled over it and dropped a bomb. They then made him land in the countryside and set fire to the machine. As a parting gesture, just when he thought he would be killed, the guerillas gave him back his gun and told him to go home.

We were later told that a junior officer had requested permission to fire on us, in accordance with standing orders, which demanded the destruction of unauthorised flights. Of course our flight was authorised, but no one had told these soldiers. The commanding officer thought about it, and decided to wait and see a little longer. This was probably poor military practice, but I have not lodged any complaint.

My family arrives

My family was waiting in Taganga, and we were able to spend a few days relaxing in the sun and swimming around the coral reefs. They needed it. The journey from London had been difficult. Their plane had been stranded in Caracas because of fog at Bogota.

The delay had become ever longer, and eventually it had dawned on the passengers that there was no reason why they should ever get to Bogota. The plane appeared to be permanently grounded. There seemed to be no crew for it. The staff had given up claiming that there would be a flight shortly.

The men began it, physically threatening airline officials. Then the women took over, screaming and raging wildly. There was real physical menace. The airline staff went into hiding, and some of the quieter male passengers withdrew, saying that they could not afford to be caught up in this. The Caracas Airport Riot of 1989 had begun.

There was only one way to save the airport from destruction, and that was for the airline to find a crew very suddenly. Later the same afternoon, everyone was in Bogota, and my wife and daughters were ready to deal with Avianca.

Avianca, after the normal inordinate delay, began loading people on to a plane to Santa Marta. Unfortunately though, as they announced, it was really now much too late at night to go to Santa Marta. So they would take everyone to Bucaramanga instead. Bucaramanga is a very nice town in the Andes. It is not recommended for Caribbean holidaymakers by anyone except Avianca, since it is a 400-mile walk to the beach.

Avianca is used to dealing with angry Colombians – that is what it does every day – but it was no match for Englishwomen who had passed through the fire of the Caracas Riot. The plane was flown on to Santa Marta. There is a moral here, but I will not dwell on it.

My family did at least arrive ready to cope with small fry like bandits and guerillas. No sweat. In fact to pass the time while I was filming, they made an expedition of their own with Frankie Rey, following one of the river valleys into the jungle. This was in an area of the Sierra below the Lost City, where few Indians live and which the colonos have only sporadically settled. It also turned out to be the area of Frankie's 'bank account', where another deserted city is located, unknown to archaeologists. Most tomb-robbers have some particular site, a cemetery or Tairona settlement, where they do a little digging when their resources are low and the ground is soft. Frankie has retired from digging holes in the ground, but it does no harm, from his perspective, to have something waiting for a rainy day.

Sarah was going to come with me on the next leg of the trip, together with daughters Kate and Ros. I had been made very conscious, after my first visit to the Kogi, that my own way of thinking and understanding the world around me was being changed, and life would be much easier for all of us if they would share in this experience. I also hoped that it would be helpful for the Kogi to see me with my family. Certainly I had the impression that Sarah's presence had been very helpful on the last trip. It was difficult for the Kogi to understand who I was or where I came from, and unless they could see me as a rounded individual, with a family of my own, I was afraid that they would find it quite easy to think the San Antonio stories were true, and I was some kind of roving bandit. The Kogi kept trying to grasp the relationship between the members of the crew in terms of tribe or family, and were not very satisfied with our insistence that we really have no kin ties.

I concluded that my intuition was justified when I heard how Mama Valencia greeted thirteen-year-old Ros, meeting her for the first time on a trackway. He stared at her without expression, looked her up and down slowly and carefully, then beamed, seized her hand, pumped it up and down vigorously and cried, 'Hanchika! Hanchika! Hanchika!' Rosalind had no idea who this tiny bouncing gnome might be, but grasped correctly that this was an effusive welcome. It was the first truly enthusiastic greeting given to any of us by the Kogi, and the first I ever heard of.

Aluako

Ramón was waiting in Santa Marta, which was a great relief. Everything seemed fine as far as he was concerned. He was a little worried by death threats from his brother, but the guerillas had not contacted him and he was very positive about the filming.

We were still without any report on the film rolls that had been sent to London from Bogota. Unable to riot, they had been stranded in Paris. Felicity would have to stay in Santa Marta for a few days after filming restarted, to perform telephone riots on their behalf.

On New Year's Day, late at night, Ricardo appeared at the Blue Whale in Taganga to tell me he was setting off at three in the morning to take the mule train with our equipment back into the Sierra. It was an emotional occasion, in which he swore undying loyalty to Sarah and the girls, and explained to the other hotel guests that no one could go near these women without his permission, unless they wanted to be sliced up with his machete. Underneath the ridiculous braggadocio there was a great deal of nervous tension. Ricardo was genuinely worried about their safety, and was deliberately making an exhibition of himself so that word would spread, and nothing would happen.

It was a long and difficult trip for him, because we were going considerably higher up the river valley than Pueblo Viejo, to a town of perhaps two hundred houses in the heartland of the Kogi. There were no colonos up here, no medical centre, nothing but Kogi. This was Aluako. It is believed that this name became corrupted to Arhuac, and is the origin of the name 'Arhuaco' in the Sierra.

We were given four buildings to live in. Two of them were large and rectangular; they had originally been built by missionaries, one as a church, the other as a dwelling. Both were now kept permanently shut. The other two were ordinary circular houses.

Ramón took us on a tour of the town, which was thronged with people. It is situated between two branches of the river, and the paved central pathway is of great antiquity, as are some of the house foundations. The Kogi trace some of their lineages back a very long way, and at least one clan group which is now in Aluako maintain that they had dwelt here in antiquity, but moved down to the coast long before the Spanish came. They had come back as refugees, possibly in the great flight of 1599, but it was not clear who was in the town when they returned to it.

The physical layout of the town also constitutes a spiritual geography. The ancient path through the town, which joins the two parts of the river, is also a path in *aluna*, a route into the spirit world for those who know how to work in *aluna*. There are patterns of large stones at the edge of the town; one such area marks out a centre of fertility, with an open circle of stones as a womb, and a single large stone sphere as a testicle. There are also groups of small standing stones among the houses, presences which protect and nurture the people. In all these places the Mamas must work, making their offerings of leaf, thread and stone, offerings which carry spiritual food, drink and firewood, the sustenance offered by man to nature.

This town is so large that it needs two *nuhues*, one for the vassals and one for the Mamas. Being on a flat valley floor between steep mountain sides, it does not need the monumental terracing of the Lost City, but it is on a comparable scale. We were impressed by the sense of orderliness. The place was planned and managed as a whole. The Kogi are, in a sense, the gardeners of the Sierra, and here one really feels that they are in full control. The people were also more relaxed and comfortable with us. Many of our friends had come up from the area where we had been filming before, but there were also a large number of new faces. Previously women and children had been rather withdrawn in our presence, but here we were constantly being made welcome. I was taken to meet people's wives and families, and whenever we were in our own dwellings we had a constant flow of visitors, including children.

We had grown used to formal hospitality, with visitors coming by to bring gifts – bananas, oranges, eggs – but this was much more casual and relaxed. Aluako is a very large town, and there were hundreds of people there. Four thousand Kogi live in this river valley, and anything up to a quarter of them were present. There were a great many children, who would cluster around our houses in the evening. Kate, Sarah and John, the camera assistant, seemed to be a cause of much ribald amusement as they walked around. We never understood why they were more comical than the rest of us, but it was common to see a small boy being shushed by his mother after making some obviously impolite joke and giggling at them.

The Kogi children would come in large groups to sit in our houses and peer in at the doors. We never saw any children playing games, or playing with any kind of toys, but they were always giggling and boisterous. Ros in particular spent a lot of time with the children. She recited 'Jabberwocky' to them, and they were delighted by the strange noises; she also whistled tunes, which they learned to whistle back immediately.

Against the very long life-span of the Kogi must be set their very high rate of infant mortality. My own estimate is that more than 60 per cent of babies die in their first year, usually from respiratory problems. The Kogi do not take this lightly – all babies are cherished – but given the choice between sustaining a sickly baby with continuous medication and allowing it to die, they will let it die.

The children that survive are much loved, and family life is close and affectionate. It was a measure of the Kogi's trust in us that their children were allowed to spend so much time in our houses, and it was a delight.

Ramón

One reason, I am sure, for the relaxed and confident reception we were given was the presence of Ramón. He was the guarantor that we were not harmful or dangerous, and he took complete control of the filming arrangements with the Mamas.

Ramón believes that his special position is the consequence of his inheritance; his mother's family see themselves as descended from one of the original Lords of Creation, Luawiko. But Luawiko was always to some extent an outsider, and so is Ramón.

The two first Lords, the first masculine forces emanating from the Mother, are called Serankua and Seocucui. Serankua was the first weaver, shaper of things, associated with the movement of the sun and with the passing of time, and Seocucui was associated with darkness and death.

Luawiko was their younger brother, an ignorant urchin who Serankua and Seocucui treated with contempt. They listened devoutly to the Mother, and treated her with the utmost respect, but, as Ramón put it, Luawiko 'did not understand. He would go out on the streets.'

One day, the story goes, the Mother was infected with a painful hook-worm. It lodged between her toes (there are limits to the daring of this story, but one bodily crevice in this context evidently symbolises another), and she pleaded for her sons to remove it. Neither Serankua nor Seocucui dared touch her, but Luawiko said, 'Mother, give me a needle and I will remove it immediately.' So she did, and he did.

The Mother gave him special powers in return, and, though Serankua and Seocucui tried jealously to destroy him, 'as the Mother herself had given him power, there was no mystery, no kind of malign power that could harm him'. In the end, they learned to take his advice.

Ramón sees himself as having inherited this tradition. He was never a *moro*, but Luawiko too learned nothing as a youth. He sees himself as irreverent, bold, and prepared to do what is necessary even if it seems outrageous to more hidebound citizens. They have, in the end, to take his advice. And though Luawiko suffered from the persecution of his brothers, out of his suffering body was produced the sugar-cane. In fact by making him suffer the two first Lords produced the one machine which the Elder Brother needs and values: the sugar-gin, or *trapiche*.

The *trapiche* is an impressive object, built of great baulks of timber bound together with vines. Two huge supports, its legs, hold a cross-bar. Extending from the cross-bar is a long pole, harnessed to a mule. As the mule walks round the gin, the bar turns a vertical cylinder, which is geared to two other cylinders, one on either side of the first. As these three drums turn, sugar cane is passed in and squeezed between them. The liquor which drips down is collected and hardens into a cake of unrefined sugar. The *trapiche* was made, they say, from the body of Luawiko.

They cut off Luawiko's leg here, both legs; they made a *trapiche*, the wooden sugar *trapiche* is made from Luawiko's legs.

Then when the grinder had been constructed, he returned, he was born again. They said they would finish off Luawiko; they cut off an arm, put it in the grinder, ground it and when they ground they got cane, white cane.

Ramón identifies completely with Luawiko.

They stopped fighting with Luawiko, they returned and all came around to Luawiko, and that is what happened to me.

The story is a way of describing a real historical process in the language of myth. Luawiko plays a complex role; in one way, he represents the Spanish, the Younger Brother who learned nothing, grew up in ignorance, and who the Elder Brothers tried unsuccessfully to kill. However many victories were won, however often the Younger Brother was cut to pieces, he was constantly renewed and could not be defeated. The sugar-gin and sugar-cane were brought by the Spanish.

Up to the sixteenth century, Tairona agriculture was based on large-scale maize growing, which demanded extensive irrigation and drainage works. The Spanish brought with them crops which were new to the Sierra, including plantains and sugar-cane. With the collapse of the ordered economic life of the Sierra in 1600, the refugees became dependent on these crops, which did not need large communal building works to grow them. They remain to this day the basis of the Kogi diet. I was also told that manioc, an important root crop, was brought originally from Africa, and came with the black slaves which the Spanish imported.

Luawiko, then, represents the invaders, seen in a surprisingly positive light. But he also represents an indigenous figure, one who is able to step outside the bounds of convention and so enable the Kogi to take what they need even though it may be novel, and find a place for it within the framework of their own culture. This puts Ramón's relationship with the Mamas in a fairly clear light. He is treated with respect and taken seriously, but always with a measure of reservation. He is very useful but not, in their terms, fully mature. Relative to them, but not to us, he is indeed a Younger Brother.

A divination

In order to teach how they worked, the Mamas demonstrated a divination, explaining the different beads and the technical process of reading the signs. Sitting on a hillside above the town, they sat with their ritual pointed hats and a divining bowl. The hats represent houses, a round house over a round skull which is itself an image of the whole of the world. The Mama in his hat-house becomes the world, and his divination is a transaction between man, the physical world, and *aluna*.

In a world which divides everything into four classes, there are naturally four classes of stone bead. These are white, black, red and green. The white beads are called *abu*, the Mother. These represent water, with all its implications of the primeval spirit-ocean. The black beads represent spirit; they 'belong' to the time before the Dawning, and are associated with death. Green beads represent plants and trees, and are used for divinations concerning vegetation; red beads represent human blood, and are used for divination concerning sickness.

The primary object of a 'technical' divination is to find out where to make the appropriate offering. The whole process is part of the Kogi concept of balancing and regulating the world by taking offerings from one place to another, of putting things back into balance in the Sierra as a whole. The stone bead is called a *tuma*.

The *tuma* was made specially for divination — it is a living being, it has life, it has its soul, it has everything.

To carry out the divination, the *tuma* is placed in a bowl made from the bottom of a large gourd. The bowl is called the *tu-tuma*.

The Mama chooses the *tuma* and gives spiritual power where the Mother of the *tuma* is, where the Mother of water is, where the Mother of divination is, he gives it power. He takes the water and pours it in the *tu-tuma* where the stone is thrown; he also blesses the water and prays. Now they are purified: the water, the *tuma* and the *tu-tuma* — the three of them — they are purified.

And all at once the Mama speaks to the *tuma*; he says that we are going to talk and straight away he throws it into the container, straight away bubbles come out, speech comes out and the Mama listens to the word of the bubbles, listens; the Mama hears clearly what is needed.

One of the alarming aspects of tomb-robbing is that it involves the theft of divining beads. These should be kept, like the golden Mothers, in their pots in the earth.

These were their houses. Four types of beads, all of them in their pots. We have always kept them in pots. We also go into pots, and everything that represents us. Now that they are pulling out the roots of the earth, the earth is being diminished. When the Younger Brother has finally stolen all the beads, everything will start to dry out.

The Kogi also claim that they had golden *tumas* and golden *tu-tumas*, which were stolen by the Younger Brother. In the Museo del Oro in

Bogota, there is a life-size model of an 'Indian' dressed in golden pieces. The golden cap on his head looks suspiciously like a divining-bowl.

Whenever the Kogi did something for the cameras, it was properly done and seriously meant. They would stage it in the sense that the time and place would be chosen to make it filmable, but it was still a real event, not play-acting. So the divination we filmed was a real divination, and the speech of the bubbles was listened to with care, and interpreted. The question put was the inevitable one: how should they speak to us? The Mamas consulted the oracle and spoke, and Ramón interpreted the interpretation.

> From the beginning in Colombia
> everything, everything remained as it always was
> among us,
> the native people;
> the same belief,
> the same mask,
> the same dance.
> Everything well organised,
> in order,
> a terrace for every animal.
>
> Younger Brother was permitted to be in other places,
> other countries.
> There was a dividing line, the sea.
>
> He said, 'Younger Brother that side,
> Elder Brother this side.
> You cannot cross it.'
> Because this Colombia was the heart of the world,
> of the whole universe.
>
> But Younger Brother came from another country
> and immediately he saw gold
> and immediately he began to rob.
> There were golden images,
> golden oracles.
> The Mama prophesied with golden bowls,
> he had a golden *tuma*,

he had everything
and Younger Brother took it all to another country.

Now the Mama grows sad,
he feels weak.
He says that the earth is decaying.
The earth is losing its strength
because they have taken away much petrol,
coal,
many minerals.

A human being has much liquid inside.
If the liquid dries up we fall with weakness.
This same thing can happen to the earth,
weakness makes you fall,
weakness.

So the earth today catches diseases of all kinds.
The animals die.
The trees dry up.
People fall ill.
Many illnesses will appear,
and there will be no cure for them.
Why?

Because Younger Brother is among us,
Younger Brother is violating
the basic foundation of the world's law.
A total violation.
Robbing.
Ransacking.
Building highways,
extracting petrol,
minerals.

We tell you,
we the people of this place,
Kogi,
Asario,

A divination

Arhuaco:
that is a violation.

So the Mamas say,
'Please BBC
no one else should come here,
no more ransacking
because the earth wants to collapse,
the earth grows weak,
we must protect it,
we must respect it,
because he does not respect the earth,
because he does not respect it.'

Younger Brother thinks,
'Yes! Here I am! I know much about the universe!'
But this knowing is learning to destroy the world,
to destroy everything,
all humanity.

The earth feels.
They take out petrol,
it feels pain there.
So the earth sends out sickness.
There will be many medicines,
drugs,
but in the end the drugs will not be of any use,
neither will the medicine be of any use.

The Mamas say that this tale must be learnt
by the Younger Brother.

9

What Must Be Done

After a couple of days, Felicity was ferried up in the helicopter with the good news that the 'rushes' – by now a term of irony – had been located in Paris and shipped to London. Sarah, Kate and Ros went down in the helicopter to begin the long journey home, carrying all the film we had shot so far. It took them four days to get back.

The daily life of Aluako was quite extraordinary. This was truly a world apart from our own. It was like being on another planet. The Kogi had kept repeating, 'We have not forgotten. We have forgotten nothing. We still know and keep the law,' and here that was self-evidently true.

To go at night to the *nuhue*, illuminated by the full moon and the four fires, is a deeply moving experience and a remarkable privilege. The cloud comes down low into the valley, until it covers the thatched roof. Behind, the mountain is shaped like a larger version of the building, with the cloud surrounding it in just the same way. Inside, the dense smoke filling the roof is a continuation of the cloud, and there are people sitting round the fire. At first you see a few, the ones nearest the flames, their white clothes reflecting the fire-light. Then, as your eyes adjust, you realise that there are at least two hundred men sitting there, some fifty at each fire. All are dressed in white, all are holding poporos.

Perhaps our Younger Brother thinks that we do not eat salt, that we are savage, wild people. No, we eat salt. We are civilised. It was our ancestors who put the salt here. So we all still come here to the ceremonial house to eat it. We are still here.

Why is salt such a universal symbol of civilisation? In my own home, as in every Jewish household, we greet the Sabbath by eating bread and salt. There is a story in the Arabian Nights of a thief who inadvertently tastes salt in the house he is robbing, and is obliged to replace what he has taken. In formal English dining, the salt-cellar marked the dividing line between honoured guests and those of lower status; the hoi-polloi sat 'below the salt'. The 'salt of the earth', a phrase describing excellent reliability and trustworthiness, appears in the Lindisfarne Gospels.

In this case, Mama Santos was speaking with the elliptical imagery common in ritual speech. He was using the image of the salt-lick, an exposed vein of salt in the rock. Animals return there to lick the salt, just as the Kogi return to the *nuhue*, to sustain themselves. He carried on with more such imagery, feeling, as did all the Mamas, that the Younger Brother was there to see whether the Kogi still merit respect.

Long ago, the Law was revealed to us. It came to us with a *cabo*, a sentinel, and a wall around it, so that we would not leave it. We still have not rebelled against that *cabo*. We must hold on to the Law and be loyal to it. We do not set one man against another, we do not struggle against each other, we share one bench, and that is why we remain undefeated. The community is the foundation, and we build on that. If we forget, then yes, the world will fall.

Then two tambours begin to play, and a pair of flautists strike up. One plays the male pipe, with just one hole, and a gourd rattle, the other plays the female pipe, with six holes. The music seems simple and repetitive, but gradually complex changes begin to develop. And then someone begins to dance, in the centre of the house. It is a slow, weaving dance, one of the dances learned by listening to the world itself. Two hundred men are watching gravely. This is not ecstatic, it has none of the pulsing throb of voodoo. It is calm, relaxed, thoughtful, dreamlike. This is the dance of the world, in the world-house at the heart of the universe.

We are here, with this mountain. And still the mountain is not empty. So we can say this is how it should be. Can't we?

Greeting ancestors

We flew down from Aluako to Pueblito with Mama Valencia, Juan Jacinto and two *moros*, into a site where the mountain was empty and things have not been how they should be for centuries. Mama Valencia took the two boys to a ring of stones where a ceremonial house had once stood. Carefully he led them round to the doorstep, and brought them in to this vanished *nuhue* as though it were still full of people holding their poporos.

> You can't just wander in like a boy. You have to think about what you are going to say then you have to speak carefully. You should go to the door and speak, you should greet the people inside. They ask, 'Where have you come from?' You say, 'I've come from such and such a place.' They say, 'And did anything happen to you on the way?' and you say, 'No. Nothing happened to me.'

They were standing in the open, under the sun.

> So they'll say, 'Is everything well with you?' and you'll say, 'Yes. Everything is well with me.' So then you can enter. You go in and you tell the Mamas what it is you're going to say.

They stepped over the threshold, into the empty circle.

> You speak. 'I've come to help, I've come to bring wood and I've come to bring food for you.' You speak and you speak and you speak. So then the Mamas will say, the ancestor Mamas will say, 'Good. Fine, come tomorrow and I will divine for you on the hill.'

He looked up. But there was nothing. Not even the echo of the past.

> But now I come here to speak to the ancestor Mamas and there's nothing, only empty holes, nothing. So who will I make my offering to here?
>   They've destroyed everything. The government and the Younger Brothers say, 'Come here and make offerings, pay tribute to the great mothers and the great fathers.' But how am I going to do that

if there's nothing here? They themselves have destroyed everything, they've stolen everything, so who do I make offerings to?'

Here I've brought food for the ancestors, but who can I offer it to? Everybody's been taken away.

The ritual would be carried out, though perhaps it was empty and meaningless. He showed the boys where to place their offerings, one on the right of the place which was once a doorway, one on the left. 'Now say goodbye properly, say "I'm going to visit over there, but I will return."'

They walked on through the ruined city. It was clean and well tended; the Kogi themselves come to look after it. There was a Kogi work-party there, arranged by Ramón, and brought in trucks from Valledupar by Inderena, the National Parks Agency. They were to build a ceremonial house so that offerings could be made there properly. Inderena had dumped them at the roadside and they had walked to the site two days before. They had not been supplied with any food, and had not eaten since they left the truck.

We fed them. And Mama Valencia led his two charges along the path, to standing stones.

Look, this was all a town. Here were the terraces; now there's nothing left. These stones are *cabos*. You shouldn't pass these without asking permission. And these *cabos* shouldn't let bad people or jaguars pass through here.

If you go through without asking permission of these stones, who knows, further on other *cabos* might grab you. And who knows what they might do to you? If you go through without permission, they will tell other *cabos*, they communicate with each other. It's as if you were going to see the President – you don't just walk in, you have to ask permission.

Tourists were strolling along in their light summer clothes, the men stripped to the waist, drinking cans of Polar beer from Venezuela. They stared at the strange figures in white, so out of place here.

So I'm going to ask these *cabos*' permission. I'm going to say, I've come from such and such a place to visit you, I've come to speak to you all.

That is what I'm going to do. So let's see if they make complaints to me. Perhaps they'll say, 'Who has come down to see us?' and when they see that I'm a chief perhaps they'll say, 'Listen: they have stolen everything, we have nothing here.' So then I'll make offerings to them, saying in spirit. 'Look I've brought you sugar, meat and coffee.' So I've brought them these things and I'll put them here, and I'll see if they take them. All these things are done in *aluna*.

Juan Jacinto stared around stunned.

Look, the ancestors had everything here, they destroyed everything. Look, they've broken all the pots. There's nothing to see here but empty holes. The same on the other terraces, they've taken everything.

Mama Valencia had known what to expect. 'Yes,' he said sadly, 'they've destroyed it all.' The Colombian tourists watched curiously, unable to understand the language.

Teaching a moro

There is a cave in Pueblito, which was used to keep the *moro* in his years of darkness. We were shown it, because Mama Valencia was going to use the ancient site in front of the camera. There was a passageway of thin stone slabs, 6 feet high and an inch thick, leading into the inner chamber. A single shaft of light fell into the back of the chamber from above, illuminating a large spider sitting on the wall. We stared at it.

'Is it dangerous?'

'It can bite.'

'What happens when it bites?'

'You can die.'

The Younger Brothers held a telepathic conference, and voted on the life of the spider. The verdict was unanimous. Bill took a large stone and slammed it against the rock. The spider joined its ancestors.

Mama Valencia took the younger *moro*, a boy who looked about nine years old, blind in one eye and with sight failing in the other, into the darkness. There he began to teach. He gave the boy an offering bundle – a piece of dried leaf, a piece of thread, a tiny package to be held between thumb and finger.

This boy was being taught how to think, how to understand, how to feel the world correctly. From the Kogi's perspective, the future health of all mankind depends on this child and the few score like him who are learning to carry the burden of caring for the Heart of the World. We are doing damage to the earth, wounding the Mother, but even if we were all to become wise and good, we could not do the work of the Mamas. This was a lesson in responsibility, caring in *aluna* for the plants and creatures of the world, as the world slides into chaos. Here were the final defenders of the Mother, an old man and a blind child, sitting in a cave among the ruins.

It was a gentle lesson. What has been hurt must be tended. What has been broken must be mended. The task is great, yet the Mamas do not believe that it is hopeless, unless we make it so.

In the time of the ancestors they made offerings to the Mother here, so now give your offerings to her, concentrate, think that this is food for her in *aluna*, this is her meat, her vegetables, firewood. Concentrate hard and give your offering.

Think too of the Mothers of the trees, of the birds, of the waters, and offer them your tribute. First do your offering on the left side, then do your offering on the right side, concentrate there on the houses of the Mothers of the birds, trees, the waters, farms and cane fields. Think of nothing else, concentrate hard, making your offering – not to one alone, but to all the Mothers.

Around here you have seen much of the way the world is. The Mother and Serankua set it up well, made it straight. Now you have seen it overthrown. They've broken all the stones. The Mother placed these stones properly, but now they've been turned over and broken. So think that it's as if they've broken her arms and legs and made her back hurt. So in *aluna* place these stones properly again and offer them to the Mother. Concentrate on the idea that all these stones are Mothers. There, over there, there's one lying on her face, she cannot rise, another has had her hands cut off, she cannot eat. Another has had a leg cut off so that she can't walk. See it in your mind, concentrate on this and cure them, think of all of them lying there suffering, and cure them with your offering.

Now put their food over there. When you have concentrated properly on all of these things put your food offering there on the right-hand side. Think that you're offering them medicines. They're sick and suffering and you're giving them medicines to cure themselves.

So what will the Younger Brother say? Will he say that it's true that he's cut off the Mother's leg and mutilated her? Let's see what he says. So put your offerings there.

Put it over there, put it over there. Now concentrate on the paths that the Mother will take to collect this food and firewood. Concentrate and make them straight and clear so that no harm comes to her. Make her a good path, with no dangers for her. Fill the holes in so that she doesn't fall and put a fence around it so that no jaguar attacks her, and no snakes bite her. Make it straight.

Now make the offering to the Mother of blood and all the things related to blood and put it on the left side. When you put it there, concentrate on the food offering you've made, and then say farewell to the Mothers.

This is like a ceremonial house; you should not be letting your mind wander, you must concentrate hard and leave your offering here. Food, water, firewood, everything that the Mother needs, leave it there.

Then think of the skies; concentrate on Father Serankua and Father Luawiko and say to them in *aluna*, 'Here I am, offering food in *aluna*, and looking after the Mother.' Concentrate and make your offering on all the other levels. Make the Mother's path straight.

They're recording this and they should understand. First they arrived and took all we had, now they are here and they are taking our photos. It's the same thing. I wonder if it's true they're recording my voice here and will listen to it later? Perhaps they'll just take away our photos. If they do that, that will make me very angry, they're not thinking like me. I come here and I see the holes and I see the broken stones, I see everything destroyed and it hurts me. To them it means nothing.

Make your offerings to the sky above and below to the earth, to all nine of them. At first we had good roads, they were straight. Now they are torn up and the stones are all scattered. Now if the Great

Mother walks on these roads she could fall, she could break her leg. Now all the roads are broken and ruined.

Does the Younger Brother understand what he has done? Does he?

Triumphs of technology

Since my first bright idea for reaching Pueblito a year before, by boat and on foot, had certain weaknesses, I was very pleased to have found a place where we could land the helicopter. We had put it down on a terrace surrounded by canopy jungle, a circular clearing. Only when we came to leave did I realise that this clearing was in a natural amphitheatre. The only way out was to rise straight up for 400 feet.

The problem, as we discovered when we had loaded the helicopter and climbed aboard, was that the machine could not lift us 400 feet straight up. It needed to fly forwards, and that would be inadvisable.

It rose about 250 feet, ran out of power, and sank back to the ground. We got out and stared at the stranded machine.

For a long time now a conflict had been building up between the film I was making and the way I was making it. It was a conflict which I had pointed out to the Mamas at the very beginning: it is impossible to make a film without using our technology, our machines. Helicopters, generators, cameras – all things which represent the dangerous world of the Younger Brother – had to be brought into the Heart of the World. The Kogi's period of mental preparation for the filming meant that they had found some resolution of this conflict which worked for them, but I had not found one which worked for me. Instead, I had dealt with it by not thinking too hard about it. Somehow I felt that if the Mamas could solve this conundrum, I did not need to worry about it.

Now I threw myself wholeheartedly back into the world I had come from. My commitment was to the machine. We would fly out of here with panache. With fewer passengers and less gear, we rose again. Just at the level of the tree-tops, the pilot rotated us, looking for the lowest tree. He aimed for it and missed by centimetres. He giggled. We were out, singing the Ride of the Valkyries.

Our base was a house which Graham had rented on the beach close to the Irotama Hotel. The pilot agreed to put us down right on the beach, which seemed an excellent idea. Not only would it mean that we did not have to transport everything from the airport; it also should impress the hell out of the sun-bathers and water-skiers.

In the event it was all quite unsatisfying. Having landed, the beach seemed tawdry and unpleasantly noisy. The sea was warm and cloying, without the refreshing clarity of bathing in the Sierra rivers. The house seemed claustrophobic, with its rigid solid walls and hard ceilings; it did not breathe like thatch, and I missed the comfortable smell of wood-smoke. But we had finished filming among the Kogi. I was going to have to settle into my own world again.

Then came the blow that rocked us all, a message from London. Every single roll of film that had been carried back to England by Sarah had been damaged by X-rays. We would have to go back to the Kogi and reshoot.

It was shattering and incomprehensible. I knew that Sarah had refused to allow airport security to X-ray the film cans when boarding. Perhaps it had happened *en route*? Or perhaps the film had been X-rayed on its way to us? In which case all our unused film was also damaged.

London assured us that the damage had been done after we had filmed, not before. The only shots which had been visibly affected were those taken in the darkest conditions (on fast stock), so we simply had to list all those sequences and reshoot them. To reduce the risk from further X-ray damage, the reshoot would be done with a larger generator and extra lights brought up from Bogota.

We later discovered that the damage had been done between Bogota and Santa Marta, and had nothing to do with the return journey; all the film had been X-rayed, and I had ultimately to devise, with the film editor and BBC engineers, a way of undoing the damage. We were, thankfully, very successful. But this did give us the opportunity to reshoot the darkest sequences in a way that we had not dared to do first time around. Bill and I had been wary about using large lights in the *nuhue*, as we felt that it would disturb the Kogi too much, but they had proved so willing and helpful in working with us that there now seemed to be no problem. It was not easy to get the equipment up there, of course, but by now we had the logistics under fairly good control. And I was not at all unhappy about having to go back to the Kogi, back to a world which I believed I had left for ever.

The Kogi were puzzled – it was obviously a difficult problem to explain – but determined to be helpful. They would arrange another reunion, and we would reshoot what we had to.

Communing with water

In the meantime the Kogi were to make a 'pagamento', an offering, at Mingeo. These offerings are a fundamental part of the work of the Mamas. To sustain the ecological balance it is not enough to work in the physical world. The Mama must also create balance in *aluna*. He is a gardener in the unseen world as well as the visible one, working in the world of memory and potential.

In the days of the Tairona, the Sierra was a patchwork of different zones of husbandry and labour, which had to be ordered as a whole. No part could survive alone. Although Kogi communities today are physically far more self-sufficient, that understanding of the Sierra as a balanced whole survives. The Mamas work to achieve a spiritual harmony and balance across the Sierra, and the welfare of the individual species, by travelling from place to place, bearing small tokens which they place at sacred sites, meditating on the Mother appropriate to the act.

As the Younger Brother has pushed into the lower parts of the Sierra, the Kogi have been cut off from some of these sacred sites, especially those nearest the sea. These are obviously of great importance, because the sea itself is so important. To people who believe that the Mother began as an ocean, and to whom the salt sea is the amniotic fluid in which the world was born, the sea must have a special place. Both the shells of the beach and the stars of the sky are referred to as the traces left by Serankua's original act of fertilising the world – his ejaculation. Both the sea and the sky are aspects of the original ocean.

The idea of both sea and sky as part of a single original continuum is common to many cultures, including our own. The creation in Genesis begins with a division 'of waters from waters'. The Hebrew for water is *mayim* (a plural), and the Hebrew for 'heavens' or 'sky' is *sha-mayim*.

The association between shells and the impregnation of the world with life is also shared between cultures. Botticelli's *Birth of Venus*, with the goddess emerging from a sea-borne scallop, draws on our own ancient mythology. In fact the story as recounted by Hesiod, in which Kronos cuts off the testicles of Heaven and hurls them into the sea, which gives birth to Aphrodite ('The Foam-born'), is quite startlingly similar to the Kogi's way of speaking about the generation of life in the sea.

The Kogi integrate this way of thinking into their total perception of the cycle of life and water. The waters of life bind the Sierra together. They are very conscious that evaporation from the sea and the rain forest rises as cloud, and is deposited again as rain, and as snow on the highest peaks. Just below the glaciers are the Kogi's sacred lakes, deep lakes of melt-water which are the starting-point of the rivers that sustain all life below. Reichel-Dolmatoff was told that the snow-fields around the lakes were called 'Gonavindua', and the lakes were the vagina of the Mother. Since *gonavindua* conveys this sense of 'quickening', the first twitch of new life, it is not hard to see what all this signifies.

In fact the Kogi speak of the new-born river water as a baby cradled in the river, and say that it begins its life being carried down the mountain, chuckling and gurgling. The life of the water becomes the life of everything, and over and over again they spoke to us of the water that is shared by plants, animals and earth – a water that is the essence of life and indeed is *aluna* itself.

They repeatedly asked the rhetorical question, 'How are we alive?'; the answer was, 'Because we have water.' 'First we were formed in water and that is why we now have tears and saliva.' Salt water, in the form of tears, and fresh water, in the form of saliva – these correspond to, and are shared with, the water of the world itself, for the world and everything in it is also alive. 'Like us trees and hills have water. The mother gave all things water. We need water to live. Without water we die of thirst. The earth has its blood and it has its water.'

The world began as *aluna*, which was the sea. This means that communing with water provides access to the memory and the potential of the universe. Divination with beads is a conversation between the bead and the water, which allows the Mamas to commune with the core of being. 'First the Mother gave us beads and we lived in *aluna*. For us the water is like a book and the bead writes in it.'

The poporo, too, is a way for water to give tongue, in this case the water of saliva. The ring of calc which builds up around the rim is saliva (the fresh water of the body) mixed with shell-dust (the seed of Serankua, *dua*, the seed of all life). Created during contemplation, by thoughtfully licking the stick and rubbing it on the neck of the gourd, this calc is also described as a book: 'We write our thoughts in it.'

Visiting the sea is therefore a most important activity for the Mamas. It is as important as visiting the mountain tops. In fact the shore and the peaks are linked: they are the opposite ends of a single structure. To maintain the balance of the structure, both must be kept in harmony. Keeping the waters in balance is fundamental to everything else.

Among the most sacred places in Kogi geography are a group of freshwater lakes behind the beach at Mingeo. These are the sea-level images of the lakes on the mountain peaks, and they represent, like the lakes of Ciénaga Grande, the meeting of fresh and salt waters. They were major centres of generative energy at the time of the conquest, and the ground around was heavily seeded with gold images in their pottery containers. The lakes were surrounded by stone guardians. This was a spiritual centre, home to many of the Mothers, which acted as a focus of thought for the protection of the species of the Sierra, and a place of shrines at which offerings had to be given.

Today, it represents a focus of energy of a different sort. The area has been cleared, the most important lake has been drained, and the guardian stones have been removed. The gold Mothers have been stolen. What stands there now, behind a high security fence, is the gleaming pipework of Termo-Guajira, a huge coal-burning power station.

This is where the 'pagamento' would be made. And while it was being made, Mama Bernardo would go to the paramo to make an equivalent offering there, binding together the opposite ends of the world.

The offering

We went first to Dibulla, to collect shells. It was very disheartening. There were even fewer shells than there had been the year before. The sea is growing barren. The Mother is visibly weak. Mama Valencia poked around angrily in the garbage washed in by the waves.

> Before, Mamas used to come and make offerings here, and the Mother brought in sea-shells, lots of them. But now they are all gone. Younger Brother is not making any payment to the Mother, not a single cent. So what can I do?

There were also offering-stones to be collected, small pebbles which must be taken from the beach to be used in caring for specific parts of the Sierra, or to be taken up to the paramo in the cycle of movement that regulates the world. One stone, *harta-ichi*, was collected because it is used for looking after coca, another, *mama-quichi*, because it contains flint for fire-making, and is used in burials. It is the stone which is the seed of light, *mama-quichi-sewa*. *Zela-quichi* was also collected, a stone used in the care of peccaries and pigs, and *noa-ichi*, 'that's good for our tobacco paste'.

From there we went on to the beach below Termo-Guajira, and in the shadow of this monument to the Younger Brother's concept of power, the Elder Brothers made their offerings to the sea. As each of the Mamas approached the water's edge, he turned around clockwise, echoing the turn of the spindle from which life and the world spin out. Standing at the waterside, concentrating on the Great Mother and all the Mothers which sustain life, the Mamas cast fragments of leaf from the paramo on to the waves. Counting the waves from one to nine, their offerings were carried out into the bosom of the sea.

> All the Mamas think about the Mother. The sea is for us. The Mother has many things for us. The sea is our Mother. She has many, many things to look after us with. She looks after the Younger Brother too, she looks after everything. Until the end of all things, we will never forget this truth.

The Mama of the Dance

It was time to go back to the Sierra, and reshoot our damaged pictures. The Sierra loomed behind the beach, a world quite apart from this tropical 'paradise'. Going back there felt like returning home. But although we now had many friends there, not everyone was pleased to see us arrive.

One Mama in particular appeared who I had never seen before. He was obviously a focus of some anxiety, and I heard that he was opposed to the filming. There had always been some people who did not want personally to be filmed, and we had respected their wishes carefully, but this seemed to be rather more difficult. I spoke to him, saying that I did not want to be the cause of problems and asking if he objected to us being there. He had been drinking earlier in the day, and had been affected by that, but this did not mean that he was incoherent. He told me that he did not object to filming, but did not want to be filmed.

While we were setting up lights in the *nuhue* he came to complain that he did not approve of us being there. I was ready to pack up and withdraw when he pulled me into the centre of the house and began stroking my hair with both hands, staring into my eyes and speaking. We were brothers. We were the same flesh and blood. His eyes were glazed and staring, his chin streaked with spittle. He squatted on the ground and invited me to sit with him. The intense staring, the hair stroking, the murmurs of brotherhood were continued. Then he asked me, do I know how to dance. No, I do not know how to dance. Come, I will teach you. We stood up, and he began to repeat the weaving, swaying movements I had seen before, but with more litheness and delicacy. I tried to follow his movements.

As everyone else worked, we danced, and the ceremonial house was gradually filling with Kogi. Dusk fell, the lights came on, and the situation was becoming very strange indeed. Mama Valencia, Mama Santos and Arregoce were going to need considerable powers of diplomacy to defuse dangerous moments as they arose. The new Mama, I discovered, was regarded as the most accomplished dancer. And dancing, especially in this slightly disconnected state, is the truest speech.* His effort to draw me into the dance was also an attempt to exert control over me, to take charge of events.

One of the vassals in the *nuhue* suggested that we should make a gift of the generator. Then they could have light every night. Mama Valencia and Mama Santos agreed, yes, that would be a good idea. Mama Valencia would tell us to give him the generator. Arregoce

* The Kogi say that their children dance first, and walk later.

211

approved. In fact, said Mama Valencia, we should leave quite a number of generators. Although, he pointed out as though a new thought had struck him, the soot from the fires would soon obscure the lights.

Yes, agreed Arregoce. In no time the lamps would give no light.

Mama Valencia pondered further. What would happen if something went wrong with the generator? We know how to look after it; the Kogi do not. He was gently defusing the situation, steering the vassals away from confrontation with us.

Mama Santos decided that, since the matter was now resolved and it might not, sadly, be such a good idea to ask for the generator, it was time to close the subject.

The dancing Mama, who was now seated and had released me, was not pleased. We had still not been brought under control.

When we receive our poporos, we have to spend four nights without eating. They'll have to do the same. We Kogi have to be able to spend seven nights without sleep and without food. They should do the same so that they understand something. Ah, all this filming, if all you think about is sleep and you spend your time sleeping you can't understand a thing.

They took everything we had, so now we'll tell them that they're going to spend seven nights without sleeping. We know they took everything, and now they've come back here to show us. Why don't they leave their things behind to help us for once? They took everything; do we wander over to their land, asking questions? No. But they come here asking questions as if it was them that had been robbed. They've seen our Mamas' hats, they've seen our ceremonial houses, they've seen everything. They keep coming up here, they keep coming, why do they keep coming? Is it that they've lost their own law?

Yes, said Mama Valencia gently. They must have lost their law and they've come back here to ask for it back, but that's all right if they help us. They've come to see if we've lost our ways. But they must help us, and go on helping us, so that we do not lose them.

The Dancing Mama went to Mama Valencia, his limbs loose, his head rolling with anger. 'I didn't steal gold from them, they stole it from us.'

Mama Valencia could not disagree.

'They've already taken so many photos.'

Yes, we had taken photos of the ceremonial house, of the mountains, of the rivers, of everything.

'For how long has the Younger Brother been coming here and taking photos of us?'

Mama Valencia suggested that what we were doing might be helpful. Perhaps we were planning to destroy them, but he did not think so.

'What? But they're robbing tombs right now in Bongar! They're destroying down there right now!'

Ah yes, said Mama Valencia sadly. He sat upright in a hammock, and the Dancing Mama was now sitting at his feet.

They steal our gold, and they steal our beads and then they sell them, they get money and they buy their houses with it. They've taken everything, and they use it to buy whatever they like.

He leapt to his feet and began moving around the *nuhué* shouting.

The Mother said that the Younger Brother would help the Older Brother, but how is he helping? All he's doing is destroying, all he's done is to dig up our precious objects in the past, right up to now.

They've dug them up, now they're all in Bogota, the museum in Santa Marta, they're not in the earth where they should be, they're outside of it.

This was becoming an embarrassment. Arregoce, who was the *comisario* of this town, decided to assert his authority, and told the Dancing Mama not to shout. The response was vigorous.

'Why not? I'm in my own ceremonial house. I can shout if I like.'

Arregoce had heard enough. 'What's the matter with you, aren't you going to show me some respect, do you want me to call the *cabos* and throw you in jail?'

'Go ahead, take me away.'

'What's this, is there no respect here? As if there were no *comisarios* here? Go and find my *cabos* so they can take him away.'

The situation was distinctly awkward, roughly comparable to a

213

policeman being told by a government official to arrest a bishop. The Mama's assistant attempted a word in Arregoce's ear. 'But he's a Mama! And that's the way he speaks all the time.'

'Not to me he doesn't! Go on, take him away.'

The *cabos* decided on a compromise solution. They sat the Dancing Mama down firmly in the darkest corner of the *nuhue*, and sat next to him, jammed so tightly together that he could not move and could hardly breathe.

But he had opened a serious issue: was it possible for us to change, or would the Younger Brother always be what he had been since the sixteenth century – a thief, a murderer, a destroyer? The original decision to make the film was based on desperation; the only alternative was to sit helplessly as the world weakens and dies. But is there any hope? What did we, the film-makers, represent? Hope or destruction?

There was a prophecy which had been referred to a number of times in the last few months, and now Juan Jacinto returned to it.

The Mother said to the Younger Brother long ago, 'One day, you will look after the Older Brother. One day.' The Younger Brother knows that he is going to have to look after the Older Brother one day. Lots of them don't think, they rob, and they don't think about the Older Brother. But some do think of Indians – for instance, the President isn't doing these things, their Mamas and *comisarios* aren't doing bad things,* they don't know what the others are doing. They also learn and teach the young. Some of the Younger Brothers do think. Remember there are so many of them, but of we Older Brothers there are only a few. I think that from now on the bad ones aren't going to come up here any more. We don't want any more of them to come up. They've robbed and destroyed so much. They're making us lose our minds, so now I'm sending this message – 'Don't come up here any more. We don't have any power, please stay there where you are.'

I had first heard this prophecy in September. 'It is said that near the time, when the world is very weak, one of the Younger Brothers will

---

* Probably a reference to the Archbishop, whose abortive Easter visit had been seen as properly deferential, and to Martin von Hildebrand, who seemed to be respectful and well intentioned

come to help us.' I had expected it; in fact when I had proposed the one-year wait before filming, I had said to colleagues that time was needed for us to be incorporated into Kogi mythology. I do not think that the Kogi really conceive of prophecy as we do. Their prophecies are descriptions of *aluna*, the possibilities which have been created. That means that their mythology is still being written, as *aluna* is reshaped by time and events. The disputes and problems which Graham had encountered were, in my view, part of the necessary process of finding the place of what we were doing.

Although the Younger Brother cuts into the Mother, gouging out the minerals, coal and oil, and stealing the gold which is the earth's blood of fertility, the potential may be there for us to change. They know that it will not be easy.

As so much oil and so many minerals are being removed, the earth is becoming weak. So the Mama has been thinking, how can we make Younger Brother understand this?

The Mama says that it is very difficult for Younger Brother to hear and listen, and even harder to give up all that; but Younger Brother must be taught to listen to the history of the Mama, the law of the Mama, the beliefs of the Mama, and that if there is a scientist like the Mama who knows the earth – I do not know what sort, but who knows about the earth – let him study the earth to see, is it declining or not? Does the world grow weak? Why is it weak? Because they take out much of its life-blood, minerals, and the Mama is frightened, it makes him fearful. They say that Younger Brother is studying more, but he is studying to destroy the world, so the Mama is somewhat frightened and that is why the Mama says they must learn our history; they must listen to our story.

'If there is a scientist like the Mama ...' The phrase is interesting. The Mamas are careful observers of their world, and they know the patterns of rainfall and of plant and animal life in minute detail. Their own oral record is longer and more precise than our collection of observations. As empirical ecologists, the Mamas simply know more than we do, because they have more facts. But they also do not have the burden of proof that our science demands.

To establish the connection between things – the chain of cause and effect – is, for us, a process of 'proof'. For a hypothesis to become 'true', it has to be demonstrated with such clarity that it will stand up in court. Eventually, perhaps, we will be able to prove that damaging the world in one way damages it in every way, but we may get there too late. A few years ago, our science regarded concern about the ozone layer, acid rain and carbon dioxide emissions as 'cranky', because the causal chains involved had not been clearly demonstrated. They would not stand up in court. Now these things are taken more seriously, but the Kogi conviction that minerals in the earth play an important part in its life is one that we have not yet considered, and which we are therefore bound to dismiss. Our science is based on new discoveries, many still waiting to be made. Kogi science is based on ancient knowledge, tested over centuries and found, in their experience, to be true.

'So I have to give them the message well,' said Mama Valencia. 'If they kill all the Elder Brothers then they too will be finished. We will all be finished. I go and give offerings at Mingeo, all Mamas do, but they come up here and they do not know how to give offerings or do anything. All they can do is look and take photographs.'

From the darkest corner of the *nuhue*, the Dancing Mama spoke. 'We still know how to call the rain, how to bless the birds, the trees and the rivers. We still know all things.'

There was a general murmur of approval. The *cabos* relaxed.

The Dancing Mama, encouraged, spoke again: 'They've got no right to take photos of me. If I got one of them and had him kneeling here, I know he wouldn't even last half a night.'

Arregoce snapped, 'Shut him up will you!' The *cabos* squashed the Dancing Mama again.

The debate went on for hours. There were many people who were becoming convinced that the Younger Brother might indeed be capable of behaving properly, and even that the making of the film was a work with real meaning in *aluna*, creating a point of harmony. Mothers had begun telling their children that it was a good thing for them to be filmed, that it could protect against sickness. And even this filming in the *nuhue* was a point of harmony, because the inhabitants of many towns had come together despite their continuous arguments, just as they had done at my first meeting in Pueblo Viejo. That meeting had drawn together only Mamas and *comisarios*, but here were vassals too.

'It's true, here we are all kin to one another, we're one family. We're always fighting among ourselves though. That's why Younger Brother has brought us here, all into the same ceremonial house, so that we should agree with one another. Even though we vassals don't know how to speak well, we should all be here supporting the Mamas. We vassals have to be united behind them.'

Gradually the talk turned to the subject of water, the most fundamental of all things.

'It is the mountains which make the waters, the rivers and the clouds. If their trees are felled they will not produce any more water.'

'We do not cut down the trees that grow by rivers, we know that they protect the water. We do not cut down huge areas of forest like the Younger Brother does, we cut small clearings for our fields. The Mother told us not to cut down many trees, so we cut very few, tiny patches.'

The world is growing hotter. They were certain of this. And the heat is a sign of serious problems. Its causes are manifold, but all the causes can be traced to the Younger Brother and the way he treats the earth. One of the clearest causes is the cutting down of trees, deforestation. By stripping the land of trees wherever he is, the Younger Brother takes away the water in the land and dries it. Then the sun will heat it and parch it.

Mama Santos, who is responsible for the well-being of the trees, was speaking: 'If the Younger Brother keeps cutting down all the trees, there will be fires because the sun will heat the earth.

'If we want to cut down trees we have to speak to the Mamas and *comisarios* first, because the Mamas know which are the sacred places, and in which places trees can be felled. So we always ask their permission first. We are the Elder Brothers so we have to think clearly.'

The Kogi see connections between everything. They cannot understand how we fail to grasp those connections.

Juan Jacinto, the Great Chief, was the man whose task should be to speak for the Kogi to the Chiefs of the Younger Brother: 'They want to sell the Mother, they sold the produce of the earth, now they want to sell the Mother herself. For millions. If only I could speak Spanish I would go to the government and tell them about this.'

Arregoce, the *comisario*, thought in terms of issuing commands to the Younger Brother. 'It is not only we who have to plant trees again, the

217

Younger Brother must also plant trees. The Mother planted trees right down to the sea shore. The Mother planted trees on the sea shore. Younger Brother must plant again there, he should also plant again up here. Plant again what he himself has cut down.'

The film itself would carry the command. But would the Younger Brother listen to it? Although the Kogi were speaking of trees in the Sierra, they were also speaking of trees all over the world. In every place, the trees need protecting, nature needs to be cared for. Surely in the lands of the Younger Brother, in England, France, Germany, the United States, there must be indigenous people saying the same? Arregoce had been thinking about how best to present what they had to say.

'We must speak these things. We should not threaten or insult, but it is good that we speak. We must think carefully, we should cooperate with these people, because perhaps they will help. We have to speak about what has happened, so that the Younger Brother listens. Perhaps there are some Kogi over there in their land, and they would say that the Elder Brother didn't speak well, they might say that he was playing about, joking. So here we have to speak well and tell only the truth. Yes, we have to think that over there in their land there may be Kogis, who will listen to this and think that we are just playing about. So we must speak the truth. So mustn't we speak straight?'

The Dancing Mama rose from his dark corner. And everyone listened as he moved forward, speaking.

> They have taken the waters.
> The waters need their food,
> they need to breathe,
> but they have imprisoned the waters,
> locked up the waters.
>
> We know that the waters need their food.
> We do not shut them away.
> We gather the water in gourds and we carry it,
> we leave the waters in peace.
>
> Younger Brother drinks water too,
> everybody needs water,
> the animals and plants need water.

If the water dries up we will all die.
All the water that they drink below
comes from the mountains.

What if it dries up here?
They too would die.
They have taken the clouds from the paramo
They have sold the clouds.

They take the stones,
but the stones have their Mothers too.

Now they must stop digging up the stones.
Now they must stop felling the trees.
Then it would be good;
if they stopped.

We do not take the stones.
We do not cut the trees.
We know that the spirit of the Mothers is in that stone.
We know that if we dig it up, the world could end.

Do I speak the truth?

There was a solemn chorus of assent.

To everything that lives,
the animals,
the plants,
we know how to make offerings.
This is how we should speak, is it not?

Then the Dancing Mama began to sing. It was a strange, wailing melody in a language new to us. He was singing in the language of the ancestors, the language of the Lost City. It was the song of all songs, in the Tairona tongue. And Jacinto said to the vassals, 'This is the song of the Mothers.'

Drums and flutes were brought. Mama Valencia rose and joined the Mama of the Dance. Together they moved and swayed in the centre of the world-house. The musicians stood with them playing. And so the Kogi spoke, in the most true way they know.

10

The End In Sight

The rest of the filming was done very quickly and easily. The Mama of the Dance played a full part in it, and we reshot weaving, spinning and other sequences which we had been told were too badly damaged to use.

We had finished working in the Kogi towns, and they symbolically closed the bridge behind us. The Younger Brother should not return, we were told. The message had been given, no one else should come. Only I was to come back, with the finished film, so that they could see that I had done what I had promised.

Formalities complete, gifts distributed, we gathered all our equipment in the landing area and waited. It was a long wait, because the helicopter did not come. That night was a depressing anti-climax. The sky had been clear, we could see a long way down the valley. Something must have gone wrong, and I began trying to work out how we could leave on foot. We did not know that down below the weather had changed for the worse and the pilot believed that we were locked in by cloud.

The following morning, to my immense relief, he arrived. As the helicopter finally landed to take us away, I was presented with a poporo – not the small, naked gourd that I had been given on my first visit to the Sierra, but a poporo that was completed, finished. I stared at the ring of calc around the top. It mixed the water of a man's body with 'the seed of all life', the sea-shell powder. The stick, which was a penis, had been inserted into the gourd, which was a woman: the powder had been taken from stick to mouth, where it burned, and was cooled by chewing coca leaf. The juncture of shell from the sea, leaf from one zone, gourd from another zone, stick from yet another zone, was itself a microcosm of the Sierra. The joining of masculine and feminine images, of what is wet and what has been dried, of what is hot and what is cool, of plant and animal, is a microcosm of Kogi thought. The gourd itself, with shells in the base and its yellow-white cap, represents the mountain at the Heart of the World, rising from the sea to the snows. And that cap has been constructed by thoughtful, contemplative stroking of the stick on the gourd: a human act, working both materially and in *aluna*. It is a statement, containing the thoughts of the man who made it.

I cannot divine, or read the thoughts embedded in the poporo. But it represents some kind of link – a *sewa*, a seed that is a token of balance and harmony.

Return to the Lost City

My involvement with the Sierra had begun with the Lost City. I had originally gone to the Kogi in the hope of understanding it. Now I was returning to it. I was intrigued to know how I would see it; what insights would come from everything the Kogi had taught me?

In fact it gradually dawned on me, as I walked through the site, that the process had been the other way around – the Lost City had helped me to understand the Kogi. The subtle engineering of the site, with its thoughtful control of water and its careful moulding to the natural contours of the mountain, had prepared me to meet a people who see themselves as the guardians of nature.

The placing of the city in a network of roads and staircases that extends over a vast area suggested that the Sierra had to be seen as a whole, and individual communities as nodal points on a complex interlocking web. The roads and stairways are themselves water channels, part of the complicated environmental engineering of Tairona civilisation. The Colombian archaeologists had recognised this clearly, and in order to grasp how the city functioned they organised a complete transect study of the Buritaca valley, from the sea to the snow peaks. The city has no meaning, and could never have survived, in isolation; it drew on the whole Sierra, on the variety of habitats and crop regions, and made its own contribution to other areas.

All this had helped to prepare me for the mental world of the Kogi – a world inherited from that network of exchange. The Lost City had been a doorway into their world, and I had not recognised how much I had learned from it.

Wandering through the lower part of the Lost City, hacking a path with a machete in the green gloom of the jungle and then coming upon massive walls and monumental stairways, I now saw the city as quite different from the impression I formed on my first visit. The periphery of the 'city' consists of groups of dwellings linked by paths and stairways; it is probably a mistake to see it as a single community at all. I have seen many small Kogi towns grouped together in this way, as close together as the groups of dwellings here, but politically quite distinct and often engaged in long-running disputes with each other.

The central section of the site, however, has an unmistakable structural unity quite different from anything which exists in a living Kogi town. A broad highway runs up a rising ridge into a series of raised platforms, whose scale is impressive and imposing. The whole of this central complex is designed theatrically; it is a place for some great drama of public life to be enacted. And here we were looking across the chasm which separates the Kogi from the Taironas. Whatever these dramas, these ceremonies were, they ended when the Tairona world was smashed. They belong to the lost world of war-lords and gold-makers, of specialists and visual splendour, which was swept away in 1600.

The Kogi have preserved a large part of the pre-Columbian civilisation which was crushed here. But there were things which they did not and could not preserve. Now, at the end of my two-year journey, I was facing the realisation that the Lost City has been lost for ever. Ramón had been meant to join us here, but he did not come. I had expected that he would disappear at this stage, and I did not know why I expected it. But in fact the answer was simple. The Kogi were not interested in talking about the Lost City. They had a different message to convey. And the reason behind it, I was convinced, would be found at our final location, on the high peaks of the Sierra.

The paramo

The snow-peaks are the most sacred area of the Sierra, and the Kogi regard all intrusions as dangerous sacrilege. It is an area reserved for those who need to be there, so that the work of caring for the world may be carried on properly, but no one else may go there. This created a dilemma. There had been many indications that the Kogi's fears were rooted in observed changes near the mountain peaks, and it was part of Ramón's task to ensure that I went there. But my visit had to be brief, and, in effect, invisible. The Mamas knew about it and did not forbid it; they simply averted their eyes.

The helicopter flight up to the peaks was spectacular. The snow shone brilliantly in the bright, crisp, thin air. We could see immediately the first signs that had worried the Kogi. Glacier moraines, scoops of rock that looked as though they had been made with a giant ice-cream spoon, were empty of ice. Large lakes of dark water showed clearly, from the colour of the rock around them, that they had shrunk dramatically. The eternal snows were melting, and the waters were evaporating.

We landed below the snow, on high tundra. We moved very slowly, affected by the sudden change of altitude. I looked down at the ground, and I felt afraid.

We had been through quite a lot on our way up here. There had been many dangers, but they were all part of the adventure, and the fear that went with them was stimulating, exciting. Besides, I had always been protected by someone else, someone who knew the ropes. But here there was no one to offer protection. There is no protection against the death of the earth.

This area – tundra, paramo, whatever the ecologists want to call it – is a great sponge. It holds the water of the snow-melt and the high rains. It fills the lakes from which the rivers are born. It is the fresh water supply of everything below; the life of every tree, every animal, every plant, every human in the Sierra depends on the fresh water that is stored in the ground and the grasses here, and that filters into the lakes.

There was no water. The grass was dead. It had shrivelled into tight dry yellow spirals, which turned to dust between my fingers. The earth was hard and dry, and covered in a mesh of fine cracks.

It is the mountains which make the waters, the rivers and the clouds. If their trees are felled they will not produce any more water.

The tiny tundra trees, inches high, which take decades or even centuries to grow, were dead, the colour of ashes. They crumbled as soon as they were touched.

Younger Brother, stop doing it. You have already taken so much. We need water to live. Without water we die of thirst. We need water to live. The mother told us how to live properly and how to think well. We're still here and we haven't forgotten anything.

The mountain sides around us were bare rock. Frankie, who has visited the peaks from time to time as a mountaineering guide, said that ten years ago they had all been covered in snow. Each year the snow had retreated. Now it was almost gone.

One hundred acres of tropical rain forest are cut down every minute. The air temperature over the whole world has been gradually rising for a hundred years. This change is felt least at the equator, most at the poles. The Sierra is truly a model of the world, and what is happening on its high peaks is happening in the Arctic and in Antarctica. The ice is thinning.

The earth is decaying, it is losing its strength because they have taken away much petrol, coal, many minerals.

The carbon trapped in the prehistoric forests, stored in the earth as coal, oil and natural gas, is being extracted, burned, and passed into the atmosphere as carbon dioxide. Five thousand million tons of carbon are being consumed each year. The destruction of living forest adds another 2,000 million tons. For ten thousand years, the atmosphere has held a fixed percentage of carbon dioxide – 280 parts per million. Now it contains 350 parts per million, and each year there is more. The air we breathe is changing, and the balance of life is altering.

The Mamas say please BBC, inform other countries – no more ransacking because the earth wants to collapse, the earth grows weak, we must protect it, we must respect it, because he does not respect the earth, because he does not respect it.

> Younger Brother thinks
> 'Yes! Here I am! I know much about the universe!'
> But this knowing is learning to destroy the world,
> to destroy everything,
> all humanity.

At the top of the Sierra, the world is dying. The water cycle has been broken.

> They have taken the clouds from the paramo.
> They have sold the clouds.

Everything below must die as a result. The rivers must decay to a trickle, the plants and trees must die from thirst. Even without any further land clearance, evaporation from the leaves will decline because there will be ever fewer leaves.

The Mamas, with their pattern of offerings carried from place to place, echo the water cycle. They have been trained to see the connections between all life, and to understand it as a whole. They feel the life of the earth as a single being, and they hear it groan.

> The Mother is suffering.
> They have broken her teeth
> and taken out her eyes and ears.
> She vomits,
> she has diarrhoea,
> she is ill.

> If we cut off our arms, we can't work,
> if we cut off our tongue we can't speak,
> if we cut off our legs, we can't walk.
> That is how it is with the Mother.
> The Mother is suffering.
> She has nothing.

I looked at the parched ground convinced that I was looking at the death of the world. But the Mamas believe that there is still time. We are close to the end, the earth is very sick, but there is still a chance of saving ourselves. That is why the Mamas have spoken.

> We know what is happening.
> They say that the world will end.
> But it will not end yet.
> If we behave well it will not end.
> The earth is still fertile.
> It is still giving crops.
> The crops are still growing.
>
> When it is going to die, there it will be barren.
>
> Father Serankua made this earth
> so that it would not end
> so that we could all go on living here.
>
> Younger Brother,
> your water is drying up down below.
> Do not think that we are responsible,
> do not think we have forgotten our work.
> When will the world end?
> We do not know.
> Neither the Younger Brother nor us can know.

The Kogi make no predictions. They say only that if we do not change, they truly believe that the world will die. It will cease to be fertile. They say that their work is futile in the face of our destruction.

They do not ask us to be like them, but they do say that we must stop taking fuels from the ground in the way we do, and we must stop tearing trees from the earth in the way we do. More than that, we need to become sensitised to the life of the earth, at least a little. And we must leave them alone. They need access to the sea, they need to recover a corridor of land that will give them that, and they need to have their ancestral sites protected from tomb-robbers. Apart from that, they want only silence. They need very little from us, except to be left in peace.

The Mother has told me how to look after her, so I do not mistreat her. I bring food and offerings to her. I look after her. The Mother gave me a single path and I followed that path without swerving. I did not wander off on this side or that. I did not harm any thing. It is the Younger Brother who is finishing everything off. Not all of them, but some of them.

So now I am sending this message over there. I want to give some advice to the Younger Brother. If they go on like this, they will see what will happen. I do not know yet on which day the world will end. But from being plundered so much, of oil and everything else, it will end.

Postscript

Now I have finally left the Sierra. But I can no longer think of the Sierra as a place, distinct from the rest of the world, cut off and separated. The paramo completed my own process of understanding. Just as the world of *aluna* is a spirit-world mirroring everything material, so the world of the Sierra mirrors the planet; it is the Heart of the World. If the Sierra is dying, it is because the world is dying.

When the filming was over, we went to Graham's favourite restaurant in Santa Marta, the Pan-American, for a farewell party. It has one dining-room which is kept very dark and very air-conditioned. It is rather like sitting in the fridge with a candle after the door has been closed and the light gone out. It probably reminds him of Canada.

It was a remarkable gathering: Arhouac Indians and tomb-robbers, archaeologists and retired guerillas, film-makers, anthropologists and government officials. The only people missing were the Kogi. They were locked away in their mountain fastness, waiting. They still wait, and watch, to see what we will do with the world.

Anyone who has read this book with understanding will realise the importance of not going into the Sierra. People of good will, well meaning travellers, are as dangerous in Kogi eyes as any other intruders. Every intrusion, by tourist, philosopher, thief or student, is another step towards the final collapse of the Heart of the World. The Mamas have spoken once. They do not intend to speak again, and no one should ask them to.

We flew back through Miami, and I took a couple of days alone, travelling down the Keys, ending up in Key West. The journey took me through a section of the Everglades. There are lakes here, once held sacred; deep freshwater pools like the sacred lakes of the Sierra. The water they contain is the water of life, *aluna*, the universal Mother. The lake of Guatavita, where El Dorado swam, must also have been such a sacred lake. Covered in the gold that is the menstrual blood of the Mother, the essence of fertility, the cacique must have been immersing himself in the primeval water of creation, returning to the womb of the world. Refertilising the Mother with his offerings, he was ensuring the renewal of life. That is the work of the Mamas today, as it was once the work of the Indians throughout America.

Florida was the first part of North America discovered by the Spanish; they came because of stories of 'The Springs of Eternal Life', but found nothing because they did not understand what they were seeking. The Younger Brother is still looking for eternal life, everlasting youth, and still does not understand what the Indians are saying.

Today, Miami drinks the water that feeds those pools, and is draining them. Salt water infiltrates, and the pools die. Miami is consuming the water that sustains the life of the Everglades, and Florida is about to face the consequences.

> The Mother is suffering.
> They have broken her teeth
> and taken out her eyes and ears.
> She vomits.
> she has diarrhoea,
> she is ill.

Down on Key West, a massive tourist complex, I stayed in the Pier House Hotel. The luxury of a comfortable bed, a proper bath, a spa pool, was just what I needed, I thought. But it was strange sitting on the tiny, cordoned beach, in a kind of up-market residential McDonald's where waitresses moved around the sun-loungers wishing people a 'nice day'.

Mel Fisher was there – I recognised him from a colleague's film – with a large golden chain and a large golden coin hanging around his neck. They were, I supposed, spoils from the *Atocha*, the Spanish treasure ship from which he had recovered, with massive publicity, a fortune in gold and silver. I wandered over to the Mel Fisher Museum across the street.

There were the ingots. They had once been golden Mothers, melted down by the Spanish and embarked for Spain in 1622. The Florida reefs had claimed the ship, and the gold was covered by the ocean. Now Mel Fisher and Treasure Salvors Inc. have brought it back to the light, and here it lies to be worshipped again. It is money, but it is more than money. It has a mystic power: people come to look at it because it is valuable, because it is ancient, but above all because it is gold.

If the Younger Brother does not listen, if the snow continues to melt and the world to grow warmer, then the seas will rise. Our scientists say this is inevitable.

The Mel Fisher Museum, on the end of the southernmost tip of Florida, will be the first thing reclaimed by the ocean. If it is swept into the sea, then we will know that Mama Valencia and his blind pupil are the end of history. The Mother will be dead, and shortly so shall we all be.

The Elder Brothers have done all they can. Now it is our responsibility.

A note on translation

All significant Kogi speeches recorded here were made in their own language. They fall into three categories from the point of view of translation:

1 Speeches made by the Mamas or group discussions in the *nuhue*. These were recorded for later translation. The work of translation was carried out by two Kogi, Juancho, who speaks reasonably good Spanish, and by an English-speaking Kogi who appeared after filming was complete. He had been taken by missionaries as a child and brought up in the United States. He now lives as a Kogi, having returned as an adult to the place where he feels he really belongs. Graham supervised this work, playing back the tapes in short sections and discussing them, elucidating the often complex meanings of phrases.

2 Speeches and statements made by Ramón. These were either made in Spanish, or more often made in Kogi and immediately translated by him. In other cases, where Ramón provided instant translations of the words of others, I have indicated this in the text.

3 General conversations between myself and the Kogi. These were normally conducted either in the halting Spanish which a number of them speak, or more often in the presence of Juancho, who acted as immediate interpreter.

There are three living native languages spoken in the Sierra, and although they are primarily identified with the three cultures of Kogi,

A note on translation

Asario and Arhuaco, many families are at least bilingual and we occasionally found that major statements were made by Kogi Mamas in Asario. There are also considerable variations in pronunciation between Kogi groups. For example, 'Serankua' in one mouth will be 'Seijankua' in another, 'Luawiko' in one speech may become 'Aluako' in another, and so on. Since none of us came anywhere near mastering the language, this makes any attempts at etymology potentially dangerous. I have used the versions with which I personally became most familiar.

A further difficulty was that the Mamas speak in a richly complex way, using elaborate metaphors whose significance was not always immediately obvious to the non-Mamas who were struggling to translate them. The Mamas made great efforts to simplify and clarify for us, but their use of language reflects a vision of the world which is itself a complex metaphorical web.

The Tairona language, which was used from time to time in a ritual context, especially in song, increases all these problems and I am afraid defeated us.

Bibliography

Acosta, J., *Compendio histórico del descubrimento y colonización de la Nueva Granada*, Paris 1848

Aguado, P. de, *Recopilación historial de Santa Marta y Nuevo reino de Granada de las indias del mar océano*, Biblioteca de Presidencia de Colombia, Bogota 1906

Aguado, P. de, *Historia de Santa Marta y Nuevo Reino de Granada*, 3 vols, Madrid 1931

Bacon, R. (attrib.), *Mirror of Alchimy*, London 1597

Bischof, H., *Die spanisch-indianische Auseinandersetzung in der nördlichen Sierra Nevada de Santa Marta (1501–1600)*, Bonn 1971

Bray, W., *The Gold of El Dorado*, catalogue of exhibition at the Royal Academy, London 1978

Bray, W., 'Across the Darien Gap; a Colombian view of Isthmian Archaeology', *The Archaeology of Lower Central America*, University of New Mexico, 1984

Castaño, C., 'Consideraciones en torno a los elementos arquitectónicos y urbanísticos de Buritaca 200', *Revista de Arqueología,* año V, no. 39, Madrid 1984

Castellanos, J. de, *Elegías de varones ilustres de Indias*, Madrid 1847

Castellanos, J. de, *Historia del Nuevo Reyno de Granada*, Madrid 1886

Celedón, Rafael, *Gramática de la lengua Koggaba con vocabulario y catecismo*, Collection linguistique américaine, vol. 10, Paris 1886

Falchetti, A. M., 'Desarrollo de la orfebrera tairona en las provincias metalúrgias del norte colombiano', *Boletin 19*, Museo del Oro, Bogota 1987

Bibliography

Groot, M. A. M. de, 'Arqueología y conservación de la localidad precolombina du Buritaca 200 en la Sierra Nevada de Santa Marta', *Arqueología de la Sierra Nevada de Santa Marta*, Instituto Colombiano de Antropología, no. 1, Bogota 1985

Hammen, T. van der and Ruiz, P. M. (eds), *La Sierra Nevada de Santa Marta (Colombia) transecto Buritaca-La Cumbre*, Studies on Tropical Andean Ecosystems, vol. 2, Berlin/Stuttgart 1984

Herrera, A. de, *Historia General de los hechos de los castellanos en las Islas, y Tierra Firme de el Mar Océano*, Asunción, no date

León, A., Lonzano M. A. and Rojas, D., *Colombia, the Set*, Bogota 1987

Mason, A., *Archaeology of Santa Marta, Colombia: The Tairona Culture*, Field Museum of Natural History, Anthropological Series, vol. XX, nos 1–13, Chicago 1939

Mason, P., *Deconstructing America*, London 1990

Mayr, J. (ed.), *The Sierra Nevada of Santa Marta*, Bogota, 1985

Moser, B. and Tayler, D., *The Cocaine Eaters*, London 1965

Ortiz Ricaurte, C., 'Lengua Kogui: la composición nominal', *Lenguas Aborígenes de Colombia: Descripciones*, Centro Colombiano de Estudios en Lenguas Aborígenes, 1989

Oviedo y Valdés, G. F. de, *Historia General y Natural de las Indias Islas y Tierra Firme del Mar Océano*, Asunción, no date

Pagden, A., *The Fall of Natural Man*, London 1982

Preuss, K. T., *Forschungreise zu den Kággaba: Beobachtungen, Textaufnahmen und sprachliche Studien bein einem Indianerstamme in Kolumbien, Südamerika*, 2 vols, Vienna 1926–7

Reclus, E., *Voyage à la Sierra Nevada de Sainte Marthe: Paysage de la Nature Tropicale*, Paris 1861

Reichel-Dolmatoff, G., *Datos Histórico-Culturales sobre las Tribus de la Antigua Gobernación de Santa Marta*, Instituto Etnológico del Magdalena, Santa Marta 1951

Reichel-Dolmatoff, G., 'Contactos y Cambios Culturales en la Sierra Nevada de Santa Marta', *Revista Colombiana de Antropología*, Bogota 1953

Reichel-Dolmatoff, G., 'Notas Sobre el Simbolismo Religioso de los Indios de la Sierra Nevada de Santa Marta', *Razón y Fábula,* I, Universidad de Los Andes, 1967

Reichel-Dolmatoff, G., 'Templos Kogi: Introducción al simbolismo y a la astronomía del espacio sagrado', *Revista Colombiana de Antropología*, 19, Bogota 1975

Reichel-Dolmatoff, G., 'Training for the priesthood among the Kogi of Colombia', *Enculturation in Latin America: An Anthology*, Wilbert, J. (ed.), *Latin American Studies* vol. 37, University of California 1976

Reichel-Dolmatoff, G., *Conceptos indígenas de enfermedad y equilibrio ecológico: Los Tukano y los Kogi*, Rome 1977

Reichel-Dolmatoff, G., 'The loom of life: a Kogi principle of integration', *Journal of Latin American Lore* 4:5, Los Angeles 1978

Reichel-Dolmatoff, G., *Los kogi: Una tribu de la Sierra Nevada de Santa Marta, Colombia*, 2 vols, 2nd ed., Bogota 1985

Reichel-Dolmatoff, G., 'The Great Mother and the Kogi Universe: A Concise Overview', *Journal of Latin American Lore* 13:1, Los Angeles 1987

Reichel-Dolmatoff, G., *Goldwork and Shamanism: an iconographic study of the Gold Museum*, Bogota 1988

Reichel-Dolmatoff, G. & A., 'Investigaciones arqueológicas en la Sierra Nevada de Santa Marta, Parte 4', *Revista Colombiana de Antropología*, 4, Bogota 1955

Simón, Fray P., *Noticias Historiales de las Conquistas de Tierra Firme en las Indias Occidentales*, Bogota 1882

Soto Holguín, A., *Informe de trabajos e investigaciones realizados en el Proyecto Buritaca 200 – Ciudad Perdida – de junio de 1976 a septiembre de 1982*, Bogota 1982

Soto Holguín, A., *La Ciudad Perdida: historia de su hallazgo y descubrimiento*, Bogota 1988

Soto Holguín, A. & Cadavid, G., 'Buritaca 200: Ciudad Perdida', *Revista Lámpara*, no. 76, Bogota 1979

Valderrama, B., *La ciudad perdida: Buritaca 200*, 2nd ed., Bogota 1981

Valderrama, B., *Taironaca: una historia de ciudades perdidas, indígenas, guaqueros, colonos y marimberos en la Sierra Nevada de Santa Marta*, Bogota 1984

Index

VINTAGE DEPARTURES

The Road From Coorain by Jill Ker Conway

A remarkable woman's exquisitely clear-sighted memoir of growing up Australian: from the vastness of a sheep station in the outback to the stifling propriety of postwar Sydney; from untutored childhood to a life in academia; and from the shelter of a protective family to the lessons of independence and tragedy.

"A small masterpiece of scene, memory...this book [is] the most rewarding journey of all."

—John Kenneth Galbraith

Autobiography/0-679-72436-2/$10.00 (Can. $12.50)

Looking for Osman: One Man's Travels Through the Paradox of Modern Turkey by Eric Lawlor

As he traverses Turkey in search of exotic splendor recorded by nineteenth-century romanticists, Eric Lawlor finds instead a modern, professional, sometimes brutal land, with unexpected remnants of the old Turkey to be encountered along the way.

A Vintage Original/Travel/Adventure/0-679-73822-3/$11.00 (Can. $14.00)

A Year in Provence by Peter Mayle

An "engaging, funny and richly appreciative" (*The New York Times Book Review*) account of an English couple's first year living in Provence, settling in amid the enchanting gardens and equally festive bistros of their new home.

"Stylish, witty, delightfully readable."

—*The Sunday Times* (London)

Travel/0-679-73114-8/$10.00 (Can. $12.50)

Maiden Voyages: The Writings of Women Travelers
Edited and with an Introduction by Mary Morris

In this delightful and generous anthology, women such as Beryl Markham, Willa Cather, Annie Dillard, and Joan Didion share their experiences traveling throughout the world. From the Rocky Mountains to a Marrakech palace, in voices wry, lyrical, and sometimes wistful, these women show as much of themselves as they do of the strange and wonderful places they visit.

Travel/Women's Studies/0-679-74030-9/$14.00 (Can. $18.50)

Iron & Silk by Mark Salzman

The critically acclaimed and bestselling adventures of a young American martial arts master in China.

"Dazzling...exhilarating...a joy to read from beginning to end."

—*People*

Travel/Adventure/0-394-75511-1/$10.00 (Can. $13.50)

Available at your local bookstore or call toll-free to order: 1-800-733-3000 (credit cards only). Prices subject to change.